THE THIRD ARAB-ISRAELI WAR

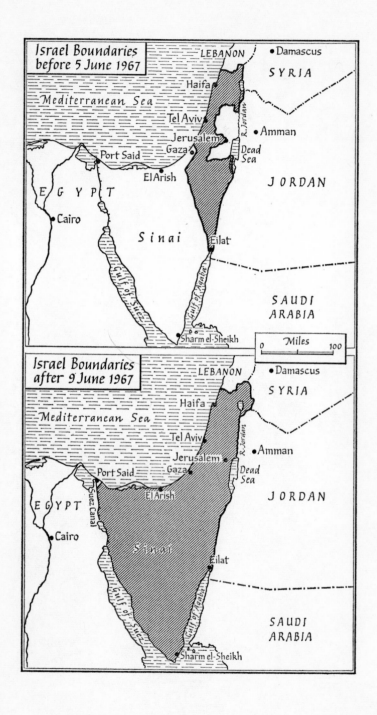

Israel Boundaries
before 5 June 1967

LEBANON
• Damascus
SYRIA
Haifa
Mediterranean Sea
Tel Aviv
R. Jordan
• Amman
Jerusalem
Gaza
Port Said
Dead Sea
El Arish
JORDAN
E G Y P T
Cairo
S i n a i
Eilat
Gulf of Suez
Gulf of Aqaba
SAUDI ARABIA
Sharm el-Sheikh
0   Miles   100

Israel Boundaries
after 9 June 1967

LEBANON
• Damascus
SYRIA
Haifa
Mediterranean Sea
Tel Aviv
R. Jordan
• Amman
Jerusalem
Gaza
Port Said
Dead Sea
El Arish
JORDAN
E G Y P T
Suez Canal
Cairo
S i n a i
Eilat
Gulf of Suez
Gulf of Aqaba
SAUDI ARABIA
Sharm el-Sheikh

THE THIRD
ARAB-ISRAELI
WAR

Edgar O'Ballance

ARCHON BOOKS
HAMDEN, CONNECTICUT
1972

Library of Congress Cataloging in Publication Data

O'Ballance, Edgar.
    The third Arab-Israeli war.

    Bibliography: p.
    1. Israel-Arab War, 1967–   I. Title.
DS127.023   956'.046   72–1059
    ISBN 0–208–01292–3

First published in 1972 by
Faber & Faber Limited, London, England
First published in the United States of America 1972 as an
Archon Book by The Shoe String Press, Inc.,
Hamden, Connecticut
All rights reserved
Printed in England

Contents

Maps

Acknowledgements

Published Sources

The following works have been consulted in compiling this book, and grateful acknowledgement is made to the authors, contributors, reporters and publishers.

Allon, Yigal, *The Making of Israel's Army*, Vallentine Mitchell (1970).

Ayalon, Lt-Col. A., *The Six Day War*, Israel Army Spokesman's Office (1967).

Burdett, Winston, *Encounter with the Middle East*, André Deutsch (1970).

Churchill, Randolph S. and Winston S., *The Six Day War*, Heinemann, London (1967).

Dayan, Lieutenant Yael, *A Soldier's Diary. Sinai 1967*, Weidenfeld & Nicolson (1968).

Draper, Theodore, *Israel and World Politics*, Secker & Warburg (1968).

Hussein of Jordan, *My 'War' with Israel*, William Morrow, New York (1969).

Kimche, David and Dan Bawley, *The Sandstorm*, Secker & Warburg (1968).

Laqueur, Walter, *The Road to War 1967*, Weidenfeld & Nicolson (1968).

Peres, Shimon, *David's Sling*, Weidenfeld & Nicolson (1970).

Teveth, Shabtai, *The Tanks of Tammuz*, Weidenfeld & Nicolson (1969).

Young, Peter, *The Israeli Campaign 1967*, William Kimber (1967).

Safan, Nadar, *From War to War*, Pegasus PB (1969).

Interavia, Issue number 11/67.

ACKNOWLEDGEMENTS

Israeli Defence Force Spokesman's Office, *The Northern Front*; *The Central Front*; *The Sinai Front*.

Israeli Ministry of Defence Publishing House (1967), Official Account, *The Six Days' War*.

I would also like to thank Lieutenant-Colonel (Res.) Elhannan Orren for his help in checking the manuscript for accuracy of detail. I regret that I was not always able to accept his suggestions, and responsibility for the contents is entirely mine.

Preface

This is, I think, the first factual, comprehensive account of the course of the Third Arab-Israeli War of 1967 (popularly termed the Six Day War), looked at coldly and analytically from the viewpoint of the military student. I have tried to produce a clear, simple and readable narrative devoid of bias and emotion. Some of my comments, opinions and deductions may be considered harsh, and perhaps there are passages that many would like omitted – but this is a 'warts and all' account. The Israelis fought and won a brilliant, almost text-book, victory, and one cannot argue with success; but the uncertainties, the often critically narrow margin of success and the minor setbacks must be woven into the skein of triumph.

I 'walked the course' over all the battlefields, on each occasion accompanied by an Israeli officer who had taken part in the action, and who explained to me how the fighting went. All that was missing was his Arab counterpart to give me his 'worm's eye' view of the 'other side of the hill'. This war illustrates many lessons, including the old one that morale is of major importance and the new one that the era of conventional aircraft needing runways is waning and that of the 'jump jet' is dawning.

Considerable assistance was given me by the Israeli Ministry of Defence and by many Israeli officers and soldiers generally. Within the limits of their security rules they answered my probing questions frankly and fully. Unfortunately, even at this late date, certain details, such as the exact designations of brigades and the individual analysis of armoured losses, are still security classified by the Israelis.

I ended my book, *The Sinai Campaign 1956*, with the words: 'There is a distinct probability that Israel will in the future

develop into a "Sparta" of the Middle East.' During the Third
Arab-Israeli War the Spartan qualities of the Israelis were amply
obvious, and it was made apparent that Israel had gained a high
place in the league table of fighting nations of the world.

EDGAR O'BALLANCE

CHAPTER I

The Years Between

In the years between November 1956 and April 1967 British and French influence in the Middle East declined sharply and American influence increased despite the fact that the USA had refused to lend money to President Gamal Abdul Nasser of Egypt to help him complete the Aswan Dam. This refusal had set in motion events that led to the 1956 War, which had involved not only Egypt and Israel but also Britain and France. The situation became overshadowed by the Soviet Union, which gradually gained a stronger grip on both Egypt and Syria. A power game was played in which the Soviet Union, in its constant cold war confrontation, sought to keep the Middle East seething and unstable, both to embarrass America, then Israel's main supporter, and to outflank NATO. This allowed President Nasser, despite setbacks, to regain his former dominant, if insecure, position in an Arab world so riddled with feuds that it could not unite against a common enemy–Israel. After a period of comparative calm, from 1965 onwards Arab terrorist activity increased with the objective of provoking Israel into a war which the Arabs were convinced they would win easily. This war was provoked partly by terrorism and partly by brinkmanship on the part of the Soviet Union and Egypt, but the result was devastatingly different from what the Arabs had anticipated.

The swift 100-Hour Campaign against the Egyptians in 1956 enabled the Israeli Defence Forces to occupy the whole of the Sinai Peninsula, from the Gaza Strip in the north to Sharm El Sheikh in the south, and westwards almost[1] to the Suez Canal. This had coincided with the Anglo-French assault on Egypt, which was halted by indignant and self-righteous American pressure. This pressure forced the Israelis reluctantly to evacuate

---

[1] The Israelis officially halted 10 miles east of the Suez Canal in accordance with an Anglo-French ultimatum.

the territory they had occupied, until they retained only the Gaza Strip and Sharm El Sheikh. On 5 February 1957 Israel was sternly warned by America that, if the United Nations called for such action, it would enforce economic sanctions unless these two places were also evacuated. As Israel could not exist without external aid, especially the considerable volume from the USA, this was the final push, and by 6 March the Israelis had pulled back from both the Gaza Strip and Sharm El Sheikh to behind their 1949 boundaries. Britain and France associated themselves with American assurances to the Israeli Government that no nation had any right to prevent free and innocent passage through the Straits of Tiran and the Gulf of Akaba. The UN Emergency Force spread out in observation positions on Egyptian territory along the frontiers with Israel, thus protecting the battered Egyptian army.

By 1965 American prestige in the UAR was rapidly being over-shadowed by that of the Soviet Union, which had already sent Nasser large quantities of arms. The Soviet Union had con-temptuously written off the various Arab Communist Parties, and instead, by becoming more friendly with Nasser, had sought to further its new policy of trying to supplant the traditional Western role in the Middle East and to outflank NATO. American assistance to Egypt had been deliberately restricted in an endeavour to bring Nasser to heel, and it was Soviet economic and technical aid that enabled work to continue on the Aswan Dam project. Khrushchev had attended the ceremonies marking the completion of the first stage of the Aswan Dam in May 1964, when his anti-Israeli remarks caused alarm in Israel. Nasser, who had visited the Soviet Union and received further Soviet arms and credits during the year, became more openly hostile towards America. Relations worsened and the US Information Offices in Cairo were burned down by anti-American mobs in November (1964). US aid was suspended, but resumed again in June 1965, when Nasser[1] promised to pay for the damage. American stock in Egypt slumped to a new low when the USA cut off its wheat supply in the hope of persuading Nasser to modify his policy in the Yemen, and the Soviet Union promptly stepped in and

[1] Nasser had been re-elected President of the UAR for a further term of six years as from March 1965.

supplied the wheat instead. America brusquely refused Nasser's request for additional economic aid in May 1966, the very same month that Kosygin, the Soviet Premier, visited Egypt and, in a speech attacking America generally and its policy in Vietnam in particular, acknowledged the 'legitimate and inalienable rights of the Palestine Arabs'.

Perhaps 1966 could be characterized as a year of even greater disunity than usual in the Arab world. Nasser was ranged against King Faisal of Saudi Arabia over the civil war in the Yemen; Jordan and Syria were at loggerheads over the activities of anti-Israeli terrorists; King Hussein of Jordan feared and distrusted the Palestine Liberation Organization (PLO); while Iraq was indulging in one of its periodic 'hate Syria' campaigns as well as snarling at other Arab states because of their opposition to its claim to Kuwait. Tunisia refused to attend a meeting of Arab heads of state held in Cairo in March, and the fourth Arab summit, due to take place in Algiers in September, had to be abandoned. Unified Arab High Command plans were also abandoned because of the refusal of the Lebanon, Jordan and Syria to allow Egyptian troops to be stationed in their countries. In October the UAR broke off diplomatic relations with Tunisia.[1] In Iraq President Aref, killed in a helicopter crash near Basra on 13 April, was succeeded by his brother, Major-General Abdul Rahman Aref, who, in July, had to face an attempt to take over the Government by force. In Syria, on 23 February 1966, a left-wing Baathist group toppled the Government that had been suspected of being too friendly with Nasser. In April the new Syrian Government concluded an economic pact with the Soviet Union, which gave it the confidence to continue a hostile policy towards Israel. In September there was an unsuccessful *coup*, led by Colonel Selim Hatoum, a Druze, who fled to Jordan; it was alleged that he had been given Jordanian assistance and that a Jordanian plan to invade Syria existed. Jordan denied these allegations, but was warned by both the Soviet Union and the UAR that they would support Syria should Jordan attempt to invade that country.

---

[1] Diplomatic relations with Egypt had been broken off by Tunisia in 1958, it being alleged that Egyptian help had been given in a plot to assassinate President Bourgiba, but they had been resumed when the UAR supported Tunisia in its Bizerta crises.

The sinister Fatah now comes prominently into the story. Since 1948 many Arab underground political and terrorist organizations based on the Palestinian refugees[1] had appeared with the vague aim of restoring Arab rule over what was formerly called Palestine. These organizations briefly flourished and then disappeared, there being usually scant liaison between them. Then there appeared the better organized and more determined Harakat al Tahrir al Watani al Falastini, the Movement for the National Liberation of Palestine, which became notorious as Fatah.[2] Its military arm was called Kuwat al Asifa, abbreviated as Asifa, meaning Storm. Initially financed by the UAR and Kuwait, and armed with Soviet and Czech small arms supplied from Egyptian and Syrian sources, Asifa was reputed in November 1966 to be about 400 strong, roughly half its members being Palestinians, and during the following months it increased in strength to over 500.

Fatah was led by Yasser Arafat, formerly of the Muslim Brotherhood, who was born and brought up in Jerusalem and whose family moved to Egypt after the 1948 War. No one seems to know much about Fatah's early history[3] except that it initially trained in Kuwait and Algeria but later settled in Syria because that country was conveniently adjacent to Israel. The first Fatah raids into Israel, with the object of sabotaging the National Water Conduit, began in January 1965. Most were made from Jordanian territory, although a few terrorists entered from the Lebanon and Syria. To gain favourable Arab opinion and universal recognition it made outrageous claims to terrorist successes and began to acquire prestige among the Arabs; it was responsible for enough real incidents, however, seriously to worry the Israelis who,

---

[1] The UN Relief and Work Agency 1966 estimates of Palestinian refugees were 700,000 in Jordan (of whom 400,000 were on the West Bank), 300,000 in the Gaza Strip, 160,000 in the Lebanon and 136,000 in Syria. These figures could not be guaranteed as there was a high birth rate in the refugee camps, and deaths were often concealed so that the vital ration card could continue to be used by the family. Most estimates vary between 1 million and 1·3 million.

[2] The initials HTF form the Arabic word for Death, and when reversed to FTH form the Arabic word for Conquest—hence Fatah.

[3] David Kimche and Dan Bawly, authors of *The Sandstorm*, who have made a deep study of Fatah, write 'We cannot point to any precise date, place or event to mark the birth of this movement.' They insist that Fatah's aim was gradually to provoke a war with Israel, which it was certain the Arabs would win.

rather than replying in kind, periodically launched reprisal raids. In October 1965 Israeli forces attacked two villages just inside the Lebanon, which caused the Lebanese Government to tighten its control over Fatah personnel in its territory. Most of the Fatah terrorists[1] continued to cross the 350-mile-long Jordanian border, where it was comparatively easy to slip into Israel undetected, and these actions provoked Israeli reprisal assaults in the Jenin and Kalkilya areas on 27 May 1965, further attacks in the Sea of Galilee region on 5 September, and another one on Kalkilya on 30 April 1966. These reprisals prompted the Syrian Government to establish a Higher Defence Committee to mobilize national resources in case of attack by Israel.

After the *coup* in Syria in February 1966, the new Baathist régime took a deeper interest in Fatah, which until then had operated independently of any Arab government, although it had published its newspaper, *Saut el Asefa* (The Voice of the Storm), in Damascus since May the previous year. The Syrian Government first gave Fatah more material aid and then, in July, took it over altogether, after which Fatah embarked on more ambitious raids into Israel. On 14 July Israeli aircraft bombed Syrian engineering equipment used to divert water from the Banias River, one of the sources of the River Jordan, and fought an air battle in which the Syrians lost one MiG. The acute friction engendered by this was eased only slightly and momentarily by an exchange of prisoners on 7 August.

In October the Soviet Union accused the Israelis of massing troops near the Syrian border, indicating that it would support the Syrian Government in this matter. Thus emboldened, on 11 October Yussef Zeayan, the then Syrian Premier, affirmed his Government's support for Fatah, at the same time condemning King Hussein's attitude towards it. Its fast-rising reputation in the Arab world forced Nasser at last to acknowledge Fatah, although he still debarred it from operating on Egyptian territory, but he became anxious lest its activities precipitate Syria in a war with Israel that might involve Egypt. He announced on 4 November that a mutual defence pact had been agreed between the UAR and Syria. A joint military command was to be set up,

---

[1] In 1965 there were 31 Fatah raids into Israel, of which 27 were made from Jordanian territory.

and in the event of operations both armies were to be placed under the command of the Egyptian Chief of Staff. The most important clause, from Nasser's viewpoint, required full consultation by Syria with the UAR before any military operation was begun, which he hoped would restrain any ill-considered Syrian action.

Continued activity by Fatah terrorists crossing into Israel predominantly from Jordan provoked Israel to mount a fairly substantial punitive raid on 13 November on the large village of Samu,[1] south of Hebron, about three miles inside Jordanian territory. As a result 18 Jordanian soldiers were killed and about 134 wounded, and many buildings in Samu, including a mosque, were demolished—all in four hours. The Israelis admitted losing one soldier killed and 10 wounded, while it was claimed that 15 Jordanian vehicles were destroyed for 22 Israeli vehicles damaged. This was the largest Israeli reprisal raid so far, and the first to be carried out in daylight.

The Samu raid had varying repercussions. President Nasser was convinced that his new defence pact with Syria had deterred the Israelis from attacking that country, which was the real Fatah base; as a face-saver they had had to hit at the much weaker and isolated Jordan, although everyone knew that King Hussein disapproved of the terrorists using his territory. The Soviet Union openly condemned the raid (Nasser correctly assumed that this would cause anxiety in the Israeli Cabinet) and so did most other Arab countries, except Syria, which was particularly vitriolic against Jordan at this period. Even the UAR condemned it, although on 19 November the Cairo newspaper, *Al Ahram*,[2] accused King Hussein of collusion with the Israelis to prevent further attacks. As a direct reprisal Jordan refused to allow supplies for the Israeli detachment in the Mount Scopus enclave in Jerusalem to pass through Jordanian territory until 12 December, when it permitted them to be carried in UN instead of Israeli vehicles. Across the border in Israel there was more discontent than satisfaction over the Samu raid, the Government being widely blamed for its seeming weakness in hitting at

---

[1] Samu then had a resident population of about 4,000.

[2] The Editor of *Al Ahram* was Mohammed Heykal, a friend and confidant of President Nasser. The paper was thought to express Nasser's views.

Jordan rather than at Syria, which was now openly supporting and directing Fatah. Inside Jordan the raid caused violent reactions against King Hussein's moderate line.

Despite the Arab states' inability to agree on anything for very long, all spoke of the day when Israel would be triumphantly wiped out by force of Arab arms. The presence of Israel was an excuse for Arab states to maintain comparatively large defence forces and a high military budget. For 14 years, until 1964, Israel's gross national product had risen about 10 per cent each year, and a new impression of the Jew as a worker, fighter and intellectual had been presented to the world, but in 1965 the economy began to slow down, partly following Government measures to stop inflation, partly because US aid had decreased and partly because Zionist fund-raising organizations found it harder to obtain money overseas for Israel. Immigration had fallen off, only 31,600 arriving in 1965 and 12,000 in 1966 (in which year some 11,000 emigrated from Israel), German reparations had ended, economic growth had stopped and a mild depression had set in with some 10 per cent of the labour force unemployed. A pay increase granted to workers under heavy union pressure had added to inflation. Israelis from the kib-butzim, the frontier farming settlements, began to move into the cities. Coincident with the growing economic depression in Israel came more Fatah attacks, which despite the salutary Samu raid increased in number and effectiveness. Public opinion demanded military reprisals against Syria, the base for Fatah, but Premier Eshkol did not wish to provoke war with any Arab state nor to offend the powerful Soviet Union which was in an anti-Israeli mood. His new Foreign Minister, Abba Eban, counselled diplomacy rather than militant action. Eshkol had plenty of domestic troubles, especially with inflation and rising unemploy-ment, and did not want to add to them by provoking war. Another important reason for Eshkol's hesitation was the real military threat from the UAR, whose armed forces had recently received quantities of modern Soviet arms. On 29 November 1966 two Egyptian MiGs were brought down over the Sinai. Syria continued cynically to direct Fatah terrorists to use Jordanian territory as a springboard for raids into Israel, knowing that Hussein could not prevent them and that the Palestinian element in his Kingdom firmly opposed measures against this organization.

In March Gromyko, the Soviet Foreign Minister, paid a visit to Egypt, which the Israelis found ominous, so after a further spate of Fatah terrorism Premier Eshkol was persuaded to authorize the largest Israeli reprisal raid mounted so far on the Syrian guns that frequently fired on Israeli farmers in the demilitarized zone on the south-east shore of the Sea of Galilee. On 7 April 1967, after an exchange of fire between tanks and artillery on both sides, an overhead air battle developed in which six Syrian MiGs were shot down.[1] Despite the fact that the UAR-Syrian Defence Pact had been ratified by both Governments and had come into effect on 9 March 1967, the Egyptians made no move to help the Syrians in this battle. All that happened was that the Soviet Union sternly warned Israel of the possible consequences of armed provocation. Tension and tempers were rising sharply between Israel and the Arab states. Prodded on by the Soviet Union, Nasser began his brinkmanship and others joined in the fatal game which got out of their control.

---

[1] Syria admitted the loss of four MiGs, but its claim to have shot down four Israeli aircraft was not confirmed by the Israelis.

CHAPTER 2

A Diary of Escalation

It is difficult to pinpoint any one event that made hostilities inevitable. My considered opinion is that the closing of the Straits of Tiran and the attempted strangulation of the southern port of Eilat made war certain. Certainly the process of escalation was in motion on 13 May, and it continued until 4 June, 23 days later, when the Israeli Government decided to strike first. I trace here the escalation in diary form to show how each step followed the other.

Saturday, 13 May 1967

Unfounded reports reached the Egyptian and Syrian Governments that the Israelis were moving between 11 and 13 brigades towards the Syrian border. Whatever the source of the information, Nasser believed it and decided to make a show of force to deter the anticipated Israeli attack on Syria, hoping that Israel would be wary of fighting on two fronts at once.

Sunday, 14 May 1967

Nasser sent Lieutenant-General Mohammed Fawzi, his Chief of Staff, who was nominated to command the joint Egyptian and Syrian forces in the event of hostilities, to Damascus to confer with Syrian Ministers and senior officers.

In Israel Premier Eshkol's statement that a serious confrontation with Syria would become inevitable if the terrorist campaign carried out by Arab infiltrators under Syrian orders continued was taken by the Israelis as a threat of larger reprisal attacks rather than outright war. Preparations were in full progress for the Independence Day Parade to be held on the morrow.

23

Monday, 15 May 1967

The Independence Day Parade in Jerusalem went off without
incident.

In Egypt troops were moving eastwards amid maximum
publicity. There was no television in Israel then, but Israelis with
sets got a good view of Nasser's marching soldiers. Iraq promised
to help Syria if that country were attacked, and that evening the
Israeli Chief of Staff ordered a state of alertness in all regular
formations and units.

Tuesday, 16 May 1967

The Syrian Government issued a statement that its armed
forces had been alerted, and a state of emergency was declared in
Egypt. Nasser sent a message[1] to Major-General Rikhye, the
Indian UNEF commander, requesting him to concentrate his
personnel in the Gaza Strip to avoid harm if hostilities broke out
and to enable the Egyptians to take action if attacked. He also
demanded the immediate evacuation of the UNEF posts at Sabha
and Sharm El Sheikh. Rikhye objected that the procedure was
irregular and he reported the demand to the UN. Immediately
following an Egyptian broadcast of this news, an Israeli tank unit
and three mechanized infantry battalions were moved during the
night towards the Egyptian frontier in the area of the Gaza Strip.

Wednesday, 17 May 1967

At the UN Headquarters in New York the day was spent in
fluttering consultations. At Gaza Rikhye refused another local
demand to withdraw his force[2] into the Gaza Strip, but already
Egyptian soldiers were trying to jostle the UNEF personnel from
their positions at some of the border posts and by evening had
turned them out of the UN post at Sabha. Egypt and Syria issued

---

[1] The message was personally delivered to General Rikhye at 2200 (local time)
by Brigadier Ibrahim Sharqami, the Egyptian liaison officer with the UNEF, it
having been brought by an Egyptian brigadier. (*The Sandstorm.*)

[2] The UNEF consisted of 432 Brazilians, 800 Canadians, 3 Danes, 978 Indians,
72 Norwegians, 528 Swedes and 580 Yugoslavs.

statements that their armed forces were in a state of combat readiness, and both made further unfounded allegations of Israeli troop concentrations opposite their respective frontiers. Jordan announced that it was mobilizing and the Lebanon cancelled a courtesy visit by ships of the US 6th Fleet. President Zalmar Shazar calmly left Israel on a state visit to Iceland and Canada.

Thursday, 18 May 1967

During the morning Egyptian and Palestinian troops forced UNEF soldiers out of positions near Kuntilla and two or three other points in the Sinai, while in the south the UNEF commander at Sharm El Sheikh was given an ultimatum to withdraw his men. Mahmoud Riad, the Egyptian Foreign Minister, cabled U Thant formally demanding the urgent removal of the UNEF. Anticipating the demand, U Thant had already consulted representatives of the countries that provided contingents for the UNEF. Canada, India and Yugoslavia intimated that they would evacuate their men as soon as officially asked to do so. U Thant sounded Israel to see if it would allow the UNEF to operate on the Israeli side of the frontier, but this suggestion was rebuffed. Merely voicing 'serious misgivings', U Thant instructed General Rikhye to withdraw the UNEF personnel into the Gaza Strip.[1] By that evening most were concentrated in the two UN camps at Rafah and Khan Yunis, their positions being taken over by Egyptian and Palestinian soldiers. Only the UNEF detachment at Sharm El Sheikh remained in position. Kuwait placed its armed forces under the UAR-Syrian Joint Command, and both Kuwait and Iraq announced the mobilization of their forces.

In Israel Premier Eshkol and his cabinet were given a hesitant military briefing by General Rabin, which did not inspire confidence.

Friday, 19 May 1967

In the morning the UNEF lowered its flag for the last time at

---

[1] Evidence since revealed seems to indicate that Nasser was taken by surprise as he had anticipated a period of bullying and bargaining over this demand. However, he was now committed—his bluff had been called.

its Gaza HQ. At Sharm El Sheikh the UNEF detachment with-drew from Ras Nasrani,[1] overlooking the narrow entrance to the Straits of Tiran. (Sharm El Sheikh was not completely evacuated by the UNEF until the 23rd.) A handful of Egyptian paratroops was flown to Sharm El Sheikh to forestall any Israeli attempt to seize this strategically vital spot. The UNEF's sudden dramatic removal came as a shock to the UN, western nations and Israel. Broadly it had fulfilled its object of preventing hostilities between the two countries. That U Thant agreed to the Egyptian demand with so little argument, although legality was clearly on the Egyptian side, caused some comment.

The UNEF's withdrawal caused especial dismay in Israel, coinciding as it did with reports of unusually large Egyptian concentrations in the Sinai. The UNEF presence had ensured the free passage of Israeli and other shipments of goods through the Straits of Tiran and the Gulf of Akaba into Eilat, the southern port vital to the Israeli economy. A tanker loaded with Iranian oil called every fortnight or so at Eilat to discharge a cargo which amounted to about 90 per cent of Israel's oil supply. For the first time in many months Egyptian aircraft violated Israeli air space when two MiGs flew over the Dimona nuclear research centre in the Negev.

Saturday, 20 May 1967

In Israel, the first phase of the call-up completed, the absence of men from their daily jobs had become noticeable. On the Egyptian side Field-Marshal Amer toured the former UNEF positions, which along the Gaza Strip were now occupied by per-sonnel of the 20th (Palestinian) Division[2] and elsewhere by Egyp-tian soldiers. He also authorized the recall of further reservists.

Sunday, 21 May 1967

General Rabin informed the Israeli Cabinet that the number of Egyptian troops in the Sinai had risen from about 35,000 to 80,000 during the past few days.

---

[1] Ras Nasrani is about 15 miles north of Sharm El Sheikh.
[2] Sometimes referred to at this stage as the Palestine National Guard.

For the first time the call-up of reservists was officially announced in both Israel and Egypt. At a Cairo press conference Ahmed Shukairy stated that his '8,000-strong PLA' had been placed under the national commands of Egypt, Syria and Iraq, but not that of Jordan.[1] In fact, his hatred of King Hussein rose to a new pitch as he called on the Jordanians to overthrow their ruler. Anxiously Jordan offered to place its armed forces under the UAR-Syrian Joint Command, but Nasser contemptuously ignored this gesture. A bellicose speech was made by Major-General Hafez Assad, the Syrian Defence Minister.

Monday, 22 May 1967

Nasser accepted an offer of Iraqi army and air force units in the event of war with Israel, and Libya and the Sudan pledged their support. Premier Eshkol, speaking in the Knesset, confirmed the news of the large troop concentrations in the Sinai. He proposed that Israeli soldiers should withdraw from the Sinai border region, where by this time about 30,000 were concentrated, if Egyptian troops did the same. Nasser's only response was to rush another 500 soldiers to implement his small garrison at Sharm El Sheikh. U Thant left New York to fly to meet President Nasser in Cairo.

Tuesday, 23 May 1967

Now occurred the step which in my opinion made war inevitable. Nasser announced the blockade of the Straits of Tiran to Israeli ships and ships carrying strategic goods to Israel. He was in a strong position; because of the many reefs in the Straits there was just one narrow navigable channel hardly more than 800 yards wide in parts, leading into the Gulf of Akaba proper, and it was commanded by the guns at Ras Nasrani, near Sharm El Sheikh, now once again in Egyptian hands. The UAR had always claimed that the Straits of Tiran and the Gulf of Akaba were a 'closed sea and within Egyptian territorial waters', and their closure had been a main cause of the Israeli attack in 1956. This

---

[1] This figure, quoted by Shukairy himself, is suspect and was considered to be greatly exaggerated.

dramatic act sent Nasser's stock rocketing in the Arab world, and led even Tunisia and Saudi Arabia to give him open support and acclaim. In Algeria a state of alert was proclaimed and former FLN fighters were called upon to volunteer for the struggle against 'Zionism'. Only Jordan remained isolated, immersed in its active quarrel with Syria, which became intensified when a terrorist's bomb exploded in a bus at Ramtha, a Jordanian border post on the Syrian frontier, killing 14 and injuring 23 people and causing King Hussein to break off diplomatic relations with Syria.

The Israeli Government's reaction to the closure of the Straits of Tiran was one of shock and anxiety. Premier Eshkol took the unusual step of consulting leaders of opposition parties. To counter Fatah terrorism, the army sowed mines on the Israeli side of the Jordanian border and erected floodlit fencing at vulnerable crossing points. Nasser's act provoked a vague statement from President Johnson to the effect that the USA regarded the Gulf of Akaba as an international waterway and considered the blockade 'illegal and potentially dangerous to peace'. A Soviet statement blamed Israel for the worsening tension. America and Britain[1] advised their nationals to leave Israel. In Moscow there was dismay; Nasser had gone too far, as such an action could bring a confrontation with America dangerously close.

Wednesday, 24 May 1967

Egypt falsely claimed that the Straits of Tiran had been closed the previous day by mines, guns, armoured patrol boats and aircraft, and threatened that Israeli ships would be fired on if they did not turn back and that all others would be searched. Advanced elements of Kuwaiti troops arrived in Egypt, as did token military personnel from the Sudan and an Algerian military mission. U Thant, now in Cairo, met Nasser, who wanted to revert to the '1948 *status quo*', which meant that Israel would have to give up certain territory, including Eilat, and the Gulf of Akaba would be recognized as Egyptian waters. He insisted that

---

[1] Britain had no diplomatic relations with Egypt. They had been broken off in 1956, resumed in 1961, and broken off again in 1965 over the Rhodesian problem.

Israel should fully observe the conditions of the demilitarized zones and that the Israeli frontiers be policed by the UN. Whilst emphasizing the rights of the Palestinian refugees, Nasser told U Thant that he would not strike the first blow.

Amman announced that mobilization had been completed and army units dispersed to their battle stations. Copying Nasser's publicity techniques, troops, tanks and guns paraded through the capital on their way to the frontier areas. A spokesman said that permission had been given for Saudi Arabian troops to enter Jordan, that already some had arrived (which was false), and that a further 20,000 were waiting near the border. Permission was given for Iraqi troops also to enter Jordan, but none moved in as the Iraqi Government had still not got over King Hussein's former refusal to have them in his country. Fresh gestures by Jordan to co-operate with Egypt were ignored by Nasser, who meant to isolate Hussein.

Premier Eshkol indignantly called the blockade an 'act of aggression against Israel'. Quoting the UN resolution of March 1957 guaranteeing the freedom of shipping through the Straits of Tiran and the assurances given by America, Britain and France, when Israeli troops had been compelled to evacuate Sharm El Sheikh, he demanded that the three Great Powers honour their pledge. He did not know how far the Soviet Union, which had armed Egypt and Syria, was prepared actively to assist Nasser. But the Great Powers concerned did not want to become involved. The British Prime Minister merely echoed President Johnson's statement of the previous day, adding that Britain was prepared to join others to secure general recognition of the right of free passage through the Straits. There was dismay in America when it became apparent that Israel was going to ask for help, so a note was sent to Premier Eshkol urging him to postpone any contemplated action for 48 hours, which the Israeli cabinet agreed to do. This suited the Israeli General Staff as mobilization was not fully completed.[1] In New York the UN Security Council met but adjourned without taking a vote.

Eshkol again consulted opposition leaders, including Ben-Gurion, who had been Premier and Defence Minister in 1956,

---

[1] It was completed that night.

and they agreed to sound out the three Great Powers before taking any other action. Abba Eban, the Foreign Minister, flew to Paris immediately where he briefly saw President de Gaulle, who was pointedly uninterested, thinking that Israel had fallen too much under American influence. This was a big disappointment as during and since the 1956 War France had been a good friend to Israel, but relations had tended to cool when Algeria gained its independence.

Thursday, 25 May 1967

After a brief, fruitless call at London, Abba Eban flew to Washington, where he horrified state officials with his demand for action. President Johnson declined to see him, but that evening sent a message to Nasser urging restraint. The Soviet Union refused to co-operate with America, Britain and France over the blockaded Straits, but Premier Kosygin sent Nasser a cautionary cable. The Egyptian Defence Minister, Shamseddin Badran, went with a delegation to Moscow to ask for more arms and equipment.

After further talks with Nasser, U Thant left Cairo without any communiqué being issued.

In Jordan senior army officers pressed King Hussein to come to terms with the UAR President. As a first softening-up measure Radio Amman stopped criticizing Nasser and approved his blockade of the Straits of Tiran. This change of Jordanian policy meant that all 13 states of the Arab League had now declared support of Egypt.

Despite growing criticism in Israel of Premier Eshkol's inactivity, and a mounting desire to hit back hard at Egypt, Eshkol's own party, the Mapai, confirmed his leadership.

Friday, 26 May 1967

Kosygin sent a note to Premier Eshkol urging restraint, but the Soviet leaders really considered him too weak a character to instigate hostilities, and thought such a danger lay with Nasser. Indeed, early that morning[1] the Soviet Ambassador in Cairo had

---

[1] About 0330 Egyptian local time.

roused Nasser from bed with a message from Moscow. Nasser assured his caller that he would not strike the first blow, but in a speech later in the day he declared that he was ready for war and confident that he could destroy Israel completely.

Saturday, 27 May 1967

U Thant, while reporting to the UN Security Council that Nasser had assured him that he would not initiate any offensive military action against Israel, deplored the closure of the Straits of Tiran as a 'serious threat to peace'. However, Nasser's inflammatory words caused the Soviet Ambassador in Cairo to warn him not to strike first, and for good measure the Soviet Ambassador to Israel advised Premier Eshkol not to take any hostile action either. In the evening the USA sent the Israeli Premier a note in similar vein.

The Israeli Cabinet sat into the small hours (of the 28th). When finally a vote was taken on whether to fight, nine voted for and nine against. Eshkol, who had voted for war, could have used his casting vote as Premier to carry the motion, but did not do so, and the Cabinet dispersed without any decision being taken.

Sunday, 28 May 1967

The Israeli Cabinet, meeting again in the morning, had second thoughts. After the meeting Brigadier Meir Amit, Director of Intelligence Services, was sent to Washington to find out what was actually happening. He soon discovered that nothing at all was being done to help Israel.

Shamseddin Badran, the Egyptian Defence Minister, returned from Moscow with the information that, if it came to war, Egypt could not count on Soviet military intervention. Nevertheless, the over-confident Nasser told a press conference that the Arabs would not accept co-existence with Israel, that he would not allow Israeli shipping through the Straits of Tiran, and that Israel must evacuate Eilat and Nitzana (both occupied after the 1948 cease-fire).

Desperately anxious to edge back into the Arab circle before it was too late, Hussein tried to arrange a meeting with Nasser through the Egyptian Ambassador in Amman, but Nasser's pre-conditions included the dispersal of Jordanian troops from near the Syrian frontier, the entry into Jordan of Iraqi forces, the acceptance of Ahmed Shukairy and his PLO, and the annulment of Hussein's intention to re-establish diplomatic relations with Western Germany, which had been broken off when Western Germany had recognized Israel. The conditions were steeper than expected, so Hussein tried to modify them, but he was in a cleft stick as his country was so vulnerable, restless and plagued with Fatah terrorists.

Monday, 29 May 1967

In Cairo the National Assembly conferred full powers to govern by decree on Nasser who, in accepting them, declared that 'our enemy is not only Israel but its backers, Britain and America'. Shamseddin Badran, the Defence Minister, recently returned from Moscow, said that Kosygin had pledged Soviet support for Egypt and its allies, and for the liberation of Palestine. Algeria announced that it would send military units to help the UAR. President Nureddin Atassi left Syria for a two-day visit to Moscow to ask for more arms and aid, while the Premier, Yussef Zeayan, made a fiery speech threatening the destruction of Israel.

In New York an emergency meeting of the UN Security Council adjourned without a vote being taken. In the Gaza Strip the PLA shelled the frontier kibbutz of Nahal Oz and fired on an Israeli patrol near the border.

In his efforts to remove Eshkol, Shimon Peres, Secretary General of Ben Gurion's Rafi Party (which held 10 seats as opposed to Eshkol's Alignment of Mapai and Ahdut Havoda, which held 45), found an unlikely ally in Menahem Begin, a former leader of the Irgun Zvai Leumi terrorist organization that operated in the latter days of the Mandate, who now dominated a right-wing group known as Gahal (a coalition of the Herut and the Israeli Liberal Party), which had 26 seats and was the second largest group in the Knesset. Begin, a long time opponent of Ben Gurion, went to Eshkol and asked him point-blank to step down as Premier and hand over to Gurion. Eshkol angrily refused.

Peres then suggested to him that Ben Gurion be included in the Cabinet, and again Eshkol refused.

Tuesday, 30 May 1967

After secret negotiations Nasser consented to receive Hussein, who dramatically flew to Cairo[1] and, during a six-hour visit, signed a five-year UAR-Jordanian Defence Pact providing for a Joint Defence Council, a Joint Command and a Joint Staff. Concessions included placing Hussein's armed forces under the command of an Egyptian general, Major-General Abdul Munim Riad,[2] and agreeing to having Iraqi and other Arab troops in Jordan.

Wednesday, 31 May 1967

In Israel support for the appointment of Moshe Dayan as Defence Minister became a talking point for the whole nation. Eshkol spent the first part of the day trying to hold on to the Defence portfolio, and when he realized that this was hopeless, the second part trying even harder to prevent it going to Dayan. He offered it to Yigal Yadin, who had been Director of Operations during the War of Independence, Israel's first Chief of Staff later, and the Premier's unofficial military adviser, but Yadin refused.[3] Eshkol then said he would accept Yigal Alon, but Yadin strongly advised him to appoint Moshe Dayan instead. Yigal Yadin tried to persuade Moshe Dayan to become Defence Minister on a non-party basis: Dayan did not agree. That same evening Eshkol made Moshe Dayan several offers to steer him away from the Defence Ministry, including that of GOC of the Southern Command (which would have effectively removed him from politics for the time being) and the post of military adviser, which would have meant responsibility without power. Dayan refused them all. Towards the end of the day most,

---

[1] 'Your arrival here being secret, what would happen if we arrested you?' President Nasser asked King Hussein on his arrival at Cairo. 'Such an eventuality never disturbed me,' replied Hussein. (*Sunday Telegraph*, 15 September 1968.)

[2] Not to be confused with Mahmoud Riad, the Egyptian Foreign Minister.

[3] Professor of Archaeology at the Hebrew University, Jerusalem.

including Eshkol, realized that a national government was essential to carry Israel through this crisis; at least Gahal (with 26 seats) and if possible Rafi (with 10 seats) must be persuaded to join the existing coalition. Neither would agree unless Moshe Dayan was appointed Defence Minister.

Thursday, 1 June 1967

General Riad arrived in Jordan from Cairo to take over the command of the Jordanian armed forces, and drew up plans that incorporated the use of a promised Iraqi division.

At long last Eshkol gave in and announced that he would relinquish the portfolio of Defence in favour of Moshe Dayan.

Friday, 2 June 1967

Moshe Dayan, as Defence Minister, dismissed the Deputy Defence Minister and brought in Major-General Zvi Zur,[1] a former Chief of Staff from 1960–1963, as his special assistant.

Saturday, 3 June 1967

Nasser suffered from indecision. He suspected that if he attacked he might have to fight alone, as he had the last time, while his Arab allies watched him take the full brunt of the fighting. America and France had warned him not to fire the first shot, and he did not know how the US 6th Fleet would react if he did. Neither did he know what support, if any, he would receive from the Soviet Union if he made the first move. He also wanted to ensure that the Iraqi division was in position in Jordan first. So, by not striking the first blow at this moment, Nasser lost his last chance of avoiding total defeat in the war that was almost upon him.

An Iraqi delegation visited Amman and Cairo to sign the UAR-Jordanian Defence Pact, which became a tripartite one. In Jordan King Hussein said at a press conference in Amman (at 1400 local time) that he expected war to break out within the next

---

[1] Sometimes spelt 'Tsur'.

two days.[1] Ahmed Shukairy, of the PLO, held a press conference in Jerusalem[2] at which he preached a Holy War against Israel.

Moshe Dayan's first press conference was disarming. He said that before he joined the Government it had embarked upon a course of diplomacy which must be given a chance. Israel, he added, would fight its own battles with its own troops; he 'did not want British or American boys to get killed in the defence of Israel'. When asked if Israel had lost the military initiative in the Middle East, Dayan replied: 'If you mean to say we stand no chance then I cannot agree with you.' Publicity was deliberately given to the mobilized reservists on weekend leave and enjoying themselves on the beaches.

That evening Dayan told the Israeli Cabinet that he thought the Egyptian forces in the Sinai could be defeated for the loss of 1,000 Israeli dead. Brigadier Mordechai Hod, Commander of the Israeli Air Force, estimated that he could destroy the Arab air forces and prevent Israel from being bombed. Most Ministers were now sure of not incurring American anger as they had done in 1956, and they calculated that the Soviet Union would not directly intervene. Discussion continued into the early hours of the next morning. The vote showed only two abstentions (these two afterwards wanted their votes recorded in the affirmative). The other 15 Ministers all favoured an immediate war against Egypt. Moshe Dayan ordered the IDF to prepare to strike.

Sunday, 4 June 1967

Swift and secret preparations in Israel throughout the day contrasted with sabre-rattling Arab announcements and troop movements. The Libyan Foreign Minister arrived in Cairo to declare that a Libyan contingent would fight alongside the Egyptians, and that the use of Wheelus Air Base would be denied to the Americans if they helped the 'Zionists'. General Riad had assumed command of the Jordanian armed forces, and

---

[1] 'Within the next 24 hours. Otherwise the Israelis will give up the idea until another time when we are not expecting them.' (*Sunday Telegraph*, 15 September 1968.)

[2] Ahmed Shukairy now disappears from the scene. He returned to Amman on 5 June, and on 6 June left for Damascus where he stayed for the rest of the war. He was subsequently ousted from the PLO.

elements of two Egyptian commando battalions[1] arrived by air in Amman. The first brigade of the promised Iraqi Division reached the northern border of Jordan by evening, with two units of Ahmed Shukairy's PLA, which had not been mentioned by Nasser but which after some hesitation King Hussein allowed to enter his country with the Iraqis. King Faisal of Saudi Arabia rescinded his order that none of his troops should enter Jordan, and one Saudi Arabian infantry brigade crossed the border by nightfall. The two other Saudi Arabian infantry brigades in camp at Tabuk, not far from Akaba, expected to be ordered to move into Jordan on the morrow. Hussein seems to have suspected that war was imminent and in the evening he told Major-General Amer Khamish, his Chief of Staff, through General Riad, to warn his tiny air force to cover Jordanian airfields as from dawn on the 5th. Nasser, still unsure, was hoping that Israel would not attack for a few days. He wanted the military staffs of the UAR, Jordan, Syria and Iraq to co-ordinate their plans and move their troops into more advantageous positions so that they could make simultaneous combined thrusts into Israel.

While the Israelis were secretly making final preparations, certain Western powers were still trying to find a solution, but they were met with indifference. Nasser boldly declared that he would never recognize their suggestions as it would transgress Egyptian sovereignty. And on that unrealistic, bickering note the eve of war slipped away.

---

[1] The 33rd and 53rd Commando Battalions.

CHAPTER 3

The Israeli Defence Forces

In nearly two decades the Israeli Defence Forces (the army, air force and navy), the IDF or ZAHAL (Zwa Haganah Le'Israel), had undergone a complete change. In 1948 the army, which had evolved mainly from the Haganah of Mandate times, had been hastily expanded with a shambling mixture of Jewish soldiers experienced in other national armies in other wars. Often in small groups, they fought piecemeal, success or failure frequently depending upon local leadership and opportunity, as initially there was little central control or direction. After the War of Independence the IDF was organized on a permanent basis to be the crucible of a new nation. Conscription, which included women, meant that practically all would serve in its ranks. During this period of mass immigration many Jews arrived from backward Arab countries, such as the Yemen, and few could speak Hebrew, the national language. ZAHAL was to become the medium to absorb, educate and mould these new Israelis. The IDF[1] was expected to take an active part in the construction of Israel, it being visualized that it would man the frontier kibbutzim, form new kibbutzim, carry out road construction, help with the harvest and assist in staffing hospitals and public services. For a few years the IDF struggled to fulfil these obligations, but it soon became obvious that they detracted seriously from its fighting ability. Ben-Gurion, Premier and Defence Minister, who had originally supported this concept of a citizen army, was persuaded that it would be better for the armed forces to shed some of these non-military tasks and concentrate on training for its primary role of defending Israel. Moshe Dayan was appointed Chief of Staff in December 1953, and it was during his term of office that the IDF

---

[1] Civilian authority over the IDF is exercised through the Ministry of Defence–in Hebrew Misrad Habitachon, literally Ministry of Security. (*David's Sling*.)

was divested of most of these civilian chores.[1] He also pruned the 'administrative tail' of the IDF considerably, but had not completed his reorganization when the Sinai Campaign was fought in 1956. In this campaign the parachute brigade, with its superior training and morale, did much better than certain other formations and demonstrated the necessity of a highly trained professional army unencumbered with extraneous tasks. After the Sinai Campaign efforts to bring other army formations up to the paratroop brigade's standard had been largely accomplished by 1967. Paratroops and infantry had dominated the Sinai Campaign. At that period there was little confidence in armour, whose role was to support the infantry. The tanks, elderly and always breaking down, usually followed the infantry on transporters, the crews accompanying them in civilian buses. Despite these shortcomings and the misuse of armour its potential had been suddenly appreciated in the Sinai fighting, and afterwards its role was changed to that of deep penetration. More modern tanks were received, discipline was tightened up, efficiency increased, and accordingly the status and prestige of the armoured corps rose steadily.

Armoured corps strategy was based on a quick, hard initial punch to break through the enemy defences, carry out deep penetration tactics, cut the enemy's rear communications and shatter morale. It was prepared to accept heavy casualties to make this vital gain. This concept had superseded that of the infantry night attack, a slow and complicated tactic that had its failures in 1956. During the training seasons of 1965 and 1966 Israeli armoured units had practised breaking through an Egyptian-type replica of the Soviet three-tier defensive position constructed in the Negev. A strong punch, in which armour and fire power were concentrated, was directed at one point. Once through the defensive lines the commanders of all armoured units, no matter how small (in fact right down to individual tank commanders), were to race forward, using their own initiative to seize every advantage within the general directive laid down by the senior commander.

---

[1] 'Moshe Dayan, who replaced Maklef in 1953, and was in command for four years, instilled into the army the art of *original warfare*, and turned it into a first-class fighting force.' (*David's Sling*.)

To improve IDF efficiency discipline was tightened up. The informal comradely atmosphere in which the soldiers called their officers by their first names continued but orders had to be strictly obeyed or punishment followed. In 1948 and 1956 opportunities had been lost and minor disasters caused by disobedience, deliberate neglect and wilful individualism; indeed, some reprisal raids had been abortive through these faults. Discipline was enforced on the recalled reservists[1] who were put into strict training during the preliminary period of tension. Several days were required before reservists were brought to the physical fitness standards of the regulars in training. The Israelis also had the problem of those, mainly from Arab countries, who had lower physical standards but who had to be accepted for service in the IDF.[2] The other main change since 1956 was that the regular infantry brigades and a proportion of the reserve ones now had a larger element of their own integral transport. In the Sinai Campaign civilian transport had often been unsuitable, had broken down or proved unable to cope with rough or sandy terrain. Civilian vehicles still had to be impressed but mainly to carry fuel, supplies and stores. 'Today nobody in the army walks,' Brigadier Sharon told me. The IDF had an extremely competent General Staff, about 15 senior officers, which had been developed since 1956. In that year there had been only a few staff officers working at GHQ under the direction of the Chief of Staff, who had practically conducted the Sinai Campaign himself, usually well forward in the battle zone. This he had been able to do as he was fighting on only one front. Had either Jordan or Syria attacked at the same time, the IDF would have been at a serious disadvantage by not having a conventional General Staff at GHQ to direct and control the war as a whole–a point not lost on the Israelis. In October 1963 a National Defence College was opened, modelled on the British and American patterns. Previously the Israelis merely had a Senior Officers' School, used

---

[1] 'Shaving was compulsory and walking around without a weapon or a helmet resulted in punishment. Prisons were built and MP platoons arrived from Beersheba.' (Yael Dayan in *A Soldier's Diary*.)

[2] Describing a visit to an infantry battalion just before 5 June, Yael Dayan writes: 'In each platoon of the battalion there were a few reservists whose standard, mostly for health reasons, was lower than the others. They could not keep pace on the march.' (*A Soldier's Diary*.)

more for teaching co-operation between commanders and the various arms on the battlefield than training for senior staff appointments. In January 1964 Major-General Rabin was appointed Chief of Staff. He had a 'staff mind' and, being an experienced staff officer, he assembled and trained a good team at GHQ, overhauling existing contingency plans and producing additional ones. The Israeli General Staff was responsible for the general military policy and operations, the Chief of Staff being directly responsible to the Minister of Defence for all three services.

The IDF had a special relationship with the state, in that although the principle that the military must be subordinate to the civilian authority was generally accepted, there were exceptions to this rule. While in domestic affairs the army never interfered, the General Staff sometimes chose the time and place for reprisal raids–a freedom that had been allowed and perhaps even encouraged–by Ben-Gurion when Premier and Defence Minister. When Pinhas Lavon was Defence Minister he had tried to make the IDF completely subservient to his control and to reduce its independence in other ways, but he had been successfully opposed by the then Chief of Staff, Moshe Dayan. Eshkol, having complete faith in the General Staff, allowed this freedom to continue, merely endorsing any General Staff recommendations to retaliate against the Arabs. This was why so much notice was taken of any utterances by the Israeli Chief of Staff, which if publicly spoken by a Chief of Staff in a Western democracy would have resulted in his removal from office.

From north to south Israel was about 260 miles in length, being only 70 miles across at its widest point, 11 miles at the narrowest part of its waist near Nathanya, and tapering down to less than 6 miles at Eilat at the southern tip of the Negev. Having no depth it was unsuitable for defensive fighting, so the strategy evolved by the General Staff was to fight offensive battles outside its borders (especially in the empty Sinai against Egypt, regarded as the main enemy). Before 1955 the chief threats to Israel had been from Jordan and Syria, but this emphasis changed when the Soviet Union began supplying quantities of arms to Egypt and adopted a pro-Arab and anti-Israeli foreign policy. In 1956 only Egypt had been involved in the fighting, as Jordan and other adjacent Arab countries had cynically stood aside, their dissensions and instinct for individual survival outweighing ideals of Arab unity.

There was a general feeling in Israel that future hostilities might follow a similar pattern. King Hussein sat on a wobbling throne. The Syrian régime had difficulty in maintaining its position. The Israelis did not think the Syrians would advance from the security of their strong defensive positions, or that Jordan would order its two armoured brigades on the West Bank–no small threat in themselves–into action against them. The basic Israeli strategy was that of a holding defence against Jordan and Syria, and indeed the Lebanon if necessary, while the bulk of the Israeli forces moved swiftly against Egypt. Then, once Egypt was defeated, if circumstances permitted and it was desirable, Israeli troops would attack Jordan or Syria individually. The object was not to fight on more than one front at a time. This offensive Israeli strategy, it was realized, would be unpopular with the UN and certain world powers and would be subject to pressures from them, so the General Staff planned on the assumption that it would most probably have only three days available in which to fight before a cease-fire was forced on it by outside sources withholding money, goods, fuel and spares, and probably imposing other economic sanctions too. Therefore all Israeli mobile formations were equipped with three days' fuel and supplies, each brigade being self-contained with its own supply column following behind. The Israeli forces planned and trained for a three-day period of all-out fighting to be continued day and night, assuming that within that time and under such strains one side or the other must give. The contingency plans formulated or amended by General Rabin were all offensive ones. Moshe Dayan's appointment as Defence Minister made little difference to them;[1] he simply urged the views of the General Staff in the War Cabinet, which consisted of the Premier and the Ministers of Defence, Foreign Affairs, Information and Finance. The course of the war and objectives were selected by the Supreme Command Council, under the chairmanship of the Defence Minister and comprising senior General Staff officers and regional commanders.

---

[1] 'He [Moshe Dayan] introduced certain changes, extending the range of the Army's activities, notably in the direction of Sharm el Sheikh.' (*David's Sling.*)

As day succeeded day the main Israeli problem was to maintain full mobilization, which was severely hampering the country's economic life. Factories had either stopped work or were running at a low production rate; crops remained unharvested on under-manned farms. Once the Cabinet decision to strike at Egypt had been taken, it came as a relief to the General Staff, the IDF as a whole and the Government. Clearly, it had either to be war or a stand-down, and demobilization to any degree would have been interpreted by the Arabs as a weakness they could exploit.

With a population of 2,365,000 Jews,[1] the Israelis were able to mobilize a total force of about 264,000 within 72 hours. The mobilization could be by stages, depending upon the degree of emergency, and had been practised so many times that it was almost perfect. Key men, such as commanders, staff officers and signallers, were telephoned and fetched by vehicle, while code words issued over the radio were used to mobilize the remainder, each man knowing only his unit's particular code word. In this way some 150,000 men could be mustered within the first 24 hours. The soldier's uniform was kept at home, and he normally reported to a nearby collection centre, to be taken from there to a base camp where his unit assembled and was issued with arms and other equipment. Most brigade and battalion formations were territorially based so that they could mobilize quickly. If a reservist went to work in another part of the country he was, unless in a specialized formation such as the signals or artillery, transferred to the local reserve formation of his arm. Women formed about 30 per cent or slightly less of the total mobilized forces; mainly they were called up on the second and third days as drivers and clerks and for work in military stores and hospitals. No women served as combat personnel. A number of Druze volunteers were intermixed in Israeli units; Druze had served in the IDF since 1948 but at first they had been in all-Druze units.

In November 1966 Eshkol had announced that the period of conscript service (previously reduced to 26 months) would be restored to 30 months for men (it was 20 months for women). All single women were required to serve; indeed, there were remarkably few exemptions. After their basic service Israelis were

---

[1] There were about an additional 300,000 Arabs living in Israel. They were not subject to conscription, although the Druze were allowed to volunteer.

allocated to a reserve formation and recalled for up to 30 days' annual training for soldiers and up to 40 days for officers. They remained on the 'active reserve' until they were 45 (40 for women if still unmarried), after which they were either posted to home defence units or to the HAGA, retaining commitments of this nature until they reached 55. The HAGA (Haganah Ezrahit– Hebrew expression loosely meaning Civil Defence) was a kind of Civil Guard, with a multiplicity of home defence duties, manned by those who were over 42 or unfit for active service. At first the HAGA personnel were organized as air raid wardens, much on the British World War II pattern. Individuals, distinguished by their green berets and arm bands, were responsible for blocks of flats and streets, but later they took over other civil defence duties. They saw only limited action.

Israel had only a small cadre of regular officers and soldiers, numbering just over 2,000, but up to 72,000 conscripts in various stages of training and recalled reservists undergoing annual training were mobilized at any given time. Apart from the basic training centres scattered about the country there were usually seven brigades in existence, one paratroop, two armoured and four infantry. The brigade (equivalent to the American regiment) had been retained as the basic formation in the Israeli army; there were 31 brigades when fully mobilized. Of these 22 were infantry (two having a paratroop capability), each with an establishment of about 4,500 personnel; eight were armoured, each with about 3,500 men; and one was the paratroop brigade, which had a strength of over 4,500. Thus the 'teeth' element of the Israeli army amounted to just over 130,000 men, and about the same number of men and women were disposed in the 'administrative tail'. This ratio of about 50:50 compares with a more usual ratio of 20:80 in major armies of the world.

The armoured brigades were usually composed of two tank units and one of mechanized infantry carried in armoured half-tracks, with the normal sub-units of reconnaissance, support and supply. Infantry brigades were formed of three or more motorized infantry battalions, but only the regular brigades, and a proportion of the reserve ones, were equipped with armoured half-tracks; in the remainder the infantrymen were carried in wheeled vehicles. According to circumstances there were differences in the composition of individual brigades. Artillery units were some-times grouped together for a special task, or allocated out to brigades as thought necessary. The brigades were all numbered, and some additionally had acquired a name made famous in previous wars, such as the Harel or Golani Brigades. (For security reasons I have been asked not to quote their official designations, but to refer to them either by the name of the com-mander or by a letter; I have chosen a letter.)

Israel was divided for defence into three regional commands. The GOC (General Officer Commanding) Southern Command was Brigadier Yeshayshu Garvish, the GOC of Central Command was Brigadier Uzi Narkiss, and the GOC of Northern Command was Brigadier David Elazar. GHQ was at Ramat Gan, in Tel Aviv. Ranks were conventional and, of course, were Hebrew, but I shall refer to them throughout by the British or Western equivalent. The highest rank of any serving officer was that of 'Raf-Aluv', or major-general, held only by the current Chief of Staff.[1]

There was no formation higher than the brigade in the Israeli army, but a number of brigades could be grouped, for a special operation or task, into an impromptu division known as an 'Ugda', a Hebrew word that can be roughly translated as 'task group'. Senior officers whose jobs were temporarily in abeyance during the war were appointed to command the Ugdas as they were formed; these included Brigadier Sharon, Director of Training, Brigadier Elad Peled, Commandant at the National Defence College, and regional commanders such as Brigadier Narkiss. The small regular officer corps was highly trained and carefully selected. Most officers were expected to retire at about the age of 40, or shortly afterwards, to take up a second career in civilian life. This system ensured that the IDF remained a young and vigorous organization.

Unable to manufacture its own sophisticated major military equipment, modern aircraft, tanks[2] and heavy artillery, Israel was dependent on the whims of major foreign countries. Much Israeli

---

[1] Since then the Chief of Staff has been made a lieutenant-general, and a number of brigadiers have been promoted to major-general.

[2] Since then Israel has produced the 'Shoot Kal', a fast tank with a 105-mm gun, which came into production late in 1970.

equipment was old, some even of World War II vintage. Obtained from any source that would supply it, it simply had to be kept in service so it was maintained with extreme care. Britain, anxious to keep the tenuous balance of arms in the Middle East, had periodically supplied material, as had America, although less generously. Premier Ben-Gurion's friendship with President de Gaulle, at a time when France was involved in the Algerian insurrection and Nasser was supporting the Algerian rebels, resulted in quantities of equipment, especially aircraft, being sent to Israel by France. Premier Eshkol, Ben-Gurion's successor, disliked placing total reliance upon any single power; in any case France would only supply items for cash, with payment usually in advance, so he visited President Johnson in 1964 and managed to some extent to soften American reluctance to send arms to Israel.

The Israeli Government wanted to obtain arms from the West German armaments industry, but Arab pressure was strong against this so West Germany decided to make reparations in cash. Israel then purchased arms from certain countries, especially France, and the West Germans paid the reparation money direct to that country instead of to Israel. This arrangement caused Egypt to break off diplomatic relations with West Germany. Hesitation and delay occurred in arms deals with Israel. For example, America had first agreed to sell HAWK missiles in October 1962, but they did not arrive in Israel until April 1965. In February 1966 America reluctantly confirmed that it had been supplying Patton tanks to Israel for some time; they were, in fact, those discarded by West Germany when America began supplying that country with the more modern M-60s. Because West Germany refused to send them direct to Israel, America had had to act as the middleman.

Israel had developed an industry to produce lesser items of military equipment and arms, and was turning out small mortars and bombs in quantity. The Israelis had ample 120-mm mortars, Uzi sub-machine guns and small arms ammunition, and they were assembling military vehicles under licence. Premier Ben-Gurion had made plans for Israel to produce its own anti-aircraft missiles as well but this project was cancelled by Eshkol when he became Premier as he thought they could be bought cheaper abroad. The country also had a strong armoured force of about 800 tanks, mainly of British, American and French origin—in round figures about 250 Centurions, 200 M-48 Pattons, 150 AMX-13s and 200 Super-Shermans. All these had been modified for desert warfare; and if variations can be counted the Israelis had in all ten different types of tank in service, so the problem of maintenance and spares was a complex one. The British Centurions were both Mark 5s and Mark 6s, and had been fitted with a 105-mm gun[1] a few months before June 1967. A stabilizing device enabled the gun to remain steady no matter how rough the terrain, an immense advantage in a quick-moving tank battle. With a radius of action of about 60 miles, the Centurion's speed was just over 20 mph and its weight about 50 tons. The M-48 Patton, with a high velocity 90-mm gun, was considered one of the most powerful tanks in the Middle East; with a speed up to 35 mph, it had for some years been the sole battle tank in the US Army, only being replaced by the M-60 when it was thought that the Soviet T-54 might be superior to it in some ways. It weighed about 45 tons, mounted a 12·7-mm anti-aircraft gun and had an infrared periscope. The AMX-13 was a light French tank, weighing about 14·5 tons, mounting a 75-mm gun and having a speed of about 35 mph. During this war the Israeli AMX-13 was seen to be fitted with a 'pod-like' object on its side, believed to be an aiming aid, which journalists were not allowed to inspect. Certainly the AMX-13 did some spectacular shooting at distances of up to one mile. This type of tank carried French SS10 or SS11 guided anti-tank missiles, and some were fitted with a 40-mm gun instead of the 75-mm one. The Israeli Super-Sherman was basically the old World War II American 30-ton M-4 tank, which had been equipped with a more powerful engine, broader tracks to obtain better purchase in sand, and a 76-mm gun. It had a speed of about 25 mph. The Super-Shermans and the AMXs were with the reserve armoured brigades, although the light, speedy and manoeuvrable AMXs usually formed the base of the reconnaissance units in most brigades, even infantry ones, together with locally-assembled Jeeps mounting the 106-mm recoilless rifle. The 106-mm recoilless rifles and the SS10s and SS11s were also mounted on other vehicles. In addition to its

---

[1] Originally fitted with a quick-firing 20-pounder gun.

approximately 800 tanks, Israel also possessed about 250 self-propelled guns, which were mainly 155-mm howitzers mounted on the M-4 Sherman chassis, and the AMX-13s, fitted with a 105-mm howitzer. About 300 armoured half-tracks completed the list of Israeli armoured vehicles. They were the American M-3 of World War II vintage which had the rear part of the vehicle resting on small rubber tracks and the front part on two front wheels that steered it. This concept had been abandoned by most major armies as it was considered that such vehicles combined the disadvantages of both tracked and wheeled vehicles without any compensating advantages, and also because they were open-topped, leaving the personnel in them without any overhead protection. Despite this, the half-track was the favourite Israeli war vehicle, used extensively as mobile command posts and for carrying infantry within armoured brigades.

Like Egypt, Israel had also experimented with rockets. Its first, known as Shavit II, was fired on 5 July 1961, beating the Egyptians by about a year. The Shavit II was an unguided, multi-stage meteorological rocket, which rose to a height of about 50 miles and made Israel the seventh nation to launch a rocket into space. The Israeli rocket development programme fell (as did the Egyptian) into difficulties, mainly concerning, it is believed, directional devices.

Israel had a nuclear research programme in operation. In 1959 Premier Ben-Gurion had persuaded President de Gaulle to build an atomic reactor in Israel. The French President imposed no conditions as to its use, perhaps because he was bridling at the many safeguards the existing nuclear powers tried to impose on French nuclear development. This reactor, able to transform uranium into plutonium, was constructed at Dimona, in the Negev, in complete secrecy, and it was some time before the Americans came to know about it. Uranium had been discovered in small quantities in the Dead Sea phosphates, and the Israelis eventually admitted that their reactor would be able to produce enough plutonium to make about one nuclear warhead a year. A security blanket lies heavily on this project. Probably by 5 June 1967 the Israelis possessed one or two nuclear warheads, but the devices and the techniques of delivery remained untested. The Egyptians alleged that the means to wage biological and chemical warfare were being developed at the Israeli Weizmann Institute at Rehovat, but while the Israelis were certainly advanced in many forms of scientific research it was doubtful whether they had gone to such extremes.

One big advantage that Israel possessed over its Arab adversaries was an extremely efficient intelligence system. Some 75,000 Jews still resident in Arab countries,[1] fluent in Arabic and usually able to pass themselves off as Arabs, formed a sound basis for espionage which was exploited to the full. On the other hand, few Arabs knew Hebrew or could pass as Israelis. Further, the Middle East had always swarmed with individuals willing to sell information, and the Israeli Intelligence Service had sifted through them to employ the best agents available. The centralized and skilfully conducted Israeli intelligence efforts were single-purposed, designed solely to safeguard their country from attack. As its agents had penetrated the defence ministries and armed forces of the adjacent Arab countries, they could gain an up-to-date and accurate picture of the Arab order of battle, equipment, strategy, tactics and intentions. Israel was able to obtain details of minefields, so that valuable maps could be produced, and to detect the 'blind spots' in Egypt's radar defensive system. But good as this intelligence system was, it was not perfect; the Israelis did not know that Egypt and Syria possessed Soviet 160-mm computer-operated cannon, which in June 1967 had not even been shown on a Soviet Army Day Parade in Moscow. In contrast the many Arab intelligence systems overlapped and, being mainly devoted to preserving or toppling an existing régime, were as much political as military.

---

[1] The 2,250,000 Jews in the Soviet Union were not allowed any official contact with any Zionist or Israeli organization.

CHAPTER 4

The Air War

The actual start of the Third Arab-Israeli War was marked by a
carefully planned, frequently rehearsed and extraordinarily well
co-ordinated surprise attack[1] by the Israeli Air Force on Egyptian
airfields and aircraft. It had astounding and devastating success,
much more so than the competent, realistic and clear-thinking
Israeli General Staff had ever dared to hope. This sudden and
massive aerial assault had a most decisive influence on the
subsequent course of the war, leaving ultimate Israeli victory in
little doubt. Before recounting and analysing the events of the
Air War, the Israeli Air Force and the air forces of the Arab
states involved will be briefly described.

THE ISRAELI AIR FORCE

During the War of Independence in 1948 the Israelis had few
aircraft and after this war they experienced considerable difficulty
in obtaining planes of any sort from suspicious world powers.
However, a few were accumulated by dubious means, including
some British Hurricanes and Spitfires and some German Messer-
schmitts from the (then) sympathetic Czechs. These enabled the
infant conventional Israeli Air Force to emerge. After a pause the
wavering foreign policies of certain world powers caused them to
dole out a few aircraft to Israel, but in numbers far short of those
required by Israel for defence against potential Arab aggressors.
It was not until France became deeply involved in the Algerian
insurrection, when Egyptian help and encouragement were given
to the Algerian Nationalists, that French friendship and co-
operation with Israel developed, enabling the Israeli Air Force to

---

[1] The term 'pre-emptive attack' is preferred by the Israelis, which indicates
the high ability of their Public Relations Directorate as it dispels any odium that
may attach to expressions such as 'Striking the first blow', 'Catching the enemy
off guard', 'A sneak attack' or 'Hitting Nasser when he was asleep'.

expand appreciably. In 1956 French aircraft and arms were sent to Israel in some quantity, although some Ouragans had been received earlier. At the time of the Sinai Campaign (30 October–4 November 1956) Israeli-French co-operation was at its height. The first French Mystères (Mark IV) had already arrived in Israel between April and August 1958. Then, receiving its first Mirage jets in 1960, the Israeli Air Force visibly expanded until by 1967 well over half its aircraft were French, the remainder being mainly home-assembled Fouga Magisters.

About half the Israeli defence budget (of over £150 million) was allocated to the Air Force, which indicated the priority accorded it. There had been many behind-the-scene defence arguments over the years as to whether large proportions of the limited money available should be spent on aircraft or on armoured fighting vehicles, but the 'air faction' had made its case. The fantastic development costs of modern jet aircraft, beyond the reach of the country's economy, had obliged Israel to purchase abroad, but a start had been made with its own aircraft industry. In 1952 a jet plane assembly factory had been set up in Israel by the French firm of Fouga which, commencing in 1962, began to turn out adaptations of the standard French Fouga Magister, but these alone were inadequate for the country's defence.

The Israeli Air Force was not an independent service, but came under the firm control of the General Staff. Commanded by Brigadier Mordecai Hod, Chief of the Air Staff, the strength of the regular element of the Air Force was about 8,000 of whom some 1,200 were pilots, or pilots in training. In emergencies this number was supplemented by a similar number of skilled reservists for ground and maintenance tasks. When fully mobilized, including the essential civilian support, the Israeli Air Force amounted to nearly 20,000. Israel possessed about 450 aircraft of all sorts, including helicopters, and its '350 front-line aircraft' were disposed into 13 squadrons–four of interceptors, five of fighter-bombers, two of transport aircraft and two of helicopters. Israel had no strategic bomber force as such, mainly perhaps because it had no long-range bombers; as most of its aircraft had a radius of action of 400 miles or less, large portions of Egypt, Iraq and Saudi Arabia were beyond effective Israeli reach.

Broken down to individual types, in round figures[1] Israel possessed 20 Super Mystères, 40 Mystères Mark IVA, 73 Mirage Mark IIIJs, 48 Ouragans, 60 Fouga Magisters, 25 Vatour IIAs, 20 Noratlas and Stratocruiser transport aircraft, and 25 helicopters that included three Super Frelons, as well as Sikorski UH34s and Alouettes. There were additionally a few miscellaneous aircraft, such as an assortment of liaison and observation planes. It is of interest to note that the French Air Force had just 'lent' 20 Super Mystère aircraft to Israel for 'training purposes'. Flown by Israeli pilots, these were used in the war, being duly returned to France afterwards, and are not included in these figures.

The French Super Mystères were the fastest and most modern aircraft the Israelis possessed, and were the only ones they considered technically a match for the Egyptian-piloted MiG-21s. The Super Mystères, fighter-bombers armed with two 30 mm cannon, equipped with air-to-air missiles and fitted with both rockets and napalm tanks, were grouped together in one squadron. This was the first West European aircraft capable of supersonic speeds in level flight.[2] About 60 French Mystère IVAs had been supplied to Israel in 1957, and at least 40 of them were still in service. French production had ceased in 1958. Classed as a ground-attack fighter, the Mystère IVA, a turbo-jet armed with two 30-mm cannon, carried bombs and napalm tanks. The single-seater French Dassault Mirage Mark IIIs, the first of which were delivered to Israel in May 1963, were delta-wing supersonic fighters, armed with two 30-mm cannon and having a speed of Mach 2·1. Grouped together into three squadrons, they were a multi-mission aircraft capable of both high-level interception and ground attack, and they had the advantage of being able to operate from comparatively short and rough airstrips. Having a combat radius of action of nearly 400 miles, the Mirage Mark IIIs were the only interceptor possessed by the Israelis capable of challenging the Egyptian MiG-21s.[3] The Israeli-assembled

---

[1] There is always a slight variation in figures such as these, as sources differ. Israeli security is good, and in several instances corrections or official figures have been refused.

[2] *Interavia*, Number 11/1967.

[3] The Israelis were pinning their interceptor hopes for the future on the 50 French Mirage Vs they had ordered and paid for (but never received), and the American A4 Skyhawks, ordered in 1966, but still not received in June 1967.

Fouga Magisters, tandem two-seater trainers, were strengthened and modified to carry bombs, rockets and napalm tanks, and were used almost exclusively in a ground-support role. The Ouragan, an obsolescent French aircraft, was the oldest fighter-bomber in service with the Israeli Air Force; it had four 20-mm cannon and could carry a bomb-load of over 2,000 lb. The French single-seater, swept-wing Vatour IIAs were an all-weather multi-mission ground-attack bomber, capable of carrying a 4,000-lb bomb load. These twin-jet aircraft, armed with four 30-mm cannon, were grouped into one squadron. The French Nord 2501, the Noratlas, was a medium transport aircraft, able to carry 45 fully-equipped soldiers or 18 stretcher cases. Vehicles and freight were loaded through a rear loading door. The American Stratocruiser, Boeing 377, was also able to carry personnel and freight, which were likewise loaded through a rear door. This aircraft was used extensively to drop paratroops and to air-drop supplies to forces on the ground in the forward areas.

Of the helicopters possessed by Israel the largest was the French Sud 321, the Super Frelon, medium-sized, for general purposes, and able to carry a payload of over 9,000 lb. Having a radius of action of nearly 300 miles and a crew of two, it could lift at a time 30 fully-equipped soldiers or 15 stretcher cases. Initially in this war it was used by the Israelis chiefly to carry assaulting troops into action, and then later for casualty evacuation. Israel had a few Sikorski S55s, a helicopter used extensively by US troops during the Korean War. They also had some American Sikorski UH-34 (S-58),[1] a scaled-up version of the S55, which was a utility helicopter with a radius of action of about 140 miles. Able to lift 18 fully-equipped troops, or eight stretcher cases, it was used for casualty evacuation from the forward battle zone, for lifting paratroops and ferrying supplies forward. The smaller French Alouette, able to transport four passengers besides the pilot, was used mainly as a command, communication and reconnaissance helicopter. It had a radius of action of about 220 miles and could lift a payload of about 1,400 lb.

Air-to-air missiles were fitted to a number of Israeli aircraft, especially the Mystères. They included the French Matra R530,

---

[1] Known in Britain as the Wessex.

which had a 60-lb warhead, an infrared homing device and a range of about 11 miles, and the French Nord AS30, which was also a heat-homing missile with a larger warhead of about 500 lb. The two units of American HAWK[1] missiles were under Air Force command. The HAWK is a small ground-to-air missile, designed to be effective against low-level attacks, having a 'slant' range of up to 22 miles and being effective as low down as 100 feet.

Additionally the Israelis had a rocket-boosted bomb for cracking the hard surface of concrete runways; later it was given prominence as a 'secret weapon' as its effectiveness was suddenly appreciated and perhaps over-played. However, it was not exclusive to Israel; several other nations had experimented with a similar device and some may indeed be developing one today. Becoming known as the Concrete Dibber Bomb,[2] it was originally a design study of Engins Matra of France, and had simply been further developed by the Israelis. About 0·3 of a second after this bomb was released from the aircraft a retro-rocket was fired and a cruciform drogue chute opened to bring the bomb to its correct penetration angle; then booster rockets drove it into the ground, the force enabling it to penetrate hard surfaces when conventional bombs might bounce off at an angle. It was also used with a fuse timed to explode some while after it had been driven into the ground. Having a 365-lb warhead, these bombs were fitted to Vatours and Mirages, which were able to make effective use of them when running in over the target at less than 600 mph and at heights of only 200 feet. Other Israeli aircraft used conventional 250-lb, 500-lb and even 1,000-lb bombs.

Because of the small size of its territory as compared with adjacent Arab countries, Israel was particularly vulnerable from the air. The majority of its some 20 airfields and major airstrips, most of them inherited from the British, were huddled together within a small radius in the centre of the country near its narrow waist. Only a few names of airfields have been released by the Israelis, and those only perhaps because they are so obvious to tourists that they cannot be concealed, but a British Ordnance Survey map of Palestine, dating from World War II or just a little later, shows them all. The Israelis simply took them over and gave

---

[1] Homing All the Way Killer.
[2] 'Concrete Dibber Bomb.' (*Jane's All the World Aircraft 1968–69.*)

53

most of them new Hebrew names. A few new airstrips had been constructed in the Negev, such as that at Hatzerim.

Israeli defence against aerial attack was weak, largely because the country was too narrow and small for an effective radar network that would give a workable warning time. For example, Tel Aviv was only about four and a half minutes' flying time from El Arish, while from Tel Aviv to Cairo the flight took only about 25 minutes. The HAWK ground-to-air missiles were few (reckoned to be about 50), of which half were dispersed to protect the nuclear plant at Dimona in the Negev, and the remainder were placed just south of Tel Aviv. In view of this disadvantage Israeli strategy was based on aerial attack as the main defence. The Air Force's primary task was to gain immediate air superiority, both to protect Israeli territory from raiding Arab aircraft and to provide an 'air umbrella' under which Israeli ground forces could operate freely. The doctrine of a massive surprise attack on Arab (especially Egyptian) airfields had been firmly adopted by the Israeli Air Force, which was convinced that Israel could best be defended over Cairo. Moreover, it had planned and frequently practised this against mock enemy airfields in the wilderness of the Negev for many years.[1]

One of the principal architects of the Israeli Air Force was Brigadier Ezer Weizmann. Chief of Operations in 1966 and formerly for eight years Chief of the Air Staff, to him belongs much of the credit for forging such a splendid instrument as the Israeli Air Force proved to be. He had devised and perfected the massive aerial assault plan, and his good work was continued by his successor, Brigadier Hod, who further sharpened the weapon.

The pilots were the cream of Israel's young men, who trained for three years before qualifying as fully operational pilots. They were dedicated professionals, being mainly long-service regulars who enlisted at 18 for a minimum period of five years. All had an impressive number of flying hours to their credit, and although their average age was only 23, many had been flying continuously for up to five years. Their morale was tremendously high. Unlike Egypt, Israel had a surplus of pilots. Great emphasis was placed

---

[1] 'For 16 years we lived with the plan, we slept with the plan, we ate with the plan. Constantly we perfected it.' Brigadier Hod at a press conference in Tel Aviv in June 1967.

in training on accurate cannon shooting at ground targets, precision bombing, navigation and low flying. Pilots had individually practised these techniques in uninhabited parts of the Negev on model enemy target sites.[1] Large-scale practices were held every four months and annually there was one involving practically all Israeli aircraft in a mass attack; wave after wave of aircraft struck at 'enemy targets' to give the crews experience in timing, control co-ordination, refuelling, turn-round techniques, and accuracy of bombing and shooting. Live bombs and ammunition were used. For many months a group of Israeli pilots was briefed weekly on the state of their pre-selected targets in Egypt.

In August 1966, after sending a note to say he was coming, a Christian Iraqi pilot in a MiG-21 defected to Israel. He claimed that as a Christian he was discriminated against in Iraq. Thus the Israeli Air Force got its hands on what was then one of the most modern Soviet aircraft in Arab possession. In fact, it was the first of its kind that certain Western powers, by courtesy of Israel, were able to examine at close quarters. This stroke of luck meant that not only were Israeli pilots able to test the capabilities of a MiG-21, but also to practise against it in mock aerial combat. In short, Israeli pilots had practical experience with, and against, the best aircraft the Arabs could put into the air, which proved a distinct advantage when it came to actual dog-fights.

Emphasis was placed on training ground and maintenance crews in rapid refuelling, replenishing ammunition and servicing aircraft, so that the turn-round time was cut to about 10 minutes, compared with the half-hour which most major air forces considered safe. Most ground staff were regulars, and their aircraft's serviceability and turn-round time were matters of individual pride and national concern. It was estimated that during the war the serviceability of Israeli aircraft was over 90 per cent at any given moment.[2]

---

[1] The Jordanians allege that the two Israeli pilots taken prisoner by them said that 'they had been training for a year and a half on models that were exact replicas of the objectives they each would have to attack'. (*My 'War' with Israel.*)

[2] After the war Brigadier Hod claimed that at the beginning his aircraft had a 99 per cent serviceability, which was maintained throughout, and that no aircraft was on the ground being repaired or patched up for more than one hour. This is probably too high an estimate and later reports indicate that a truer percentage was nearer 90—which, of course, was extremely high by any standards.

THE EGYPTIAN AIR FORCE

Commanded by Lieutenant-General Mahmoud Sidki, an experienced officer, the Egyptian Air Force was larger than that of Israel, but it differed in being made up almost entirely of Soviet aircraft. A large proportion was quite modern, as in 1958 the Soviet Union began to supply supersonic aircraft, such as MiG-21s and Sukhoi-7Bs. Like the Israelis, Nasser had tried to develop an aircraft industry, but with little success. In 1950 the Egyptians had produced a small trainer, the Goumhouria, but it was not very robust. In 1962, with Spanish and German technical assistance, a grandiose plan was announced to develop and produce a supersonic fighter, the HA 300, but no visible progress was made. A few other prototypes were produced, all pale copies of existing Soviet or foreign aircraft. The infant Egyptian aircraft industry, like other Egyptian armament projects, was deliberately stifled by the Soviet Union to prevent Nasser becoming too independent in this sphere. The Air Force consisted of about 20,000 personnel, practically all regulars, and it possessed about 450 combat aircraft. Broken down by types, the Egyptians had about 120 MiG-21s, 80 MiG-19s, 180 MiG-17s and MiG-15s, 20 SU-7s, 30 TU-16s and 40 Ilyushin-28s. There were also about 90 transport aircraft; these included 60 Ilyushin-14s and 25 Anatov-12s, as well as about 60 helicopters, of which there were at least 12 Mi-6s and 20 Mi-4s. About 120 mixed trainer aircraft were available, some of which could be armed and used in battle. It was estimated that about 60 of these aircraft were still in the Yemen, and should be deducted from the overall totals.

The MiG[1] series were developments of the original MiG-15, a single-seater jet fighter, armed with two 23-mm cannon, that made its appearance during the Korean War. The MiG-17 was simply an improved version, while the MiG-19 was a fast, twin jet-engined fighter, armed with two 37-mm and two 23-mm cannons: the first to go supersonic in level flight. The delta-wing MiG-21, a short-range fighter, carrying two air-to-air missiles, was the most modern aircraft the Egyptians possessed, and was firmly believed by them to be more than a match for the Israeli

---

[1] Compounded from the initial letters in the names of its two designers, Mikoyan and Gurevich.

Super-Mystères, but it had a radius of action of only 200 miles. The single-seater Sukhoi-7B was a swept-wing fighter armed with two 30-mm cannon, able to carry both bombs and rockets. The Ilyushin-28, with a bomb load of up to 10,000 lb, was a standard Soviet twin-jet light bomber which formed the backbone of the Egyptian strategic bomber force, its radius of action being about 850 miles. These were supplemented by the more modern TU-16s,[1] twin turbojet aircraft classed as medium reconnaissance bombers and capable of carrying a bomb load of up to 20,000 lb. Having a crew of seven, they were armed with up to seven 23-mm cannon, the rear two being radar-controlled, and they carried air-to-air missiles and anti-shipping missiles.[2] The TU-16s were the bombers regarded apprehensively by the Israelis as, with a radius of action of 2,200 miles, they out-ranged any aircraft the Israelis possessed. In the transport class the Ilyushin-14 was a piston-engined, light transport aircraft. The Antonov-12 was the standard Soviet military load-carrier, able to lift 100 troops and carry tracked and wheeled vehicles. Having a radius of action of 1,000 miles, it had a payload of 44,000 lb and could be used for dropping paratroops or stores. The Mi-6[3] was the largest helicopter in the world, able to carry 70 fully equipped soldiers. Its radius of action was 200 miles, it had a crew of five, and it could lift a payload of 40,000 lb. The Mi-4 was a smaller helicopter, with a crew of two, that could carry 14 troops or small vehicles, its payload being 3,800 lb.

The Egyptian Air Force operated from about 25 airfields,[4] the majority clustered around Cairo and in the Delta region; the others were in northern Sinai and more widely dispersed into the southern and western parts of Egypt. Cairo and the Delta were protected by a radar warning system whose installations extended right into the Sinai. In the event of attack by the Israeli Air Force, the Egyptian Air Staff planned to hold back the bulk of its interceptors for the immediate defence of its cities and airfields, and to use its strategic bomber force for retaliatory raids into

---

[1] Tupelov.

[2] The NATO code-name is KENNEL.

[3] From the name of the designer, Mikhail Mil.

[4] King Hussein speaks of '32 Arabian bases' in the Arab countries involved. (*My 'War' with Israel*.)

Israel. Its bombers had a far longer radius of action and carried heavier bomb loads than any Israeli aircraft, so on the face of things the Egyptians had the technical advantage in any counter-bombing contest. Israeli vulnerable targets, such as cities and industrial complexes, were more concentrated. Hard blows against them would disrupt the government and economy of the country, and might indeed cripple the capability of Israel to continue a war. On the other hand, although four million Egyptians lived in Cairo, generally the population, airfields and industry were more widely dispersed, and it was doubtful whether bombing alone would knock Egypt out of a war. In short, the main strategic concept was to harass and destroy Israeli airfields and protect its own.

In addition to the conventional Egyptian anti-aircraft capability, Egypt had about 150 SAM-2[1] missiles on about 18 sites, to protect the main airfields within range of an Israeli air strike; but only one near Bir Gifgafa, however, was on the east side of the Suez Canal. These were in a special command, firmly under Soviet control. The SAM-2s were the standard Soviet air defence missile, designed to bring down aircraft flying at medium and high altitudes. This two-stage missile had a warhead weighing 288 lb and automatic radio command guidance; the target was tracked by radar, it had a 'slant range' of about 28 miles and a ceiling of about 60,000 feet. It was not very effective against low-flying aircraft, being slow to get off the launching pad and slow to accelerate initially.

Like the Israelis, the Egyptians had offensive aerial plans which they practised periodically, although not with the same thoroughness and intensity. These plans catered for surprise air strikes on all Israeli airfields and certain military installations. They also had plans to bomb Israeli cities such as Tel Aviv, Haifa and Eilat, but it is thought that they intended only to put them into operation if the Israelis first bombed, or seemed about to bomb, Egyptian population centres. After the war the Israelis produced captured documents, one of them an Egyptian battle

---

[1] This is the American designation, SAM meaning Surface-to-Air Missile. The NATO code-name is Guideline. The Soviet designation for the missile itself is V750VK, and for the whole missile system V78SM. (*Jane's All the World Aircraft 1968–69.*)

order, dated 18 May 1967, which called for '27 fighter-bomber sorties and three light-bomber sorties' to support the land forces detailed to cut into the southern Negev to capture Eilat. Another captured document, signed by the Chief of Staff, Eastern Air Region (that is the Sinai), gave a list of Israeli targets and their priorities around Eilat. The Egyptian Air Force had completely separate channels of command and communication from the ground forces, the only close liaison between the two being at high-level headquarters. Orders for aerial operations went from the Supreme Command Council to the Chief of Operations at GHQ, and thence direct downwards to the Chiefs of Staff at each subsequent operational or field headquarters.

A notable feature was the huge transport capability the Egyptians had developed to drop paratroops, lift troops forward and keep them supplied by air. It was estimated, for example, that the Egyptian Air Force was able to drop some 3,000 paratroops in one flight, and to follow this up shortly afterwards with another of 4,000 troops and 600 tons of stores. None of the Egyptian aircraft was equipped for a night ground support role.

Egypt had an acute shortage of pilots as the sudden expansion of its Air Force had outpaced their training. There were about 500 trained pilots, just about enough to fly all the aircraft Egypt possessed, but this meant that although approximately another 100 were in various stages of training, none was in reserve for any emergency. The Israelis later issued figures indicating that Egypt at the outbreak of war had only 350 trained pilots; this must refer to combat pilots only, as opposed to pilots of transport and other aircraft, including helicopters. The training techniques and procedures, the aerial strategy and tactics, were those of the Soviet Air Force and were taught by the large Soviet Military Mission and training teams. Contrary to the impression that has since become current, the standard of training of the Egyptian pilots was fairly good, although as the medium was English the instruction lost something in the translation. The Soviet instructors certainly told their pupils that they were good; basking in this praise, the Egyptian pilots considered themselves more than a match for their Israeli opposite numbers. Their morale was high and they had great confidence in themselves and their aircraft. Some observers have said, although usually in retrospect, that their standard of training was rather indifferent and that Egyptian pilots tended to lack that aggressiveness so essential for successful aerial combat, but as so few of them had the opportunity to prove themselves in battle these views must be treated with reserve. A Soviet report, later produced by the Israelis, showed that on 26 May 1967, when Soviet inspection teams checked Egyptian airfields, they found that some Egyptian pilots had not been airborne for days, that the dummy aircraft on or near runways were unconvincing, and that the real aircraft were often massed so vulnerably together as to make good targets. Perhaps these were merely harsh routine training comments designed to keep the Egyptians up to scratch, that could be applied to the Israelis to a lesser degree. Both the Israelis and the Egyptians used dummy aircraft, usually balloon-like rubber replicas that could quickly be inflated and deflated. A proportion of the Egyptian pilots, perhaps one-third or slightly more, had flown on active service in the Yemen, but as the Yemeni Royalists had no air force, they had not been engaged in aerial combat but merely on bombing and reconnaissance missions. Even so they had suffered losses from ground fire, which inclined them to fly high over their targets and not to linger over enemy territory.

Soviet training teams had instructed Egyptian ground crews in Soviet techniques. Their aim of a two-hour turn-round for an aircraft between sorties had largely been achieved and was considered adequate. In fact, ground crews had reached a fairly high state of efficiency, although it was estimated that up to 20 per cent of Egyptian aircraft were not serviceable on 5 June 1967. The situation was ascribed mainly to unfamiliarity with the new types of Soviet aircraft, and only to a lesser extent to poor maintenance. The hot, dry climate certainly added to this unserviceability in machines designed to operate in Russian sub-zero temperatures.

THE JORDANIAN AIR FORCE

The Jordanian Air Force was extremely small and was acutely short of pilots. According to King Hussein[1] it had 22 Hawker Hunters with only 16 pilots available. In fact, it additionally had three Doves, three Dakotas and three helicopters.

---

[1] *Sunday Telegraph*, 15 September 1968.

The British Hawker Hunter is a ground-attack fighter aircraft which carries bombs, rockets or napalm, and is supersonic in a shallow dive. With four 30-mm cannon, its main characteristic is its superb manoeuvrability. The British Dove is a light, two-engined transport plane, able to carry about six passengers or the equivalent weight in freight.

In November 1966 America had promised to deliver to Jordan 36 F104 Lockheed Starfighters in June 1967, but at the outbreak of war they had not arrived. A number of Jordanian pilots were training in Britain and America. The training, tactics, techniques and ground maintenance methods were modelled mainly on the RAF pattern. However, six F104s, with US instructors, had reached Amman airfield, the first on which Jordanian pilots were to train. Hussein states that he sensed the danger to them, and asked for them to be removed from Jordan; the Americans were reluctant to comply because they thought there was no danger. Hussein persuaded them and the aircraft were removed from Amman on the afternoon of 4 June.[1] Having a strength of about 2,000 personnel, the Jordanian Air Force was largely centred on its two major airfields at Mafraq and Amman. About half-a-dozen smaller airstrips were scattered about the country. Its strategy was to take part in limited bombing operations of certain Israeli military targets in conjunction with the Syrian and Iraqi Air Forces. A British radar defence system had recently been set up in Jordan. The main radar installation, sited at Mount Ajlun, near Jerash, was intended to give warning of an Israeli attack so that Hawker Hunters could intercept it over Jordanian territory. In the past the Jordanian Air Force had been shaken by defections of senior officers to other Arab countries, and its morale was accordingly uncertain. King Hussein was trying to rebuild it.

THE IRAQI AIR FORCE

The Iraqi Air Force, with a strength of about 10,000, was equipped with some 220 aircraft, about half Soviet and half British, which included 60 MiG-21s, 15 MiG-17s, 15 MiG-15s, 6 TU-16s and 10 Ilyushin-28s. It also had 50 British Hawker

---

[1] *My 'War' with Israel.*

Hunters and 20 Provost trainer aircraft, two squadrons (about 26) of British Wessex helicopters and approximately 40 mixed British and Soviet transport planes. Training and techniques were a mixture of British and Soviet methods. The Iraqi Air Force had only just enough pilots to fly the aircraft it possessed. Many had seen active service during the Kurdish Rebellion, which had spasmodically been in progress for some six years. Iraq had a small strategic bomber force, whose strategy was to take part, with other Arab air forces, in raids into Israel should war break out, and to keep its fighter and interceptor planes at home to protect its own cities and airfields.

THE SYRIAN AIR FORCE

The Syrian Air Force had a strength of roughly 9,000 men, with about 120 Soviet aircraft including 20 MiG-21s, 20 MiG-19s, 60 MiG-17s, six Ilyushin-28s, a few transport and trainer aircraft and some helicopters. Soviet techniques and tactics were being taught to pilots and ground crews, but the Soviet training teams had made little progress towards efficiency and Syria too had a chronic shortage of trained pilots. Syrian strategy in case of war with Israel was to use its tiny bomber force in conjunction with other Arab air forces, to hit targets in Israel, and to keep back its fighters for home defence. Morale was shaken by previous losses in action against Israelis. SAM-2 missile sites were under construction, but none was activated in time.

THE INITIAL ISRAELI AIR STRIKES

Monday, 5 June 1967

The political decision having been taken, the time selected to make the massive aerial strike at Egyptian airfields was 0745 (0845 Egyptian time).[1] The Israeli General Staff calculated that it had about four hours in which to destroy or neutralize the Egyptian Air Force before it might have to turn and face the air forces of Syria, Iraq and perhaps other Arab states. The time was shrewdly

---

[1] All times mentioned are Israeli local time unless otherwise stated.

chosen as the moment when the Egyptians would be least on their guard. The usual dawn stand-to, when flights of MiGs, with their engines warmed up, waited poised on the end of runways ready to take off, and when other flights were actually airborne at high altitudes ready to pounce on intruders,[1] was over, and most pilots and ground crews were breakfasting. The ground mist was dense until about 0730, but began to clear at about 0745. By 0800 it had cleared completely.

Senior Egyptian commanders, officers and key executive personnel had not reached their offices. The Israeli pilots, who anticipated a long day ahead, had been able to have a good night's sleep. Another advantage to Israel, although not anticipated and taken into account by them, was that Field-Marshal Amer, with the Commander of the Air Force, had intended to fly that morning from Cairo to visit the airfield at Thamed and to start a tour of inspection. To ensure his safety instructions had been given not to open fire on any aircraft over the Sinai. There had been a state of 'constant alert' in the early morning of the 3rd and 4th, but not on the 5th.[2] Further, the Egyptians had always conventionally assumed that in any such attack Israeli aircraft would first try to hit the radar installations to black out this warning system, which would be a form of warning in itself; unconventionally, the Israelis had chosen to ignore the radar stations all the morning. Lastly, elaborate electronic deception tactics were used by the Israelis, of which no details have yet been released. At 0730 the Ilyushin-14, carrying Field-Marshal Amer and his party, appeared on the Israeli radar screens just as Israeli aircraft were setting out for their targets. This caused some concern to Brigadier Hod as it might have been a reconnaissance flight that would within minutes detect the mass of attacking aircraft and warn the Egyptian Air Force and air defences. However, this did not occur. Once aware of the situation, the pilot sought altitude to get above the battle.

Under cover of a high 'air umbrella' of about 40 Mirages, the

---

[1] According to Brigadier Hod, the Egyptians had sent a patrol of 12 planes to the Israeli border at dawn (about 0400) and this was followed by three others, each of 12 MiGs, at half-hour intervals over the Mediterranean and the Suez Canal. (*Paris-Match.*)

[2] Brigadier Hod.

first Israeli wave of about 40 aircraft, mainly Mystères in small groups, each of four aircraft acting in separate pairs, struck at nine airfields. Some Israeli Mystères flew in very low from the Hatzerim airfield in the Negev, screened by the low Sinai hills from radar detection, to hit at Egyptian airfields in the Sinai at El Arish, Jebel Libni, Bir Thamada and Bir Gifgafa, while others from airfields in central Israel flew westwards low over the Mediterranean and then turned successively southwards towards their targets, the airfields at Fayid and Kabrit on the Suez Canal, Abu Sueir in the Delta area, and Cairo West. Beni Sueif, about 60 miles south of Cairo on the River Nile, was first struck at 0815. At precisely 0745 the Israeli radio announced that Egyptian armoured forces had moved at dawn towards the Negev and that radar had detected numerous Egyptian aircraft approaching Israel. This was not true, but it alerted the civilian population to the fact that war had started. The Israelis admit being a few minutes behind schedule in hitting the airfield at Fayid. Their aircraft could not find it for several minutes as it was still shrouded in heavy mist, but they claim that the other seven were struck simultaneously on time. The Egyptians do not agree that this synchronization was as perfect as the Israelis claim, but hold that timing varied by as much as 15 minutes in the initial wave and that some targets were completely missed. However, considering that the Israeli aircraft had to take off from different airfields at different times in order to strike together, the organization and timing were extremely good.

The attacking Israeli aircraft flew in very low over the sea and land to keep beneath the effective radar screen, or they moved in through the 'gaps' in the radar detection system. It was only as they approached close to their targets that they climbed and suddenly became visible on Egyptian radar screens. The object was to warn the Egyptians at the last moment so that their pilots would belatedly get into their aircraft and be destroyed with the aircraft on the ground. The waves of Israeli aircraft were each allowed 10 minutes over their targets which, provided they found it at once (which not all did), enabled them to make three or four runs. During the first two runs heavy cannon fire was poured into any aircraft on the runways or aprons, while usually on the third bombs were dropped on the runways themselves. If there were no navigational errors, or they did not become involved in a dog-fight, they were able to make additional runs until their time was up or their ammunition expended. Because of the fuel problem, the 10-minute period had to be rigidly adhered to.

When the first attacking Israeli aircraft hit the Egyptian air-fields the defending anti-aircraft gunners were caught by surprise, but most of them quickly recovered and fired back at the second and successive waves. The only Egyptian aircraft airborne at this moment of the initial strike were four unarmed trainers, which were shot down. Only two flights, each of four MiG-21s, managed to get airborne to succeed in downing two Israeli Mirages before they too were brought down themselves. The Egyptians say that seven of these pilots got their aircraft off the ground and were shooting back at the Israelis before they had reached a height of 60 feet. The Israelis claim that at least eight formations of MiGs were destroyed while taxiing to take off. Invariably at each Egyptian airfield the aircraft were neatly lined up on the runways and aprons as though for inspection, and despite the state of emergency no attempt had been made at dispersion or camouflage. Waves of attacking Israeli aircraft, each still consisting of about 40 planes, followed one another at 10-minute intervals, the second appearing near the target just as the first was leaving it, the third then being on its way, while the fourth was getting airborne and the fifth was on the ground waiting to take off. In this way five waves of Israeli aircraft successively and continuously struck at the Egyptian airfields until within 50 minutes the same aircraft were again over the same targets. This pattern was maintained without respite for 80 minutes, when there was a 10-minute break from 0905 until 0915. At 0915 the same pattern recommenced, this time with the Israeli aircraft aiming at the same Egyptian airfields. At 1000 three additional airfields were struck, those at El Mansura and Helwan in the Delta area, and El Minya on the River Nile. The 10-minute pause was unexplained by the Israelis, but it was most probably in anticipation of a possible Egyptian counter-attack with bombers from bases beyond Israeli reach. The Israelis were not sure at this stage how many Egyptian bombers were being brought back from the Yemen, or whether any more had returned to southern Egyptian bases overnight. In fact, none had arrived. By 1035, after another concentrated 80 minutes, it was all over—the Egyptian Air Force had been practically wiped out. From 1035 until noon the Israeli Air Force paused to refuel, undertake repairs and reorganize. Only a few protective patrols flew overhead in Israel, while most pilots relaxed waiting for another mission. At noon Israeli aircraft attacked the Egyptian airfield at Bilbeis, at 1215 Hurghada, and at 1230 Luxor. Much later the Israelis hit at Cairo International (at 1715) and at El Banas (at 1800), thus making a total of 17 Egyptian airfields on the First Day. During this respite the Egyptians worked frantically to move any aircraft they could to airfields out of Israeli reach. They succeeded in flying a few out of harm's way, while workmen toiled to repair shattered runways and ground crews tried to salvage what machines they could. Many Egyptian soldiers and Air Force personnel were hastily mustered to put out fires.

Just prior to 5 June the Israelis had caused the Egyptians to move 12 MiG-21s and 8 MiG-19s south to their airfield at Hurghada[1] on the Red Sea. They achieved this by planting false intelligence and by sending several strong air patrols out in the vicinity to lead the Egyptians to think that an Israeli aerial attack might not necessarily come from the north-east but would be aimed through the southern part of Egypt. Shortly after the Israeli attack began these Egyptian aircraft took off, heading northwards to join in the battle, but they all fell to the attacking Israeli planes. It is thought that they were the original '20 enemy aircraft' claimed shot down in dog-fights in this initial phase.

The Israeli Air Force had disrupted the 17 major Egyptian airfields and destroyed nearly 300 aircraft, including all 30 TU-16s caught on the ground at Beni Sueif and Luxor. It claimed to have killed about 100 Egyptian pilots, and admitted to losing only 10 aircraft. The Israelis had gambled everything on this surprise attack, and had won. They say that only 12 aircraft were kept back for home defence, of which eight were continuously flying, with the other four ready on the runways to take off at a moment's notice. As the 60 Fouga Magisters were allocated to the ground forces from the beginning, they cannot be included, which means that the aircraft involved in the attacks on Egypt, if one counts the

---

[1] Sometimes spelt Ghurduka.

'air umbrella', must have amounted to about 240. Apart from the 19 aircraft shot down either by Egyptian MiGs or ground fire, practically every Mystère–the bulk of the attacking planes–was hit by shrapnel or anti-aircraft fire; many had to be patched up as they refuelled and the Israelis claimed that none took more than one hour to be made airworthy again. The majority of the Egyptian aircraft were put out of action by cannon fire from Israeli Mystères deliberately flying low and comparatively slowly over the target area. The accuracy of the shooting was extremely high, as photographs later released by the Israelis showed. The Israelis dropped bombs to disrupt runways, but at first the Egyptians quickly made them passable again. The continual and spasmodic explosions of the delayed action fuses, however, soon rendered this repair work impossible. The supply of Concrete Dibber Bombs must have been limited, as the majority of bombs dropped were conventional types; they were not used against Egyptian airfields in the Sinai, which the Israelis hoped to capture speedily to use for their own aircraft. One of the few Israeli claims not later substantiated was that they had deliberately not destroyed the runway at El Arish as they wished to use it themselves once it had been taken by the ground forces. Eyewitnesses insist that it had been made unusable, and had to be repaired by Israeli bulldozers before the first aircraft could land on it.[1]

A number of SAM-2 missiles were released against attacking Israeli aircraft[2] but failed to hit their targets, mainly because they were slow to pick up speed and were designed for action against medium- and high-flying planes. The Israeli aircraft flew too low and too fast for them. Their intelligence had been accurate, as the Israelis knew precisely which airfields to strike at and which to leave alone. Their target identification was very good as in most instances the dummy aircraft were not touched. However, the Israelis admit to hitting dummy aircraft at Abu Sueir. The news of this tremendous success was held back by the Israelis for some time to avoid provoking the United Nations into forcing a cease-fire on them before their ground forces had made impressive

---

[1] The first Israeli plane did not land on the El Arish airfield until 1345 on the second day of the war (Tuesday, 6 June).

[2] The drawbacks and limitations of the SAM-2 have since been confirmed by American pilots fighting in Vietnam.

advances. Just after noon rumours that the Israelis had destroyed about 200 Egyptian aircraft were played down, and an Israeli official spokesman condemned them as 'premature, unclear and utterly unauthorized'.[1]

The Egyptians also concealed their huge disaster; communiqués boasted of the destruction of over 75 per cent of the attacking Israeli planes. By the end of the day the Egyptians claimed to have accounted for 160 Israeli aircraft. It seems that for some time no one dared tell Nasser the bad news and that he did not learn the real facts until nearly midnight. By a misfortune of war Egypt now had far more pilots than aircraft, as only about 100 had been killed; thus about 400 survived, although some of the survivors were wounded, to fly about 200 planes. A contributory factor from the Egyptian side was the passivity at the nine airfields that were not hit until 0915 or afterwards and on which there were many interceptor planes. For 90 minutes, while the first nine airfields (those detailed to be at instant readiness) were being pounded, they showed no sign of aggression and as far as I can discover not a single sortie was launched from them against the attacking Israeli aircraft. This is explained by the fact that the key senior officers were 'marooned in the air' for that period and were unable to issue orders. The Ilyushin-14, carrying Field-Marshal Amer, Lieutenant-General Sidki and other senior Air Force staff officers, had to stay in the air for an hour and a half[2] before managing to land at Cairo International Airport again. Thus the Egyptian Air Force and air defence organization were absolutely paralysed and without orders until it was too late. This unplanned Egyptian misfortune was to the Israelis' great advantage.

THE JORDANIAN AIR WAR

At 0900 on Monday, 5 June, King Hussein received a message from Field-Marshal Amer that fighting with Israel had com-

---

[1] 'He [Moshe Dayan] ordered that Army spokesmen remain silent on the progress of the fighting for the whole of the first day, but let the Arabs do all the talking. The Israeli Broadcasting Service relayed the Arab communiqués without comment and announced only a few innocuous communiqués.' (*David's Sling*.)

[2] *My 'War' with Israel.*

menced and that already 75 per cent of the attacking Israeli aircraft had been shot down. The message urged the King to begin hostilities against Israel according to plan at once. But now it had come to the crunch there was hesitation in the Jordanian camp. Further claims of Egyptian successes were followed by boasts that Egyptian aircraft were strongly attacking Israel. At about this hour the Jordanian radar screens on Mount Ajlun showed a mass of aircraft flying from Egypt towards Israel, which were actually returning Israeli planes. The Egyptian reports plus the picture on the radar screen convinced Hussein that the battle was going wildly in the Egyptians' favour, and he decided to enter the fray. At 0930 he spoke on Radio Amman, saying that Jordan had been attacked (which was not true), calling on his people to join in the war against Israel, declaring that the 'hour of revenge had come', and announcing that the Jordanian armed forces had been placed under the command of General Riad (the first time the Jordanians were made aware that they had an Egyptian commander). Hussein then agreed that General Riad should take action against Israel in conjunction with Syria and Iraq. The necessary orders were just about to be issued when a message purporting to come from Field-Marshal Amer was received asking the King to take no action but to wait for further information. It was a false message fed in by Israeli intelligence, and it was only discovered to be false when more signals were received in rapid succession from the Egyptian GHQ demanding to know why General Riad was not taking action as ordered. This confusion took some time to sort itself out. Then followed another period of waiting for messages indicating that the Syrians and Iraqis had taken off, so that the Jordanian aircraft could also move into action with them.

Just before 1100 another message came from the Syrians that their aircraft were not ready to strike at Israel.[1] At about the same time a message was received from the Iraqis stating (falsely) that their aircraft were already over Israel on a bombing mission.

---

[1] 'They [the Syrians] said they had been caught off guard: their aircraft were not ready for the strike, and their fighter pilots were on a training flight. They asked us to give them first a half-hour, then an hour and so on until 1045 when they asked for yet another delay, which we also granted. At 11 o'clock we couldn't wait any longer.' (*My 'War' with Israel*.)

Hussein believed the latter signal and, deciding to wait no longer, he told General Riad to order his aircraft to attack Israel. He has stated that he had only 16 pilots available for his 22 Hawker Hunters, and that all of them immediately took to the air to drop bombs on Nathanya, the airfield at Kfar Sirkin, Kfar Sava and certain other road junctions. Hussein claims that his Hawker Hunters attacked the Nathanya airfield three times. The Jordanian pilots reported that they destroyed four Israeli planes on the ground, which were all they saw.[1] Their main success was to destroy an Israeli Noratlas on the ground at Kfar Sirkin. At about 1130 the pilots all returned safely and began to refuel. The Jordanian turn-round time was about two hours.

The Israelis had hoped that Jordan would stay out of the war, but this attack, together with signs of aggressive land movement in the Jerusalem sector, indicated the contrary, so it was decided that at least the Jordanian Air Force must be eliminated. Israeli aircraft had been mainly resting and refuelling since 1035, and were now again ready for action. Commencing at 1215, two flights each of four Mirages attacked the two main Jordanian airfields at Mafraq and Amman and, making repeated runs, poured cannon fire into the Hawker Hunters as they were refuelling and into other aircraft on the runways. Then bombs, including a few of the Concrete Dibber type, were dropped on the runways themselves. Another flight of four Mystères attacked the Mount Ajlun radar station, partially destroying the installations. Owing to the much shorter distances involved the Israeli aircraft were able to stay over their targets for about 20 minutes, and in this brief period Hussein lost all his aircraft. The Israelis lost only one plane hit by anti-aircraft fire; the Jordanian gunners had stuck to their guns but the pilot was able to eject while over the Sea of Galilee, where he was picked up by an Israeli patrol boat. On their return journey the Israeli pilots took pot-shots at moving vehicles. During this raid, the Jordanians alleged, the Israeli aircraft deliberately flew low over Amman and machine-gunned the Basman Palace, Hussein's normal Amman residence, riddling the King's apartments with bullets. The King was absent at the time.[2]

---

[1] King Hussein: *My 'War' with Israel.*

[2] An account of the initial Israeli air raid(s) on Jordan is given by King

Only two Jordanian pilots were killed in this strike, which destroyed beyond repair 18 Hawker Hunters.[1] King Hussein states that he personally saw off the 14 survivors whom he sent by bus to Iraq that night to fight with the Iraqi Air Force. They were given Hawker Hunters to fly at H-3 air base, and Hussein claims that during the remainder of the war they brought down nine raiding Israeli Mystères and Mirages. The King claims that but for the Syrian hesitation and reluctance to act with the Jordanian Air Force his planes could have taken to the air much sooner, intercepted Israeli aircraft returning from the initial Egyptian air strikes when short of fuel and ammunition, and caught others on the ground refuelling. Had this course been taken a few Israeli aircraft might have been lost in combats with the highly man-oeuvrable Hawker Hunters, but the ultimate result would have been the same.

About the time of the Israeli air raids on Jordan, the Israelis discovered the Iraqi brigade and the Palestinian battalion moving across country from Mafraq to Irbid and Jerash. Flights of Mystères attacked these formations until darkness set in, completely disorganizing them and causing many casualties of personnel and vehicles.

THE SYRIAN AIR WAR

It seems that the suspicious Syrians had not the slightest intention of allowing their Air Force to act in conjunction with Jordan's and that they most probably held back their aircraft in the hope that the Jordanian aircraft would be destroyed by the Israelis before they committed their own to battle. Even at this critical juncture Arab rivalries were paramount. Like the Jordanians, the Syrians believed the false reports of Egyptian successes given out during the morning; they too wanted easy pickings and to be in at the death, so they decided to act alone. At about 1145 12 Syrian MiG-21s flew over northern Israel, dropping

Hussein in his *My 'War' with Israel*, but his timings and details do not coincide with Israeli accounts.

[1] 'Only two Alouette helicopters were undamaged' according to King Hussein in *My 'War' with Israel*. Other reports indicate that one Hawker Hunter was untouched and another four were later repaired.

a few bombs near the Haifa oil refinery and near Tiberias. They also flew over the Israeli airfield at Megiddo where they shot up some dummy aircraft on the aprons. Syria immediately issued a war communiqué boasting that the Haifa oil refinery was in flames—it had not been touched.

The Israelis were ready to hit back. At 1215 (the same moment as they struck at the Jordanian airfields) four flights of Mystères, each of four aircraft, attacked four targets in Syria: the main base at Damascus, airfields at Marj Rial south of Damascus, 'T-4' (a desert station on the oil pipeline) and Seikal. The Israeli aircraft stayed over their targets for about 20 minutes, during which time they destroyed many aircraft on the ground by cannon fire and disrupted runways by bombing. All returned safely. Later Brigadier Hod boasted: 'We were able to deal with Syria and Jordan in 25 minutes.'[1]

REMAINDER OF THE FIRST DAY IN THE AIR

The pause by the major part of the Israeli Air Force between 1035 and noon, apart from being used for repairs and refuelling, was mainly a period of tense waiting to see whether there would be any bombing attacks on Israel by the strategic bomber force of the Egyptian or any other Arab air force. Undoubtedly there was a sigh of relief when these did not materialize. Numbers of Israeli aircraft had remained airborne over Israel just in case. As soon as the Syrian Air Force had been hit and the Jordanian destroyed, the Israelis turned their attention back to Egypt, and (using similar techniques but not at the same hectic rate) resumed attacks against the airfields hit during the morning. This time they also concentrated on knocking out the Egyptian radar stations, which had so far been left alone. By the end of the day they had put all 16 radar installations in the Sinai out of action, as well as others in the Delta and Canal regions. Israeli air raids continued at intervals, after dusk and throughout the hours of darkness, harassing men trying to repair runways and salvage aircraft. Delayed action bombs exploding at unexpected moments shook ground staffs' morale. Arab aerial resistance had died down, and during the afternoon and evening Israeli aircraft

---

[1] Press conference, Tel Aviv.

practically had the freedom of the skies, only occasionally encountering anti-aircraft fire. At 1500 Israeli aircraft made a single devastating raid on the Iraqi airfield at H-3, damaging and destroying some aircraft.

COMMENTS ON THE FIRST DAY OF THE AIR WAR

The surprise aerial blow by the Israelis had succeeded. The Jordanian Air Force had been smashed, the Egyptian knocked out for the time being, and the Syrian stunned. The decision to strike, and when, was known to only the necessary few, and even members of the Knesset were surprised.[1] One reason the Israelis were initially so reluctant to disclose the magnitude of their victory was the suspicion that when Nasser found their claims were accurate he would demand UN intervention or an immediate cease-fire to save himself from more losses and so baulk the Israelis of further progress. The Israelis successfully banked on the fact that his staff would hesitate for some time to tell him of his losses. They were also apprehensive of Soviet reaction when the Soviet Union discovered the quantity of their aircraft and other material in Egyptian hands that had been destroyed. A side-effect of this non-disclosure was that the Arabs were allowed to believe their own false news bulletins, and so were kept in optimistic darkness. Unfortunately Israelis too could listen to Arab broadcasts and were understandably anxious. To some extent they were soothed by Brigadier Haim Hertzog, the official military commentator, who developed the thesis that it was better not to lift the fog of battle too soon but to keep the enemy in a state of confusion.

The first official Israeli press conference was not held until 0100 on the Second Day (Tuesday, 6 June), when Lieutenant-Colonel Moshe Perlman, Defence Ministry spokesman, said: 'We engaged the air forces of Egypt, Jordan, Syria and Iraq. We

---

[1] 'Early on Monday morning, 5 June, members of the Knesset Foreign Affairs and Security Committee assembled at a small airfield near Tel Aviv to take off on a visit to troops in the south. The members of the Knesset were asked to step into the open-trench shelters and a few minutes later Minister of Defence Moshe Dayan appeared and told them that the war had begun.' (*David's Sling*.)

destroyed for sure 374 planes, with another 34 possibles. Our losses—18 planes. The war in the air was won in less than 12 hours. The Israeli Air Force has undisputed command of the air over the Middle East.' He was largely correct, except that the air war had been won in far less time. Brigadier Hod claimed that the Israelis had destroyed '52 in Syria, 20 in Jordan and some in Iraq'. During this First Day until midnight, the Israelis stated, they flew about 1,000 sorties which, assuming the pilots remained with the same aircraft throughout (as they had more pilots than planes this was probably not so), averages less than four sorties per pilot that day. However, as it is claimed that some pilots (obviously piloting Mystères) flew seven or more sorties, others must have flown fewer. Of these sorties perhaps 750 were against Egyptian airfields and radar installations and included the overhead protective patrols, while most of the remainder were against Syrian and Jordanian targets and on general patrol. Only about 30 sorties were flown in support of the ground forces, which had been warned not to expect much close air support on the First Day, although all 60 Fouga Magisters were placed at the disposal of the GOC, Southern Command, whose forces were heavily engaged with the Egyptians in the Sinai.

The Israeli success was achieved by surprise, thorough training, skilful pilots and good identification. A few, but not many, Arab dummy aircraft had been hit by Israeli cannon fire. Praise must also go to the Israeli Intelligence Service, whose information had enabled the Israeli Air Staff to know exactly where to strike and when. About 20 Egyptian airfields were within reach of Israeli aircraft, but the nine most vital (those on instant alert) were picked out, as were the next eight, where pilots were on more lengthy period of standby duty. The others were ignored. But while the Israeli intelligence system was undoubtedly the best in the Middle East it cannot claim all the credit for gaining accurate information. Part should go to the Israeli Air Force itself, as it had been flying reconnaissance missions over Arab territory for at least five days beforehand. These missions were unadmitted by the Israeli Government. While the Egyptian Air Staff knew of at least some of them, it was silent, perhaps because no one was prepared to tell Nasser, or perhaps because Nasser, if he knew, did not like to admit that Israeli aircraft could fly freely in

Egyptian air space. Israeli intelligence agents, infiltrated into the Egyptian High Command, had also helped considerably by revealing several gaps in the Egyptian defensive radar system.

In the opening minutes of the air strike many Egyptian pilots at the nine airfields that were, or should have been, on the alert, tried to fight back, and a number lost their lives gallantly attempting to do so. Egyptian anti-aircraft gunners accounted for a high proportion of admitted Israeli losses, it being they who perforated practically every attacking Israeli aircraft with shrapnel or bullets. The ground crews and other personnel stayed at their posts for hours trying to make good damaged runways, despite continually exploding bombs and periodic Israeli cannon fire. Many Egyptians bravely worked under these hazardous conditions to put out fires and salvage aircraft; through their efforts several Egyptian aircraft fluttered into the air during darkness to airfields beyond Israeli reach, while trucks evacuated other planes, spares and salvaged equipment.

In Tel Aviv the first air raid warning sounded at 0800, but the inhabitants were reluctant to take shelter. Similarly in Jerusalem and other places the HAGA (civil defence organization) personnel had difficulty in persuading people to take this warning seriously. However, at about 0900 the mood changed drastically as radios, both Israeli and Egyptian, announced the opening of hostilities, and the Israelis listened to successive boastful Egyptian claims that were not positively denied by the Israeli Government. Many citizens then scrambled for places in air raid shelters, and a large number slept in them for the next three or four nights. The air raid warning, for example, sounded 12 times in Tel Aviv on the First Day; the longest alert was about noon, mainly because Jordanian shells began to fall on or near the city. Windows were blacked out, and windows, doorways and apertures were buttressed with sandbags. The Israeli civilian was now also at war in the front line, or was prepared to be.

THE SECOND DAY OF THE AIR WAR
THE IRAQI AIR INCIDENT

Although it had falsely claimed on the First Day that its aircraft had raided Tel Aviv and 'destroyed seven Israeli aircraft on an airfield', so far the Iraqi Air Force had remained passive, even though its single brigade in Jordan had suffered badly at the hands of the Israeli Air Force. However, at dawn on the Second Day (Tuesday, 6 June), a single Iraqi TU-16 bomber flew low over Nathanya and dropped a few bombs, hitting a factory and causing a few casualties. This aircraft was shot down on its furtive return journey by Israeli ground forces in the Jezreel Valley, just as the morning mists were clearing. About an hour later, at 0500, four flights of Israeli Mystères hit hard again at the Iraqi air base at H-3 (a desert station on the oil pipeline), near the Iraqi-Jordanian border. Most Iraqi airfields, of course, were beyond the effective reach of Israeli aircraft.

THE LEBANESE AIR INCIDENT

In company with other Arab states (although its population was approximately half Arab and half Christian), the Lebanon had declared war on Israel, issued fictitious war communiqués, including one on the First Day claiming that a Lebanese pilot had shot down an Israeli aircraft over the Lebanese coastline, and stopped the flow of oil to Britain through the pipeline running across its territory. In fact, it remained quite passive. The Israelis regarded its declaration as empty and conventional, made merely to placate Arab public opinion. The Lebanon had a population of about 2·17 million and an area of some 4,300 square miles. It had briefly and unsuccessfully fought against Israel in 1948, but since had been Israel's least aggressive neighbour. The army[1] amounted to only 12,000 soldiers and its Air Force, of about 1,000 men, had only 12 Hawker Hunters, 6 Vampires and 10 Alouette helicopters. Its Chief of Staff, General Bustani, knew that his forces were no match for those of Israel, and was firmly against commencing hostilities. As the country had a mixed agricultural and trading economy its strategy, such as it was, was purely defensive, and its Government had done what it could to curb Fatah activities within its boundaries.

Impressed by Arab claims of success and wishing to be in at the kill, on the Second Day the Lebanese Premier, Rashid

---

[1] The army consisted of eight infantry battalions and two armoured units; it possessed about 40 British Centurions and 40 French AMX-13 tanks.

Karame, ordered his armed forces to take action against Israel, but General Bustani refused to comply. The Premier ordered the arrest of his Chief of Staff, but no one would obey this order either. For several hours there was stalemate, with the Premier wanting war and the soldiers refusing to fight.[1] This impasse lasted until the bad news of the Arab defeats and losses began to trickle through, when Rashid Karame realized what a lucky escape he and his country had had. The whole matter was hushed up. However, there was one exception to this passive Lebanese attitude. At about 0900 on the Second Day, somewhat to the surprise of the Israelis, two Lebanese Hawker Hunters flew over Israeli territory just to the north of the Sea of Galilee. They were immediately engaged by Israeli aircraft, and one Lebanese plane was shot down. This was the only clash between Lebanese and Israeli forces during the war. Presumably the two Lebanese pilots had been of the tiny minority in the armed forces who favoured joining the Arab attack on Israel, and had acted on their own initiative.

ISRAELI AERIAL ACTIVITY

Two Egyptian MiGs machine-gunned Israelis at a refuelling point between the Jiradi Pass and El Arish, causing casualties, just after dawn on the Second Day, and there were three or four Egyptian air attacks on Israeli troops in the Sinai, but otherwise no Arab aircraft ventured over Israeli territory, or intervened on or near the battlefields, on the Second Day. Israeli freedom of the air was practically absolute. Israeli strikes continued at intervals on airfields previously hit, especially Egyptian ones, and other aircraft flew over adjacent Arab territory mainly on interdiction and reconnaissance missions. Although opposition from anti-aircraft fire was far less than on the First Day, occasionally resistance from airfields deterred low flying by the Israelis. On the Second Day massive air support was given to the ground forces, the Fouga Magisters being reinforced with other aircraft with ground support capabilities. Further attention was given to the Iraqi brigade and the Palestinian battalion, scattered between

---

[1] *The Sandstorm.*

Mafraq and the Upper Jordan Valley, which were trying to recover themselves and bring some order to the chaos caused by the Israeli air strikes on the First Day.

ISRAELI AERIAL CLAIMS

By the end of the Second Day the enormity of the Israeli aerial victory was becoming obvious, despite the modest and vague official communiqués, so in the late evening of that day (6th) the Israelis issued detailed figures of their claims for the first two days of the war. They will not divide these figures into separate totals for each day, but insist on lumping them together. This perhaps indicates that there was more Arab resistance on the Second Day than they wished to admit. They did admit to losing 15 aircraft on the Second Day, but declined to give details.

These figures are:

Egypt	Bombers:	TU-16s	= 30
		Il-28s	= 27
	Fighter-Bombers:	SU-7s	= 10
		MiG-15/17s	= 82
		MiG-19s	= 20
		MiG-21s	= 95
	Transports:	An-12s	= 8
		Il-14s	= 24
	Helicopters:	Mi-4s	= 1
		Mi-6s	= 8
		Others	= 4
		Egyptian Total	= 309
Syria	Bombers:	Il-28s	= 2
	Fighter-Bombers:	MiG-15/17s	= 23
		MiG-21s	= 32
	Helicopters:	Mi-4s	= 3
		Syrian Total	= 60
Jordan	Fighters:	Hawker Hunters	= 21
	Transports:	Doves	= 3
		Others	= 3
	Helicopters:		= 2
		Jordanian Total	= 29

Iraq	Bombers:	TU-16s	= 1
	Fighters:	Hawker Hunters =	5
		MiG-21s	= 9
	Transports:		= 2
		Iraqi Total = 17	
Lebanon	Fighters:	Hawker Hunters =	1
		Lebanese Total = 1	

Grand Total = 418

Further information given by the Israelis indicated that of this number, that is 418 Arab aircraft destroyed in two days, 393 were destroyed on the ground, which indicates that 25 must have been brought down whilst airborne. This was proof that the Egyptians put up some resistance initially. The Israelis are thought to have lost 26 aircraft, of which six were Fouga Magisters armed with rockets and used for close ground support, and 21 pilots. These massive claims, largely substantiated by aerial photographs that left little doubt as to their authenticity, meant that the air war had been won by the Israelis, who had the skies to themselves for the rest of the war. Dominance had been achieved and maintained although Egypt still had operative some 200 aircraft, which either had been at airfields too remote for the Israelis to reach, had been flown to such airfields or taken there by road during the first night, or were in the Yemen. The Second, Third and Fourth Days were spent by the Egyptian Air Force in salvaging, dispersing and reorganizing what aircraft it had left. At least 100 Soviet aircraft just delivered to Egypt, still packed in crates, were flown with other equipment to airfields at Hodeida and Sana in the Yemen to be stockpiled out of reach of Israeli aircraft. Syria had over 60 combat aircraft intact, and Iraq over 200, but both remained passive.

ARAB CLAIMS OF FOREIGN INTERVENTION

By the late evening of the First Day gloom had settled on the Egyptian General Staff, deepened by the unexpected frequency of enemy sorties attacking airfields and installations. The Egyptian Air Staff had planned that in the event of war with Israel it would have its attacking aircraft over Israeli targets about once in every three hours; this allowed comfortably for a turn-round time of two hours, with which the Egyptian ground staff and pilots could cope, and for aircraft to make two or three sorties a day. They expected the Israelis to work on much the same timings. But as Israeli aircraft were over Egyptian targets once in every 50 minutes (in the initial strikes only, of course, as neither men nor machines could have kept up such a pace), a great many more aircraft appeared to be attacking Egypt than was actually the case. At the end of the First Day the Egyptian Air Staff estimated that at least 1,500 aircraft were in action against it, and it estimated that Israel possessed well under 500 planes of all types. Egyptian intelligence was aware that aircraft carriers of the US 6th Fleet were in the Mediterranean and that Britain had aircraft stationed in Cyprus. These factors combined to foster the belief that America and Britain were intervening in the war against the Arabs, a theory at which Nasser—now informed of most of the details of his aerial disaster—eagerly grasped, perhaps in the hope of bringing the Soviet Union into the conflict.

King Hussein of Jordan was easily persuaded that the Israelis were receiving foreign support, as during the morning of the First Day his radar screens at Mount Ajlun (before they were put out of action just after midday) were supposed to have detected groups of aircraft[1] flying from stationary objects in the Mediterranean towards the region of Lydda airport. This information, which was passed on to the Egyptian General Staff later that day, no doubt influenced Hussein in agreeing with Nasser that foreign powers were helping the Israelis.

At 0545 on the Second Day the Israelis monitored a radio-telephone conversation between Nasser and Hussein. Both agreed to say, the Israelis alleged, that America and Britain were participating in the war against the Arabs,[2] the vital passages being spoken by Nasser: 'I will make an announcement and you will make an announcement . . . that American and British aircraft are taking part against us from aircraft carriers.' The American

---

[1] 'Hawker Hunters had similar silhouettes to Mystères.' (*My 'War' with Israel*.)

[2] This version, alleged by the Egyptians to have been 'doctored', was released to the press by the Israelis on the fourth day, by which time the outcome could no longer be in doubt. Even on the fifth day Nasser was still loudly asserting that the Israelis were operating an air force three times as strong as normal.

and British Governments denied this allegation, but the repeated invitations from both countries for the UN to send observers to the airfields and ships concerned were ignored all the week. King Hussein's later explanation, admitting that there was no foundation for the claim of foreign intervention,[1] was the lame one that atmospheric conditions over the open sea in the early morning reflected objects on to the radar screen that were difficult to identify. He also later allowed the American Ambassador in Amman to deny on the radio the allegations of American intervention. The nearest British aircraft carriers were at Malta and Aden, well out of range. No such activity was reported from the US 6th Fleet. Soviet warships were intensively monitoring the 6th Fleet, and would presumably have made any gesture of intervention known to the UN. On the Second Day Syria made an unfounded announcement that it had identified British aircraft flying over its territory. Despite the lack of evidence and the firm denials, the Arabs somehow believed, and indeed perhaps still do, that even if American and British aircraft did not actually fly on operations with the Israelis, at least they formed the protective umbrella that enabled Israel to send all its aircraft into battle and hold only a tiny handful back for home defence.

REMAINDER OF THE WAR IN THE AIR

From the Second Day onwards none of the Arab states involved made any move of importance against the Israelis in the air. Minor attempts to hit back were made by Egypt. On the afternoon of the Third Day six Egyptian MiGs attacked the Tal Ugda as it was closing in towards the Ishmailia Pass and shot down one of the Israeli counter-attacking planes. Only one Egyptian MiG was accounted for. In the evening there were attacks on Israeli armoured formations by Egyptian MiGs during the tank battle with the escaping Egyptian 4th Armoured Division for possession of the Ishmailia Pass. The main Egyptian effort on the Fourth Day was made against the small Israeli column that had

---

[1] Much later, on 4 March 1968, in an interview with Mr William Attwood, Editor-in-Chief of the US *Look* Magazine, Nasser admitted that he had been mistaken in accusing America and Britain of giving air support to Israel. The charges made at the time were the result of 'misunderstanding based on suspicions and false information', he said.

penetrated westwards along the northern route into the Sinai, and which was approaching the Suez Canal. From dawn to mid-afternoon the Egyptians flew 32 sorties against this force. Israeli aircraft intervened and during this period 21 Egyptian aircraft were shot down, practically all in aerial combat. The other Egyptian attempt to support their counter-attacking forces between the Great Bitter Lakes and Port Suez was also on the Fourth Day, when five Egyptian aircraft were shot down by Israeli planes. The Israelis had claimed that another two had been shot down on the previous day (the Third Day) 'somewhere in Sinai'. Over Egypt some SAM missiles had been released against Israeli aircraft on the Second Day and a few more on the Third Day—but none had hit their target. Throughout the remaining period of the war Israeli aircraft made frequent flights over Cairo, parts of Iraq, Syria and Jordan, and, of course, over the Sinai until it was all in Israeli hands. Apart from bursts of hostile anti-aircraft fire they met with little opposition. Hussein claims[1] that on the Third Day, when six Israeli aircraft raided H-3 air base, his Jordanian pilots, manning Iraqi Hawker Hunters, brought down four of them and that two Israeli pilots were killed and two taken prisoner. The Israelis say that in this (eight plane) raid they lost two Vatours and one Mirage.

The Israelis later commented that on 5 June there were 18 encounters with Egyptian aircraft in which the Egyptians lost 26 planes, and 16 encounters with other Arab air forces in which 12 Arab planes were lost. Between 6 and 9 June there were a further 26 encounters with Egyptian aircraft in which 35 Egyptian planes were lost, and eight with other Arab air forces, in which four more Arab planes were lost. In all the aerial combats, the Israelis say, the Egyptians lost 61 aircraft and the other Arab air forces 16, making a total of 77 brought down in the air. The Israelis are still officially silent about their own losses in aerial combat but they are believed to have lost at least 40 aircraft during the war, of which perhaps a dozen were shot down in dog-fights. The final Israeli claim is that 338 Egyptian, 61 Syrian, 29 Jordanian and one Lebanese aircraft were destroyed during this short war, of which 79 were brought down in aerial combat.

---

[1] *My 'War' with Israel.*

Although these figures do not exactly tally in careful analysis, they do indicate that a large number of Egyptian aircraft were shot down by Israeli planes in aerial combat for tiny Israeli losses. Conversely they also reveal that a small unpublished number of Israeli planes were shot down by Egyptian pilots. Perhaps this latter point is reinforced by the Israeli insistence that the only Israeli aircraft brought down were hit by anti-aircraft fire or were 'jumped on' from above when striking at ground targets. Nine Israeli pilots were taken prisoner by the Egyptians, two by the Syrians and two by the Jordanians, making a total of 13, so in all it seems that only eight were killed. On the Second Day the Egyptians released pictures of a captured Israeli pilot being interviewed on television. Five of the Israeli pilots who had to bail out over Arab territory were killed on landing, three in Egypt and two in Syria.

SUMMARY OF THE AIR WAR

Israeli victory in the air was the key to the swift victory on land. The Egyptians had been outclassed and the Iraqis[1] and Syrians cowed. There can be no doubt that even if the Israelis had not made this massive surprise assault on the Arab air forces they would still have won the war, but it would have taken longer and there would have been many more Israeli casualties. The several reasons why the Israelis were so successful have been mentioned and must have become apparent, so let us briefly consider why the Egyptians lost. Generally, Egyptian failure has been attributed by the West, and also by the Soviet Union to a degree, to Egyptian inefficiency, inherent lack of application and an unrealistic attitude towards basic priorities. But this is a general condemnation that conveniently makes the Egyptians the scapegoats.

Clearly, the Soviet Union, or rather its Military Mission in Cairo, must take a share of the blame. The possibility of an Israeli surprise attack must have been obvious, but no serious measures were taken to lessen its impact. For example, there was no 'second strike' capability as most of the combat aircraft were

---

[1] 'In fact, according to the Israeli Air Force, the Iraqi pilots proved to be the most skilful of all the Arab air forces that were engaged in the June 1967 War.' (*New Middle East*, August 1970.)

clustered closely together on a few airfields; they included the vitally strategic TU-16s on two airfields, all within range of Israeli aircraft. There was no carefully planned dispersal of aircraft so that some should always be available at remote airfields ready to hit back. Surely it would have been elementary to have at least a proportion of the TU-16s out of Israeli reach. Anti-aircraft locations were primitive, leaving their crews exposed to attack from the air, and few were 'hardened' in concrete gun emplacements with underground bunkers so as to be able to withstand heavy assaults and still function. Also the type and locations of the Egyptian radar installations which must have been a Soviet responsibility were open to criticism. The failure of the much-vaunted SAM-2s could not be blamed on to the Egyptians. The powerful Soviet radar installations on their ships in the Mediterranean undoubtedly gained much instant and valuable information, but there seems no evidence of radio or other communication between the Soviet ships and any Egyptian operational headquarters.

On the Israeli side there was no powerful secret weapon or mystical formula; it was sheer hard-headed realism, clever planning, intelligent training and an immense amount of detailed work. Perhaps the best and most logical explanation is that the Israelis managed to get the utmost from their machines, pilots and ground crews, and that the comparative lack of over-sophistication of their aircraft expedited refuelling, repairs and maintenance. One Israeli Air Staff regret has been that it did not heavily bomb the Egyptian Research Centre on the outskirts of Cairo, which produced armaments and allegedly poison gas, and did research on missiles. Israeli pilots regard with satisfaction the fact that their country ended the war with its supply of HAWK missiles intact.

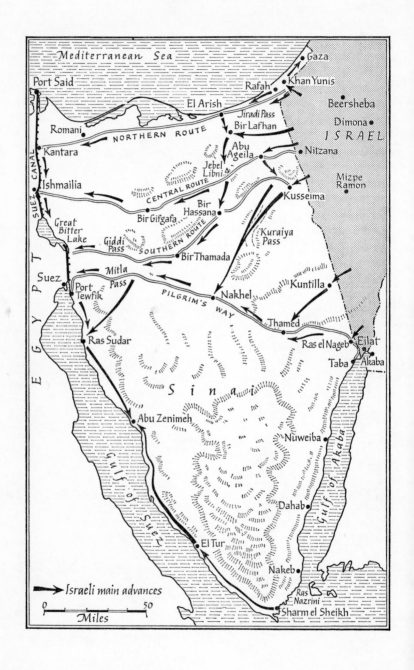

Mediterranean Sea

Gaza

Port Said

Khan Yunis

Rafah

Beersheba

El Arish

Jiradi Pass

Dimona

Romani

NORTHERN ROUTE

Bir Lafhan

ISRAEL

Kantara

Abu Ageila

Nitzana

Ishmailia

Jebel Libni

CENTRAL ROUTE

Mizpe Ramon

Kusseima

SUEZ CANAL

Bir Gifgafa

Bir Hassana

Great Bitter Lake

Kuraiya Pass

Giddi Pass

SOUTHERN ROUTE

Bir Thamada

Mitla Pass

Kuntilla

EGYPT

Suez

Port Tewfik

PILGRIM'S WAY

Nakhel

Thamed

Ras el Nageb

Eilat

Taba

Akaba

Ras Sudar

Sinai

Abu Zenimeh

Nuweiba

Gulf of Suez

Gulf of Akaba

Dahab

El Tur

Nakeb

Ras Nazrini

Israeli main advances

Sharm el Sheikh

0   50

Miles

CHAPTER 5

The Sinai Front

On Monday, 5 June 1967, the Israeli army moved into action against the Egyptian forces in the Sinai very soon after the Israeli Air Force had first struck against Egyptian airfields. The army drove a wedge into the Gaza Strip and then punched through the Rafah, El Arish and Um Katif defences, to bulldoze its way westwards, trundling the Egyptians before it until it reached the Suez Canal in the early hours of Friday, 9 June, when victory against Egypt was complete.

First, a brief description of the Sinai battleground, the land-bridge between Africa and Asia across which armies have marched and counter-marched through the ages. Comprising roughly 22,000 square miles, it is about 240 miles from its northern Mediterranean coastline to its southern tip, and about 120 miles across its northern portion that lies between the Israeli Negev and the Suez Canal. The Sinai can be divided into two distinct parts, the northern and the southern. The northern part, rectangular in shape, consists of undulating desert that includes several treacherous sand-seas, areas of hard sand, rocky outcrops, some quite massive, and low hills as well as stretches of salt marsh in the north-west. Running between 30 to 40 miles to the east of and parallel to the Suez Canal is a low line of hills, higher in the south, which flatten and broaden out as one progresses northwards until they merge into the salt marshes a few miles south of the Mediterranean coast, forming a natural barrier partially protecting the Canal, which for clarity and convenience in this narrative can be called the Central Ridge.[1] There were few motorable passes through the Central Ridge, the principal ones being the Ishmailia,[2] Giddi and Mitla Passes.

Routes across the northern Sinai are inexorably channelled by

---

[1] Although strictly speaking it is to the west of centre and rather indefinite in parts.　　　　　　　　　　　　　　　[2] Also for clarity and convenience.

hills, passes, rocky outcrops and sand-seas. The four chief routes from east to west can be known as the Northern Route, the Central Route, the Southern Route and the Pilgrims Way respectively. The Northern Route leading from the Gaza Strip follows fairly close to the coast, going through El Arish, Misfak and Romani, and on to the Suez Canal at Kantara. The Central Route, starting from Nitzana, just inside the Israeli border, passes through Abu Ageila, Bir Hamma, Bir Gifgafa, the Ishmailia Pass and on to the Canal at Ishmailia. Both these routes had metalled surfaces[1] in reasonably good condition, and were fully used by the Egyptians for military purposes. The Southern Route was not metalled, its surface being rough and the going difficult in many places owing to rocky outcrops and drifting sand. Stretches of it had been constructed by the Egyptians since 1957, largely by improving existing camel tracks, and it ran from Kusseima, near the Israeli border, to Bir Hassana and Bir Thamada, through the newly-cut Giddi Pass to meet the Suez Canal near its southern end, at a point where the Egyptians operated a heavy pontoon bridge. These three main routes were connected by a number of lateral secondary roads which had either been specially constructed or were improved camel tracks, some of which, especially near the static camps and supply installations, had metalled surfaces. The main junctions of this network were at El Arish, Abu Ageila, Jebel Libni and Bir Thamada, but there were others. In short, the Egyptians had extended and improved existing roads and tracks, especially in the north-east corner where their main defences lay. Additionally, a railway line ran from the Gaza Strip to Kantara on the Suez Canal, roughly following the alignment of the Northern Route for much of the way.

Farther south, running at a slightly different angle, is the Pilgrims Way,[2] an age-old route followed by Egyptian pilgrims to Mecca since the Middle Ages and in use by camel trains and merchants until recent decades, which ran from Ras en-Nageb, near the head of the Gulf of Akaba, through Thamed and Nakhel, where it was joined by a branch road from Bir Thamada

---

[1] The metalled surfaces of all roads in the Sinai had been destroyed by the withdrawing Israelis in 1957, but the Egyptians had resurfaced them.

[2] Also known as the Sultan's Way.

(on the Southern Route) just before it entered the Mitla Pass to reach the Canal near Port Tewfik. The Pilgrims Way was passable for wheeled vehicles but with difficulty in many places because of loose sand drifting on to the roadway. There was also a United Nations patrol road, or rather jeepable track, which ran along most of the west side of the Israeli border from the Gaza Strip southwards to Ras en-Nageb.

The settled population of the Sinai was in the region of 30,000, centred primarily at El Arish, where ground water enabled some agriculture to develop, and on the east bank of the Canal opposite Kantara and at Port Fuad, opposite to Port Said. These were the only habitations of any size, as most of the other places frequently named in this narrative had ceased to be inhabited, except perhaps as temporary transit accommodation for wandering Bedu or as Egyptian military encampments. For example, all the Arab houses in Abu Ageila had been destroyed in the 1956 fighting, and the tiny population had fled, leaving merely a desolate road junction. The nearby Rouffa Dam, damaged in the 1956 fighting, had not been repaired, and the foundation stones of the once-prominent house of the former British Governors of Sinai and the Government buildings were hard to trace, the stone having been removed for other purposes. On and near the site of Abu Ageila had sprung up a large Egyptian camp area of huts, tents and shelters. In fact, in many places in the Sinai Egyptian military camps had been constructed, either on or near the defunct villages or oases they were named after. A few Bedu in the Sinai watered and fed their animals at the few scattered wells and small oases, some of which were far from the main routes.

The Gaza Strip, which must be included as part of the Sinai for this narrative, was a narrow length of territory protruding into Israel, varying in width from three to nine miles, slanting north-east, resting on the Mediterranean coast and extending for about 25 miles; it was all that remained in Egyptian hands of the former Mandated Palestine. The city of Gaza was about 50 miles from Tel Aviv, the other population centres being Khan Yunis and Rafah. Most of the 135,000 inhabitants relied upon settled agriculture for their living, but also packed into this small space were an additional 315,000 refugees who existed mostly on UN charity.

The southern part of the Sinai, triangular in shape, consists mainly of barren mountain massifs that progressively rise in height to nearly 10,000 feet as one moved southwards; one of the better-known peaks is Jebel Musa (7,497 feet), where traditionally Moses received the Ten Commandments, and at the foot of which nestles the 6th-century Monastery of St Catherine. Few Bedu wandered into this inhospitable part of the Sinai in which there were few tracks of any sort. A motorable road went southwards from Port Tewfik along the coast of the Gulf of Suez, through Ras Sudar, Abu Durba and El Tur (where there were oil wells), round the southern tip of the peninsula to Sharm El Sheikh, near where the island of Ras Nasrini guards the Straits of Tiran some 15 miles away. A motorable track forked off eastwards near Abu Durba to the Monastery of St Catherine. From there a dubious jeepable track continued on to Dahab, a tiny fishing habitation on the shores of the Gulf of Akaba. A similar jeepable track ran from Ras en-Nageb near the head of the Gulf of Akaba, southwards along its shore through Nuweiba, Dahab and Nabek (tiny fishing villages) to Sharm El Sheikh.

EGYPTIAN ARMED FORCES

In 1956 the Egyptian army in the Sinai had been routed by the IDF and lost most of its equipment, then a mixture of British and Soviet material. The Soviet Union had rearmed Egypt, sending between 1957 and 1967 some $1,000 million worth of arms and equipment. A 500-strong Soviet Military Mission was resident in the UAR to train Egyptians, give technical advice and teach Soviet strategy and tactics. By 1960 the sovietization of the Egyptian army had been completed, and Nasser was very proud of his army and its modern Soviet arms, which on paper at least became the most powerful in the Middle East. By June 1967 he had in round figures about 1,180 tanks, 200 self-propelled guns, 1,160 armoured personnel carriers and well over 1,000 guns. His tank force was made up to 220 T-55s, 280 T-54s, 450 T-34s and 60 Stalins, all Soviet models, as well as some 90 American Shermans, 30 British Centurions, 20 French AMX-13s and some 30 others, which included some Soviet PT-76s and SU-57(2)s. The self-propelled guns included SU-100s, JSU-152s and

ASU-57s, and the armoured personnel carriers included the BTR-40, BTR-152 and the BTR-50(P).

The Soviet T-34, which had seen action in World War II, was a 32-ton tank with good mobility, a speed of about 33 mph and a radius of action of about 180 miles. Its 85-mm gun had an effective range of just over 1,000 yards, and was capable of a high rate of fire, but it lacked an adequate fire-control mechanism. The T-54 was a 36-ton tank, with a 100-mm gun, which had an effective battle range of up to 2,000 yards. Mounting three machine guns, the T-54 had a radius of action of about 180 miles. It was the standard battle tank of the Soviet Army, but as yet had not been proved on active service. The T-55 was merely a T-54 with improvements and modifications, having slightly thicker armour in front, infrared direction-finding and fire-control devices, and a 100-mm giro-stabilized rapid-fire gun. Usually referred to as the Stalin was the Soviet JS-3, which weighed 46 tons, had a speed of only 23 mph and lacked mobility; its 122-mm gun had an effective battle range of over 2,000 yards. The Soviet PT-76 was an amphibious reconnaissance tank, weighing about 14·6 tons, with a 76-mm gun that had a battle range of up to 1,500 yards. Its radius of action was about 220 miles. The SU-57(2) was an anti-aircraft tank, mounting twin radar-controlled 57-mm anti-aircraft guns, which had a rate of fire of 150 rounds per minute and an effective range of 2,500 yards. The SU-100, a self-propelled 100-mm gun, was a 'tank destroyer' weighing about 30 tons, with a speed of about 35 mph and a radius of action of about 180 miles. The JSU-152 was a similar vehicle with a 152-mm gun. The Soviet ASU-57 was a light airborne self-propelled anti-tank gun, lightly armoured, with a low open-topped compartment for the crew. The BTR-40 was a four-wheeled armoured reconnaissance vehicle weighing 6 tons with a 7·62-mm gun and having a radius of action of about 170 miles. The BTR-152 was a six-wheeled armoured personnel carrier, also with a 7·62-mm gun, weighing about 8 tons, and having a radius of action of over 250 miles. The BTR-50(P), the first Soviet tracked armoured personnel carrier (being based on a PT-chassis), had a 12·7-mm gun, weighed just over 14 tons and had a radius of action of over 200 miles. Trucks and transport vehicles were the same as those in service with the Soviet Army.

Soviet field guns possessed by the Egyptian army included one of 130-mm with a range of 20,000 yards, a 122-mm howitzer with a range of 8,000 yards, and a 122-mm gun with a range of over 14,000 yards. Its ground anti-tank guns were of two models, each of 57-mm calibre (one with an effective range of about 1,000 yards and the other of about 2,000 yards), one gun of 85-mm with a range of 1,200 yards and another of 100-mm with a range of 2,500 yards. Many of the guns were radar-controlled. The Egyptians had plenty of Soviet mortars of 82-mm, 120-mm and 160-mm calibre, and also 82-mm and 107-mm bazooka-type recoilless anti-tank rifles. Small arms, grenades and mines were the same as those in use in the Soviet Army. The anti-aircraft guns included one of 37-mm, capable of firing 160–180 rounds a minute, with an effective range of over 2,000 yards, one of 85-mm, capable of firing 15–20 shells a minute, with a range of from 6,000 yards to 10,000 yards, and one of 100-mm, also able to fire 15–20 shells a minute and with an effective range of nearly 11,000 yards. Another Soviet weapon in Egyptian use was an anti-tank guided missile system, consisting of four missiles, usually mounted on a GAZ-69 truck. The missiles had a minimum effective range of 600 yards and a maximum of over 1,500 yards, the warhead being able to penetrate up to 350 mm of armoured plate. This was known as the Schmel, and was also mounted on armoured vehicles. The Egyptians had a rocket-launcher mounted on a truck, known as the Katyusha, which could fire up to 12 rockets, either in a salvo or in single rockets, at distances of up to 7,000 yards.

Much of this modern Soviet material had arrived during the previous 18 months, and familiarization training had not gone as well as it might have done, mainly because of language difficulties. English was the common tongue, and all instructions and manuals had to be translated into that language from Russian. The Soviet Military Mission did not seem unduly worried at the slow progress, but told the Egyptians that they were bound to win against the Israelis because of the superiority of their tanks, guns and vehicles. Through lack of Soviet experience in desert warfare the Soviet instructors had an unrealistic approach to problems of fighting in the Middle East; for example, one wonders what the Soviet Military Mission had in mind for the amphibious armoured vehicles. In general the Soviet material was technically superior and more modern than that possessed by the Israelis.

Nasser's manpower losses in 1956 had been negligible. With a rapidly expanding population[1] that numbered about 30 million in 1967, and with a three-year period of conscription in force, manpower presented no problem. The strength of the Egyptian armed forces was around 190,000 men, the army consisting of about 160,000, which at this stage included some recalled reservists. Other classes of recalled reservists, together with para-military bodies such as the 60,000-strong National Guard, brought the total number of trained and semi-trained men to just over 240,000. In addition there were the hastily enlarged civil defence organization and other special emergency services temporarily carrying out full-time duty, which increased the number of Egyptians mustered into some form of service to about one million. But this huge figure was deceptive as there was a big efficiency gap between the latter categories and the actual servicemen and reservists, and an even bigger one between them and the Fellaheen, the peasants, who had no idea what to do if the country were attacked. Egypt was not geared to total war to anywhere near the same extent as was Israel.

The 1956 war had revealed shortcomings. The officer corps tended to be static-minded, ill-trained and lacking in initiative – perhaps a 'hangover' from the days when the force was merely a garrison army under British control. Some progress had been made in rectifying these faults, but even in 1967 the Egyptian army was still short of good regimental officers. The officers as a whole were not keen on training hard for a war they thought they could win easily anyway, and they tended to resent the Soviet Military Mission's suggestions that they should rise early, go out and stay out in the desert with their soldiers. There were officers and senior commanders who worked and studied to attain a high standard of competence, but there were not enough of them, and as had been shown in the Yemen, most of the officers settled for a quiet, safe life and did not look for trouble. The morale of the Egyptian army which, of course, rested with the officer corps has frequently been criticized, often with hindsight. The fact was

---

[1] Expanding by about three-quarters of a million annually.

that in June 1967 morale was fairly good, but it rested on the false premises of supremacy of weapons and numbers. Morale varied from formation to formation, depending upon the calibre of local commanders.

With patience and good training the Egyptian could be turned into a good soldier. He lacked imagination and initiative, but was sturdy and had a certain tough endurance. Contrary to popular opinion, considerable emphasis was placed on physical fitness, and selective conscription ensured that only the best were taken, an important factor in a country with an endemic low standard of health. Properly led, he responded well, but a wide social gap separated him from his officers; it had narrowed a little within a decade, but not nearly enough. Generally, Egyptian officers tended to be indifferent to their men's welfare. About one-third of the mobilized Egyptian soldiers had seen active service in the Yemen, where some had behaved well and others indifferently.

The Egyptian chain of command was rigid, and command and staff superstructure solid and conventional. As Supreme Commander Nasser handled all major questions himself. Immediately under him were the Defence Minister, Shamseddin Badran, who dealt with administration, and Field-Marshal Amer, who executed Nasser's directives. Directives passed down the chain of command were so framed as to leave divisional and lower commanders little or no initiative. While the Egyptian higher political organization was considered exceptionally good, the same could not be said of its military counterpart. Staff procedures were slow and cumbersome, and geared to static defence requirements rather than to mobile warfare.

The army's fighting element was basically composed of three armoured divisions (one in process of being formed) and four infantry divisions, all on the Soviet pattern. Twelve artillery regiments (or brigades) were distributed out to the divisions. Egypt had a prestige brigade of paratroops, and also 15 small battalions of commandos. There were the usual supporting, supply and administrative services, which call for no special comment, except to say that the Egyptian ratio of 'teeth' to 'tail' was the surprisingly high one of 40:60.

When rebuilding his army Nasser had faced the problem of

whether to give it an all-round (including an expeditionary) capability or to condition it primarily to fight Israel. Nasser tended to favour the first alternative, while Field-Marshal Amer, whose military ability Nasser held in high regard, favoured the latter. The result was an unsatisfactory compromise. Egyptian strategy had fallen completely under Soviet influence, being based on enticing the enemy forward away from his defences or bases and then hitting him hard in the exposed flank with a weight of armour. Defence was rigid, frontal and three-tiered, while flanks were largely ignored, cross-country moves through difficult terrain being discounted, perhaps because of the civilian vehicles in the Israeli supply echelons that tied them to roads. This was a strategy that had been evolved for an East European rather than a Middle East theatre of war. Individual initiative was discouraged in junior officers, and tactics had to be fought 'according to the book'.

Since 1960 Egypt had been trying to produce its own long-range missiles capable of striking at Israeli urban centres, and with a great flourish the first rocket was fired in July 1962. It had been developed by West German scientists, who were later frightened away by Israeli intimidation. Two rockets were eventually produced, the Al Zafir, which had a 1,000-lb warhead and a range of up to 235 miles, and the Al Kahir, with a larger warhead and a range up to 375 miles. An even larger prototype was produced, but no details were released. The hurried departure of most of the West German scientists in April 1963 caused this programme to end before any of the rockets became operational, and in any case the guidance system had not been perfected. The Soviet Military Mission dismissed the Egyptian rocket project contemptuously, and imported its own surface-to-air missiles, the SAM-2s, which it kept together in a special command under strict Soviet control.

Egypt had several factories producing shells, ammunition, small arms, vehicles and certain items of military equipment, mainly under Soviet licence. There was also a large research centre on the outskirts of Cairo, where it was suspected that the Egyptians were experimenting with bacteriological, chemical and nuclear projects, but these suspicions were never properly substantiated although there must have been an element of fact in them. From June 1963 there had been allegations that the Egyptians were using poison gas bombs in the Yemen. The Egyptians denied this, but the major powers seemed reluctant to pry too deeply into these charges, and there was more reluctance still when in early 1967 rumours circulated that the Egyptians possessed stocks of nerve gas. West German scientists had been employed at the research centre. It was known that West Germany was very advanced in chemical warfare techniques and had a degree of collaboration in this field with America. Egypt denied possessing nerve gas, and stated that the West German scientists who remained were employed as lecturers and on aircraft development only. However, all Egyptian soldiers in the Sinai were equipped with gas masks, which raises the question whether Nasser really had the means to wage chemical warfare or was trying to alarm the Israelis by giving the impression that he had.

Nasser had been actively engaged in the civil war in the Yemen since it began in September 1962, when he rushed paratroops to Sana to bolster up Colonel Sallal, the leader of the Revolution, who became his puppet. In the spring of 1963 Field-Marshal Amer went to the Yemen with about 20,000 Egyptians and conducted a brilliant three-week offensive, known as the Ramadan Campaign, which brought over half the country under his control and drove the Royalists back into the mountains to the north and the east. Saudi Arabia provided money to enable the Royalists to hit back, but the war soon bogged down in a military stalemate. Field-Marshal Amer continually urged Nasser to pull out of the Yemen, but Nasser was reluctant. At its height the Egyptian Expeditionary Force in the Yemen amounted to over 90,000 soldiers, supported by over one-third of Egypt's armour, guns and aircraft. On 4 June two infantry brigades and some logistic units, about 10,000 soldiers, were in transit back to Egypt, leaving behind only five other brigades, which with supporting arms and services amounted to just over 20,000 men. Tanks, guns and aircraft had been thinned out correspondingly.

EGYPTIAN DISPOSITIONS

The fighting element of the Egyptian forces in the Sinai, commanded by Lieutenant-General Abdul Mohsen Murtagi,[1] with main headquarters at El Arish, was composed of an armoured division, a smaller armoured formation and five infantry divisions. One, the 20th Palestinian Division (sometimes referred to as the Palestine National Guard), which was stronger in manpower[2] but weaker in armour and guns than the other divisions, was based on the Gaza Strip, from Khan Yunis northwards, with an almost rigid defensive role. Although the personnel in its ranks were Palestinian volunteers, recruited from refugee camps, the officers were Egyptian; it was regarded as part of the Egyptian army, and should not be confused with the PLA of Ahmed Shukairy, although he had nominally placed his PLA under its command. Infantry divisions were in north-east Sinai blocking the routes in that region. The 7th Infantry Division, reinforced with armour and guns, sat heavily on the eastern part of the northern route between Rafah and El Arish, while the eastern parts of the Central and Southern Route were held by the 2nd Infantry Division, based on Abu Ageila and Kusseima. Behind these two divisions, still astride both the Central and Southern Routes, to give depth and form a second line of defence, lay the 3rd Infantry Division, spread out between Jebel Libni and Bir Hassana. To the south, blocking the Pilgrims Way, was the 6th Infantry Division, based on Kuntilla and Nakhel. The infantry divisions consisted of three infantry brigades, each of which had a unit of T-34s or SU-100s, and a unit of Schmel anti-tank missiles.

Lying well back almost in the shadows of the Central Ridge, behind the forward screen of infantry divisions, was the 4th Armoured Division; equipped with the newest and best Soviet armour, vehicles and weapons, it was dispersed between Bir Gifgafa and Bir Thamada, ready to deal with any enemy forces that broke through the Egyptian first and second lines of defence.

---

[1] General Murtagi had undergone senior officer training in the Soviet Union, and had commanded the Egyptian Expeditionary Force in the Yemen in 1964.

[2] Most reports indicate that it was around 30,000 strong, but about half its manpower was either scattered in small defensive detachments or employed on static guard duties.

Just to the north of 6th Infantry Division, and due east of Bir
Thamada, in the undulating and rugged territory between the
Southern Route and the Pilgrims Way, in the area of the Kuraiya
Wadi and Passes,[1] facing Mizpe Ramon in Israel, was the smaller
second armoured division with about 200 tanks and self-
propelled guns.[2] It had no number and was known as Shazli
Force, as it was commanded by a major-general of that name.
(The third armoured division still in the process of formation
remained to the west of the Suez Canal.)

The offensive plan, such as it was, envisaged local attacks by
the 7th Infantry Division to cut into Israel just south of Rafah to
capture Kerem Shalom, Bir Yitzhak and other settlements near
the border, while elements from the 2nd Infantry Division were
to cross the frontier to seize Nitzana and the road junctions just to
the east of it. The major offensive task was to go to Shazli Force,
which was to dash eastwards to take Mizpe Ramon, where the
Israelis had a large camp and training area, cut off Eilat, take
Dimona and then cross the Negev to make land contact with
Jordan, it being anticipated that a Jordanian force would probe
south-west to meet it. Thus Eilat would be completely cut off, to
be either starved into submission or taken by assault. Nasser
calculated that if this could be achieved before the UN could
intervene to impose a cease-fire, he would have gained a great
territorial and strategic advantage, which could be put to good use
as a bargaining counter or to strangle Israel further. If, as he and
his General Staff thought, this first phase could be quickly
accomplished, a second and more ambitious one could be launched
in conjunction with emboldened Arab states, that might be totally
victorious.

Nasser knew the Israelis might strike first. Indeed, it was part
of his brinkmanship to bait them into doing so as he believed such
action would be to their political and strategic disadvantage. He
estimated that they would be able to make only limited inroads
into his north-eastern defences, and that his counter-attacks

---

[1] Also spelt Qreya.

[2] Shazli Force consisted of four tank battalions, a motorized infantry brigade,
a commando battalion and three artillery units. It was about 9,000 strong, had
over 450 armoured and other vehicles, and had first concentrated near Sheikh
Zuweid, being ordered to move south on 27 May.

would tumble them backwards. He did, however, believe—through Israeli deception and faulty Egyptian intelligence—that this time the Israelis would make a major effort to strike out quickly for Sharm El Sheikh so as to free the blockaded Straits of Tiran. In that event the waiting and well-placed Shazli Force was to dash forward and hit the Israelis in the flank.

Of some 90,000 Egyptian soldiers in the Sinai, perhaps just under one-third were recalled reservists, of all ranks up to and including company commander level. Just over one-third were conscripts, most of whom had barely completed their training. The other third was made up of regulars, or those on some sort of regular engagement, such as technicians, tank crews and gunners. Almost half had seen 'active service' in the Yemen.

Apart from the 20th Palestinian Division, permanently stationed in the Gaza Strip, only one Egyptian division had been in the Sinai before Nasser began his brinkmanship—the 7th Infantry Division, which had been spread out well forward near the Israeli frontier. Protected by the UNEF, it had manned defences at Rafah, El Arish, Abu Ageila, Kusseima and Kuntilla, relying upon desert patrols to watch the 139-mile frontier. Escalation had caused a hurried and not too well ordered build-up, with Egyptian formations and units being rushed across the Suez Canal at great speed into the Sinai. A degree of operational and administrative chaos resulted. An indifferent communications system exacerbated this situation, as units were moved from one place to another one day and then elsewhere the next. Few units knew where their ultimate defensive position was to be, how long they would stay where they happened to be at the moment and who was on their flanks. Most officers did not really expect war to break out, complacently recalling that Nasser had carried out a similar brinkmanship manoeuvre in 1960 and that nothing had come of it. They tended to sit down listlessly whenever their units were halted, to await the next move and for the confusion to sort itself out, instead of energetically applying themselves to ensuring that their men and equipment were ready to fight instantly. There seemed a lack of co-operation and communication between the operational and logistic staffs, and so the supply system, based on El Arish and to a lesser extent on Jebel Libni, was not working at the optimum efficiency it might have achieved had not war come so suddenly. There were rations, fuel and stores in plenty, waiting to be distributed, but as the logistics staff did not know the locations, strengths or requirements of units, many were without food, water or fuel—some for long periods. When the Israelis struck it was estimated that at least 20 per cent of roughly 950 Egyptian tanks and 250 armoured personnel carriers were 'non-runners', because of fuel shortage, mechanical breakdowns (Shazli Force in particular was 'out of breath'), unsuitability for desert conditions, or excessive mileage consequent on pointless moves from one place to another. A slightly greater percentage of all other types of vehicles and up to one-quarter of some 1,000 guns were not ready for action for similar reasons. The roads were crowded with vehicles of all sorts.

In short, the picture was not that of a huge, well-armed, efficient army poised to strike deep into Israel, which Nasser was projecting to the Arabs and the world. On the contrary, the true picture was one of confusion and unreadiness. Formations and units were fumbling around trying to find out where they ought to be or where they should go. Many were short of rations and fuel, a proportion of vehicles and weapons were not yet ready for action, and a general feeling prevailed amongst officers and soldiers that there was no need to worry as it might not come to war.

ISRAELI DISPOSITIONS

The Israeli forces about to invade the Sinai were grouped into three Ugdas known by the names of their commanders: Brigadier Israel Tal, Commander of the Armoured Corps, Brigadier Ariel Sharon, Director of Army Training, and Brigadier Avraham Yoffe, a reservist but a former regular officer. The Tal Ugda consisted of two brigades: S Armoured Brigade, which had a Centurion, a Sherman and a Mechanized Infantry Battalion,[1] and L Armoured Brigade, which had a Patton, an AMX and a Mechanized Infantry Battalion. The Tal Ugda had about 300 tanks, 100 half-tracks and over 50 guns, some of which were self-propelled. All Israeli armoured brigades had a fairly strong reconnaissance unit, mounted on light tanks, half-tracks and

---

[1] The term 'battalion' is used throughout to describe a major unit of any arm, whether infantry, artillery or armour.

jeeps. The Sharon Ugda consisted of M Armoured Brigade, composed of a Centurion, a Sherman and a Mechanized Infantry Battalion, Y Infantry Brigade (of three infantry battalions), a paratroop battalion, and six battalions of artillery.[1] In all the Sharon Ugda had over 200 tanks, 100 half-tracks and about 100 guns.

The Yoffe Ugda consisted of C Armoured Brigade and K Armoured Brigade, each of which had two Centurion battalions and a small battalion of mechanized infantry. It had about 200 tanks and 100 half-tracks, but no artillery.

Another formation to fight on this front was P Paratroop Brigade under the command of Tal Ugda, which consisted of three battalions (one being detached to Sharon Ugda) of paratroops in half-tracks and a battalion of Pattons. Each Ugda had its own integral engineer, signal, mortar and medical sub-units, which made them self-contained. It also had its own supply vehicles with three days' supplies; most were impressed civilian vehicles popularly known amongst Israeli soldiers as 'Tnuva trucks', Tnuva being a well-known Israeli dairy marketing organization.

Held ready for exploitation or defence were other forces which came into action to a greater or lesser degree at some stage in the Sinai fighting. These were X Infantry Brigade, positioned opposite the Gaza Strip, N Armoured Brigade opposite Kusseima, and W Armoured Brigade opposite Kuntilla. There was a small group of units, based on an infantry battalion, whose task was to defend Eilat.

The commander of the Israeli striking force was Brigadier Yeshayahu Gavish, GOC, Southern Command, who was more of a director than an operational 'front commander', as he gave his Ugda commanders general directives rather than precise orders. The first directive he gave to Brigadier Tal was to break into the Gaza Strip, storm the Rafah defences and then move towards El Arish, while Brigadier Yoffe was to move across the desert to block the movement of Egyptian reinforcements in preparation for a combined night operation against El Arish involving Q Paratroop Brigade and the navy. Meanwhile, Brigadier Sharon

---

[1] An Israeli artillery battalion usually had three companies, each of four guns.

was to crash through the Um Katif defences to seize the Abu Ageila road junction and so get behind Kusseima. Each Ugda commander made his own plans, which were then communicated to Brigadier Gavish for his approval, before being passed on to the General Staff for co-ordination. Once the plans had been agreed, their execution was left entirely to the Ugda commander.

An Israeli deception plan existed to lead the Egyptians to assume that the Israelis were primarily concerned with opening the Straits of Tiran and would make a dash along the dubious coastal road, in conjunction with naval support, to seize Sharm El Sheikh. A brigade's worth of dummy tanks and vehicles was positioned near Mizpe Ramon, which was in an eight-mile-wide depression, flanked by 1,000-feet-high cliffs in places and not far from W Armoured Brigade, to give the impression of at least two armoured brigades ready to move southwards.

Personnel of the striking forces had been in positions just a few miles back from the frontier for nearly a fortnight. Unlike the Egyptians they were facing, they felt that war was inevitable, and so the precious days had been spent in making thorough preparation. The communication network had been properly tested, the supply system perfected, and attention given to stocks of fuel, water, ammunition and food. Special care was given to the maintenance of tanks and vehicles, which were started up and checked daily. Instead of sitting around and doing nothing the soldiers rehearsed infantry and armoured co-operation tactics, practised communication and carried out weapon training, while the infantry marched 10 kilometres daily in full equipment, carrying extra ammunition. Recalled reservists soon regained their fitness. In short, the Israeli troops were prepared and poised.

The First Day (Monday, 5 June 1967)

THE TAL UGDA

Brigadier Tal, with the Tal Ugda in the north, decided to break into the Gaza Strip opposite Khan Yunis, at the junction of sectors held by the 20th Palestinian Division and the Egyptian 7th Infantry Division, and once inside turn left and move along

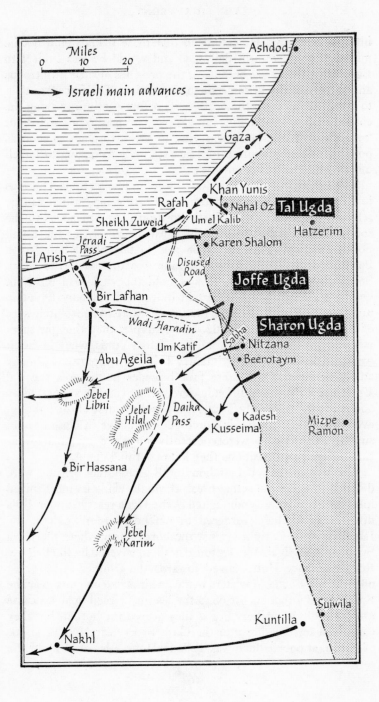

internal roadways. He estimated that these roads would not be mined as they were in daily use and would be less subject to Egyptian artillery fire because of the presence of their own troops and the proximity of the civilian population. The force was then to attack Rafah from the north-east, before continuing along the coastal road to Jiradi. This initial operation was to be carried out 'regardless of cost' as it was vital to break through as soon as possible and any failure might be extremely damaging to Israeli morale and chances of success.

The Egyptian defences at Rafah were in two sections. One was just to the west of the town and military camp, which can be referred to as the Rafah North Position. The other was to the south of the road junction, which can be known as the Rafah South Position. The Tal Ugda was to take the Rafah North Position, while P Paratroop Brigade was to assault the Rafah South Position to get on to and hold the vital road junction. Owing to the frequent uncertain movement of many Egyptian units right up until H Hour, the Israelis were not absolutely sure of the enemy order-of-battle. For example, they thought there was just one Palestinian battalion at Khan Yunis, when in fact it was held by a reinforced infantry brigade, supported by many anti-tank guns. There were four brigades in the area the Tal Ugda and P Paratroop Brigade were going to attack, supported by about 200 tanks, mainly T-34s. During the course of the fighting, even when the Israeli Air Force became active in close ground support, the Israelis were constantly surprised by small, well-camouflaged gun positions they knew nothing about.

The two armoured battalions of S Armoured Brigade were detailed to make the actual break-through, while its mechanized infantry battalion was nominated as the Ugda reserve under Tal's direct control, being ordered to defend Kerem Shalom, the Israeli settlement right against the border near where the Gaza Strip met the Sinai. The Patton Battalion, covered by the Brigade Reconnaissance Unit, moved towards the frontier at 0815. At 0830 Israeli Fouga Magisters made an air strike on guns near the Rafah Road Junction. At 0840 the leading Israeli vehicles came under desultory artillery fire as they neared the border, but they continued on crossing into the Gaza Strip near Nir Oz, south of Nirim, at 0900, which was Tal's H-Hour. Also at H-Hour the forward elements of one battalion of P Paratroop Brigade crossed the Egyptian frontier south of Kerem Shalom, making for the Rafah Road Junction. There was no special code-name for this operation, although a general one, Beni Or ('Sons of Light' from the Dead Sea Scrolls theme), was initially given to the whole Sinai offensive. The code-name 'Strike Zion' afterwards became vaguely prominent, but as Jordan came into the war, and operation succeeded operation, general stress caused all thoughts of formal code-names to vanish. The code-word for starting the attack on the Egyptians was 'Sadin Adom' (Red Sheet).

The distance from Nir Oz to Khan Yunis is about four miles, the terrain being part extensively cultivated and part open stretches of loose sand. As the Patton Battalion entered the Gaza Strip proper, Egyptian shelling from Khan Yunis, although not really heavy, became more accurate. In the initial bustle to get through the narrow alleys of the frontier hamlets, both the Brigade Reconnaissance Unit and the Patton Battalion lost vehicles, some floundering in the soft sand or being baulked by steeply banked 'walls' around the small fields as they tried to get behind houses, while others were hit or suffered damage from mines. The Patton Battalion emerged into more open country, moving in two parallel columns, the tanks following in each other's tracks to avoid mines. The Centurion Battalion followed a short distance behind. Progress was slow as many anti-tank obstacles were encountered and deviations made. Israeli covering artillery now came into action, being directed from one of the leading Pattons, causing the defenders to withdraw from some of their outlying posts. The original directive to the Patton Battalion, which had only three companies (Brigadier Tal having taken one to be his immediate battle reserve), was to crash forward to hit the Khan Yunis railway station area. One company was to deviate to take Beni Souhila, a suburb on a ridge to the east which dominated the Israeli line of approach, while the following Centurion Battalion was to sheer off slightly westwards to avoid the town and to get quickly on to, and race down, the main road to Rafah, about 10 miles distant, which Tal had correctly calculated was not mined. A considerable and unexpected volume of artillery and anti-tank fire came from Beni Souhila, and the Patton company and the Brigade Reconnaissance

Unit suffered losses as they approached, both becoming dangerously immersed in its outer defences. A machine gun post on a
water tower was demolished with a shot from a Patton, and a
school building that contained anti-tank guns was demolished as
well. The two other Patton companies also came under fire and
for a short period there was confusion because of the failure of
radio communication within the formation. At this stage Brigadier
Tal realized that his intelligence was faulty, and that Khan Yunis
was far more strongly held than he had supposed. Quickly
changing his plan, Brigadier Tal ordered the Centurion Battalion, which had only two tank companies (the other two being
nominated as the Brigade Battle Reserve), to charge forward and
assault Khan Yunis instead of bypassing it, and then to engage the
Egyptian defences at Rafah at long range to tempt them to
reveal their positions by firing back. The two Patton companies
were told to change direction and outflank the Beni Souhila ridge
from the north, and the ridge itself was to be cleared by the
Brigade Battle Reserve of Centurions. The Pattons swung round,
bypassed Beni Souhila, hit the road from Gaza, and raced south-
westwards into Khan Yunis, which was held by a strong
Palestinian brigade. As they pounded through the streets,
Palestinian soldiers fled before them or went underground, and
white flags appeared at windows. In the same movement the
Centurions forced their way into the market square, where both
met. The town was suddenly deserted; it was not until some time
later that sniping broke out and resistance again stiffened. The
Brigade Battle Reserve dealt with the Beni Souhila ridge and
managed to extricate the now badly battered Brigade Reconnaissance Unit. Next, the Centurion Battalion, with the Brigade
Reconnaissance Unit and a mechanized infantry company, was
temporarily left to look after Khan Yunis, while one of the Patton
companies moved along a track parallel to the coastline towards
Rafah. It made good progress, encountering only some small arms
fire as it approached the northern corner of Rafah Camp, which
caused it to remain on the metalled road on the north side of the
railway line. The Second Patton company moved westwards
along the railway line, which ran between the coast and the
metalled road, but its progress was slower and more costly; at
least four tanks were disabled by mines before it arrived to help

the other Patton company to clear the Rafah Camp area, which was not strongly defended.

After clearing the Souhila ridge the Centurion Brigade Battle Reserve moved closer to Khan Yunis. It remained to the south of the town astride the metalled road until its restless commander[1] pressed forward along the road westwards until he hit up against a small Egyptian-defended post at Um El Kaleb, at a junction where a camel track led off directly to the Rafah Road Junction,[2] and which was in fact the south-eastern corner of the Rafah Camp defences. The Centurions quickly rode over the Egyptian position and continued along the road, halting only briefly, where the railway line crossed it, to crush another small Egyptian position. Several civilian cars had been parked outside the Rafah railway station, and along the roadways, and already a few were in flames. The Centurion Brigade Battle Reserve then carried on along the road until it reached the Water Tower, a prominent landmark adjacent to Rafah Camp, where it made contact with the Pattons, and where it was later joined by the Brigade Command Group, the Centurion Battalion and the Brigade Reconnaissance Unit from Khan Yunis. It had been the intention that the Mechanized Infantry Battalion of S Armoured Brigade from Kerem Shalom should move into the Gaza Strip and seize Um El Kaleb, but as P Paratroop Brigade had not achieved its objective (positions near the Rafah Road Junction), to be on the safe side Brigadier Tal ordered it to remain where it was, and so this Egyptian position fell instead to the S Brigade Battle Reserve.

Most of S Armoured Brigade was now approaching the Water Tower, some three miles to the north of the vital Rafah Road Junction. Brigadier Tal expected the road junction to be heavily defended and, as he had little precise information on the actual Egyptian dispositions, he sent his S Brigade Reconnaissance Unit[3] down the road to find out. The main part of the Egyptian

---

[1] The Centurion Brigade Battle Reserve, consisting mainly of 18 Centurions, was led by the brigade second-in-command, who (according to the *Tanks of Tammuz*) fought this and other engagements with brilliant inconsistency, and also without a map.

[2] The Rafah Road Junction was in fact a cross-roads, but this 'track' had become disused because it ran so close to Israeli territory.

[3] This now consisted of two Pattons, three half-tracks and four jeeps. (*Tanks of Tammuz*.)

Rafah North Position was to the north-west of the road junction, being laid out amid rolling sand dunes, somewhat in the form of the widely-spaced points of a diamond, and all very cleverly concealed. The actual road junction was not held, the main positions, with good fields of fire, all lying back from the road-ways.

The Brigade Reconnaissance Unit moved southwards down the road and was fired upon, when only about 100 yards from the road junction, by an Egyptian position just to the west of the road, which the Israelis knew nothing about. The Israeli offensive was still at the 'regardless of cost' stage as it was essential to break through quickly, so the unit turned and charged the position with all guns firing. It proved to be a costly assault. In crossing the protective minefield one Patton, two half-tracks and two jeeps were disabled, but the position itself was overrun and the infantry trenches cleared with small arms fire. This unit was now in deep trouble, as the Egyptians brought down fire on to their former position, so it had to be hurriedly evacuated. The withdrawal across the minefield was slow, the sole surviving Patton leading the way with other Israeli vehicles carefully following in its tracks. The Patton hit a mine just before it reached the roadway, and only two half-tracks and one jeep got back safely to the shelter of the sand dunes. Over half the men of the unit had become casualties. The ambush of the Brigade Reconnaissance Unit had been the signal to the Egyptians, who opened up with their guns on whatever Israeli vehicles they could see; they thus revealed their main positions and enabled Brigadier Tal to plan accordingly. Four main defended localities in the Rafah North Position were exposed—two in the north and two in the south, held by a brigade of Egyptians (of the 7th Infantry Division), together with a Palestinian battalion, with extra guns and tanks. The Israelis afterwards estimated that there were over 150 tanks, including 30 Stalins and over 90 guns, in the area of Rafah town and Camp and the Rafah North Position. Again the Israelis were surprised by such strength of troops and weapons and by such good camouflage. When Brigadier Tal realized what was facing him he called for an air strike, which was made at 1100 by Fouga Magisters. While the Israeli aircraft were overhead, the Eygptian gunners left their guns and took cover, but when the aircraft went away they returned to their posts and recommenced firing at the Israeli tanks, up to ten anti-tank guns shooting in salvoes.[1]

The Patton Battalion was ordered to assault the two northern Egyptian-defended localities just south of the railway line. Two Patton companies made a pincer movement on to them, one drawing the fire and losing in the process three tanks, while the other came in from behind just in time to save it from further punishment, although it too was fired on from unsuspected Egyptian artillery positions on the way. This action was fought amid some confusion as radio contact between tank sub-units, and indeed in some instances between tanks themselves, had been lost; the commanders had to use signalling flags manually from their turrets. After this costly but unsuccessful battle the Pattons moved westwards across country towards the road to El Arish.

At the same time the Centurion Brigade Battle Reserve went southwards from the Water Tower, one company on either side of the road, moving through a barrage from Egyptian guns situated in the flanking sand dunes. It reached the Rafah Road Junction and raced across it to the west. Moving just to the north of the roadway, it next encountered and overran the south-western defended locality of the Rafah North Position, after which it continued on towards Sheikh Zuweid, where the railway again crossed the road. (During this move the Centurions moving westwards just north of the road passed a Patton company from P Paratroop Brigade, then fighting a battle to the south, moving along in the sands to the south of the road, in the opposite direction, to attack Egyptian positions south-west of the Rafah Road Junction.)

Once the Rafah Road Junction had been crossed all the tanks of S Armoured Brigade turned westwards. The two groups of Centurions met near the roadway just to the east of Sheikh Zuweid, where they narrowly avoided shooting each other up; the situation was saved only at the last moment by the Israeli tank commanders standing up in their turrets and signalling with

---

[1] 'The artillery [Egyptian] positions were dug in low. They fired ten rounds at a time and with each volley a tank went up in flames. We left there [at Rafah] many of our dead soldiers and burnt-out tanks.' Commander of S Armoured Brigade, Press Conference, Tel Aviv, 12 June 1967.

flags. This was something the Egyptians never did, and the practice came to distinguish the two sides in the heat and dust of battle, as by this time radio contact between Israeli tank groups was extremely unreliable. The Centurions crashed through the main street of Sheikh Zuweid, an Egyptian supply centre, completely taking the defenders by surprise. Then two Centurion companies remained in Sheikh Zuweid, while the Centurion Brigade Battle Reserve moved westwards a short distance, where it was able to ambush an unsuspecting Egyptian convoy moving eastwards into Sheikh Zuweid and set its vehicles on fire. After this successful ambush it continued on, to halt briefly before the mouth of the Jiradi Pass, about 10 miles from Sheikh Zuweid, arriving there at about 1220. The Jiradi Pass is long, narrow and about seven miles in length, running between low hills and soft sand which are impassable to vehicles. The eastern part was strongly held by an infantry brigade (of the 7th Infantry Division), supported by artillery and a unit of T-34s, which were mostly dug-in; the actual defences consisted of bunkers, emplacements and trenches, covered by a forward minefield, all facing either eastwards or inwards in the usual Soviet 'three deep' pattern. The pause was very brief, and then with all guns blazing the Centurions rushed through the defended part of the Pass, again completely catching off guard the defenders, who quickly hid in their bunkers and trenches. The Israeli tanks[1] were almost through the defences before the Egyptians reacted, only the last two being hit as the gunners recovered and returned to their guns. The now-alerted Egyptian defenders turned their guns on to the leading vehicles of the Brigade Reconnaissance Unit, which had been closely following the Centurions and which was just about to enter the mouth of the Pass. Their fire caused casualties and forced the unit to withdraw. The Brigade Command Group arrived a few minutes later to find the Jiradi Pass again blocked and the Centurion Brigade Battle Reserve cut off on the far side. Not knowing the true situation, the Centurions continued on westwards until they came within sight of the outskirts of El Arish, where at about 1600 they halted briefly before moving in and destroying four Egyptian T-34s. The Centurions quickly

---

[1] Seventeen Centurions and two Pattons, according to *Tanks of Tammuz.*

withdrew some distance to wait for the remainder of the Brigade to catch up with them. They expected El Arish to be shortly subjected to aerial bombardment preceding the anticipated dusk paratroop assault. At 1100, while at the Water Tower, Brigadier Tal received information of the successful destruction of the Egyptian Air Force, so he knew he had nothing to fear from its remnants. This enabled him to plan more boldly on the ground as armoured vehicles in open desert terrain are particularly vulnerable to attack from the air. He ordered L Armoured Brigade, his reserve brigade, to cross the border and move through country in the direction of El Arish airfield, just south of the town itself. To avoid mines this brigade was told to follow a course just to the south of the main road. Brigadier Tal also moved his Ugda Command Group forward to Sheikh Zuweid, now held by two Centurion companies. As soon as he realized what had happened at the Jiradi Pass he ordered the Patton Battalion (of S Armoured Brigade), then painfully grinding across desert expanses, to concentrate at Sheikh Zuweid preparatory to attacking the Egyptian position. Meanwhile, to act as a holding force, he sent one of the Centurion companies from Sheikh Zuweid to the mouth of the Pass to join S Armoured Brigade Command Group and the depleted Brigade Reconnaissance Unit. By 1330 Brigadier Tal realized that P Paratroop Brigade's battle to the south was not going well, and at 1400 its commander called for assistance. As the Rafah South Position was one of the 'regardless of cost' objectives he detailed three battalions to rush to its aid. These were the Patton Battalion of S Armoured Brigade (just detailed to attack the Jiradi Pass), and also the Brigade's Mechanized Infantry Battalion, still in position at Kerem Shalom. The other unit was the Mechanized Infantry Battalion of L Armoured Brigade, somewhere in the loose sand near the Rafah Road Junction.

To the south P Paratroop Brigade, consisting of a Patton Battalion and one battalion of paratroops in half-tracks, had crossed the frontier at 0900 (H-Hour) some five miles south of Kerem Shalom, making across country towards the 'disused' Nitzana Road, which led from Nitzana on the Israeli side of the border to the Rafah Road Junction. The other paratroop battalion had been detached to help X Infantry Brigade, which had been detailed to follow S Armoured Brigade in the initial break-through to mop up both Khan Yunis and Gaza. P Paratroop Brigade had been stationed near the Gaza Strip and employed for the previous week on border patrols along its frontier, having been converted to mechanized infantry and given half-tracks.[1] In Mandate days the Nitzana Road had been a good metalled one, but its surface had been destroyed by the withdrawing Israelis in 1957. Unlike most others, this road had not been subsequently repaired and used by the Egyptians, because it was no good to them. The Israelis thought the main defence must be based close around the road junction (where there were some dummy and abandoned old positions), and that there would be only light resistance to the south, which consisted of expanses of loose, shifting sand. In fact, the Rafah South Position was almost as strongly held as the Rafah North one—by an infantry brigade (from the 7th Infantry Division), supported by about 100 guns, a battalion of Stalins (about 35 tanks) and a number of dug-in T-34s. The actual defensive positions were well camouflaged in the sand dunes within the valley on either side of the disused roadway. Other strong defensive localities lay to the west of the Nitzana Road, the most westerly near the village of Kafr Shan, which had some 20 T-34s, and was close to the Northern Route. The P Paratroop Brigade Reconnaissance Unit turned south to form a warning and protective screen, while the Paratroop Battalion, led by a company of Pattons, moved directly across the sand towards the Nitzana Road. At 0915 the leading Pattons unexpectedly ran head-on into Egyptian defensive localities and in the exchange of fire the Patton company commander was killed. His company hesitated in confusion.

The second Patton company (there were four in this battalion) was ordered to change course and rush to its aid, which it did. In the process it completely lost touch with its Battalion HQ, and did not regain contact for the remainder of the battle. This company crashed through the Egyptian perimeter positions and, crossing over the roadway, hit up against another strong enemy position,

---

[1] 'A few days before the fighting broke out we received orders to move south, take delivery of half-tracks and deploy ourselves as a defending armoured brigade.' Second-in-Command of P Paratroop Brigade, Press Conference, Tel Aviv, 28 June 1967.

supported by Stalin tanks, in the southern part of the Rafah South Position. In the fire-fight that ensued the Pattons knocked out a number of Egyptian tanks. Backing away from this Stalin position, the Patton company changed course and moved over undulating desert in the direction of what it thought was Kafr Shan, on the Rafah to El Arish Road. But its navigation was faulty, and it eventually ended up at Sheikh Zuweid, a few miles further west along the road, where it contacted elements of S Armoured Brigade at 1300, and where it was ordered to stay for the time being.

Meanwhile, the Paratroop Battalion, with the third Patton company in support, swinging further southwards to avoid the now-discovered Egyptian southern defensive localities to the east of the Nitzana Road, reached the roadway and commenced a northward movement to 'roll it up'. The paratroops found themselves in a bad tactical position, coming up against Egyptian flanking guns, which brought down heavy fire that caused casualties of both men and vehicles. By 1200 the paratroops were trapped, unable to advance or withdraw. The Patton company moved to the west side of the road, and at once ran into fire from a strong Egyptian position, which cost it three Pattons and forced it to withdraw.

The fourth Patton company, which had with it a paratroop company, began an odyssey on its own. Originally detailed to protect the southern flank, it crossed the roadway after an exchange of fire with an Egyptian artillery position. Having quickly lost contact with brigade HQ, it veered off in the direction of Kafr Shan and, weaving between two other enemy positions, moved across the desert until it finally bumped hard up against a strongly defended locality about three miles south of the Rafah–El Arish road, where a fight developed. By this time the Egyptians had swung the battalion of Stalin tanks, in small groups, into action in this area. These were prowling and firing at any Israeli vehicles they could spot.

The actions of these Patton company commanders have been criticized as they all lost contact with their HQ, and the widely-dispersed unit was temporarily lost to the brigade commander when he was fighting a hard, and still unresolved battle; but they reflect the value of the policy of giving general directions to commanders of all ranks in such mobile operations, so that all knew the overall aim, which in broad terms was to get to the Rafah Road Junction and open the road westwards. Although out of contact and not knowing how anyone else was faring, they all did something, whereas if they had done nothing but sit down and wait for orders, the battle would have ground to a halt.

With his Patton Battalion 'lost', after having beaten off one Egyptian counter-attack and expecting another any moment, with his men pinned down in an unfavourable position by enemy fire, the commander of P Paratroop Brigade signalled at 1400 to Brigadier Tal that he needed urgent help. As we have seen, Tal detailed three units to rush to his assistance. What is more important still, Tal, who knew the true air situation, gave the paratroops close ground support from the air. Under successive heavy strikes from Fouga Magisters, the Egyptians deserted their tanks and guns, taking to the desert for safety. This enabled the paratroops to get into a better tactical position to push northward along the valley. As they forced their way along the roadway they became involved in a series of small infantry battles against pockets of resistance formed by Egyptian infantry in trenches, but they found most of the guns unmanned. The Paratroop Battalion's progress was such that at 1600 the brigade commander signalled that he no longer required assistance.

Meanwhile the Patton company, with the attached company of paratroops in half-tracks, overran the Egyptian position it had bumped into south of the Rafah to El Arish road, and then turned westwards to assault Kafr Shan, where it quickly destroyed some 22 enemy tanks, while the paratroops dealt with the infantry defenders. Radio contact having been momentarily restored, this company was ordered to turn about and race eastwards south of the road to aid the other Patton company, which was in serious trouble as it had run up against a strong Egyptian position near the Rafah Road Junction. (In this move eastwards the Patton company passed the Centurions of S Armoured Brigade, which were moving to the north of the road in the opposite direction.) The two Patton companies encircled and out-fought a group of Stalin tanks, but lost several tanks in the fighting. The Pattons then moved forward to cover the actual road junction, remaining there until the forward elements of the Paratroop Battalion reached and occupied it at about 1900.[1] From the Road Junction the battalion commander counted at least ten disabled Stalins with smoke pouring from them.

When, at 1600, Brigadier Tal knew that P Paratroop Brigade was no longer in serious danger, he recalled the three units he had dispatched to its aid, none of which had actually got very far, and instead concentrated upon forcing the Jiradi Pass. The distance from Rafah to El Arish was nearly 30 miles. He ordered the Sherman Battalion of L Armoured Brigade, somewhere in the sands to the south of the road, to continue westwards towards the El Arish airfield, and the AMX and Mechanized Infantry Battalions of that brigade to concentrate just south of Sheikh Zuweid to be ready for a night assault on Jiradi if necessary. The Patton Battalion, of S Armoured Brigade, was ordered to make all speed to the mouth of the Jiradi Pass to join the Brigade Command Group, where it arrived at about 1700. Spreading out on a wide front the Pattons moved into the attack, but several tanks were either hit by Egyptian gunners, who this time stayed with their guns and fired back, or became stuck fast in the sand. When this attempt obviously failed the Pattons were exposed to real danger, so they were ordered back to the roadway. Then, at 1800, under a heavy Israeli mortar and artillery barrage and an air strike, the Patton Battalion, this time on a very narrow front, charged into the mouth of the Pass.[2] Under this heavy fire and aerial bombardment the Egyptians again took to their shelters, enabling the Israeli tanks to speed through the defiles. Once through the Pass they continued on to join the Centurions near the outskirts of El Arish. When Israeli aircraft disappeared from overhead and the mortar and artillery barrage ceased, the Egyptians returned to their guns, thus again blocking any further movement through the Jiradi Pass.

Brigadier Tal therefore had to continue with his plans for a night assault, for which he intended to use the AMX and Mechanized Infantry Battalions of L Armoured Brigade, but at

---

[1] In the battle for the Rafah South Position, P Paratroop Brigade lost '40 killed and 40 wounded'. (*Tanks of Tammuz*.)

[2] Four Pattons had been disabled and another 18 had to be left behind because they were either out of fuel or sunk in the sand.

1930 he received signals that both were hopelessly stuck in the sand somewhere to the south of the roadway, with most of the vehicles in need of fuel. The infantry had dismounted to try to march, but the sand had been so soft and deep that the commander recalled them to their half-tracks. Brigadier Tal was left with only the Mechanized Infantry Battalion of S Armoured Brigade, now mopping up around the Rafah Road Junction after being held at Kerem Shalom for so long, so he ordered it forward. But this was easier said than done.

As the Rafah Road Junction was made secure and darkness fell, supply vehicles in number moved forward, and the single roadway became choked with them. Units were calling desperately for fuel, water and ammunition, while helicopters fluttered to and fro overhead picking up and evacuating wounded.[1] The drivers of the two-wheel drive 'Tnuva trucks' were reluctant to get off the roadway, partly for fear of mines and partly in case they got stuck in the sand. Drastic measures had to be taken, which included using a bulldozer to force the supply vehicles off the road to let the Mechanized Infantry Battalion through. This clearance was a slow business, however, so the whole unit left the road to make a successful detour in the sand. Bypassing the gigantic traffic jam, it arrived at Sheikh Zuweid, from where it was able to move freely along the roadway again. The Centurion company had already left Sheikh Zuweid and was actually fighting a gun duel with the Egyptian positions, when the Mechanized Infantry Battalion arrived at the mouth of the Jiradi Pass just before midnight.

By midnight on the First Day the situation in Brigadier Tal's sector was that his men had successfully forced their way through the Rafah positions, the first line of Egyptian defence, but were held up before the second line at the Jiradi Pass. S Armoured Brigade Centurion Battle Reserve and the majority of the Patton Battalion had rushed successively through the Pass, and were on the outskirts of El Arish waiting for the anticipated paratroop assault, but the Pass was blocked for the third time. Brigadier Tal was about to make a night assault on it with the only unit he was able to bring to battle, others being out of fuel or stuck in the

---

[1] 'About 1,000 wounded were removed by helicopter' (in the whole war). (*Six Day War.*)

sand. To the south, P Paratroop Brigade had overrun the Rafah South Position but was exhausted, scattered, and urgently in need of fuel and reorganization before it could be made ready for action again. Brigadier Tal had a threat to his rear, as the Gaza Strip was actively holding out.

The Rafah to El Arish road itself was littered with burnt-out, destroyed and disabled Egyptian vehicles, guns and equipment. Because of the rush to use it supply vehicles were slow in getting forward; indeed, it took practically all the hours of darkness until dawn the next day to complete the refuelling. Helicopters were used by commanders for briefing and liaison. Egyptian prisoners, although few as yet, were already an embarrassment. No one quite knew what to do with them, nor could men be spared to guard them. They were simply left in small groups by the roadway under a light escort, only senior officers being flown back for instant interrogation.

Egyptian casualties had been very heavy, especially in the opening hours of the fighting, as most stood by their guns and tanks and fired back. The Israelis claimed that over 1,500 were killed in this initial breakthrough in the north; they gave their own losses as 70 dead and 34 tanks destroyed. The loss of Egyptian tanks and equipment grew suddenly heavy from midday onwards, as during the afternoon Israeli air strikes by Fouga Magisters became more frequent. For example, Israeli aircraft saved P Paratroop Brigade from disaster in the Rafah South Position, and decidedly helped to win the Rafah North Position too.

THE GAZA STRIP

Meanwhile, after the dashing breakthrough by S Armoured Brigade, the Gaza Strip was scheduled to be reduced by X Infantry Brigade, supported by one paratroop battalion. From Khan Yunis northwards it was held by the 20th Palestinian Division, assisted in an embarrassing way by tiny groups of irregulars with small arms, such as the PLA. This division had ample anti-tank weapons, especially bazookas. One infantry battalion had followed S Armoured Brigade into Khan Yunis with the intention of mopping up, but as soon as Brigadier Tal's tanks moved westwards Egyptian and Palestinian reaction set in, and a stubborn resistance developed which brought the Israeli infantry up short. The defenders were supported by T-34s in static positions, and small arms fire and sniping began. The Israelis could make no headway, and the centre and a large part of the outskirts were in Arab hands. The Sherman Battalion (of X Infantry Brigade) and the attached Paratroop Battalion sheared off round Khan Yunis, advancing northwards along the main road, where opposition became progressively stiffer owing to the multiplicity of anti-tank defences alongside the roadway. Meanwhile, the other infantry battalion, setting out on foot from Nir Oz, made for the Ali Muntar Hill, a tactical feature which shielded Gaza from the east, where it was also held up. Foiled in their attempt to break into Gaza along the main road, the Sherman and Paratroop Battalions turned eastwards and went across country to the Ali Muntar Hill, approaching it from the rear. By 1800 hours, after a short fight, it was in Israeli hands. Thus by darkness the Israelis were effectively holding the feature that blocked the approaches into Gaza, but Gaza, and indeed Khan Yunis as well, remained firmly in Egyptian and Palestinian control.

THE YOFFE UGDA

The Yoffe Ugda was to operate just to the south of the Tal Ugda. One of its brigades was to cut across country to block the El Arish to Abu Ageila road near Bir Lafhan, where it would be in a good position to prevent Egyptian reinforcements being sent to El Arish, or to cause a diversion, or to move to the aid of either the Tal Ugda or the Sharon Ugda (the latter detailed to operate near Abu Ageila), or to help with the airborne assault on El Arish, or to exploit westwards. K Armoured Brigade crossed the border at 0900 (H-Hour) and its Centurions moved along the old frontier road from Nitzana for a little way before turning off westwards along a camel track which followed the Wadi Haradin for much of its length. This proved to be a slow crawl through the loose sand and it took the Centurions about nine hours to cover a distance of some 30 miles. Apart from a fleeting glimpse of a few Egyptian reconnaissance vehicles near the frontier, there

was no sign of the enemy until, at 1400, the leading tanks
bumped up against an outpost position known as El Haradin,
about 10 miles from the El Arish to Abu Ageila roadway, which
was held by an Egyptian infantry company supported by a few
anti-tank guns. After an exchange of fire the Egyptians withdrew,
but during the skirmish four Centurions became stuck in the
sand and had to be towed out, which further delayed the advance.
It was not until 1800 that the leading Centurions reached the
road, hitting it about one mile south of the Bir Lafhan road
junction. As the Israeli tanks moved to take up a blocking position they came under fire from a 'radar position', which caused
them to halt and hesitate. Radar positions, all on the same
pattern, were scattered about the Sinai, usually situated on
higher ground, the actual radar instruments being housed in a
protective concrete building and guarded by an infantry company with anti-tank and anti-aircraft guns. Next the Centurions
came under fire from the main Bir Lafhan position, just to the
north of the road junction facing south, being the outer defences
on the southern approach to El Arish, about 12 miles to the north.
Failing daylight, and the extreme range (which was about 3,000
yards) were to the Israelis' advantage, enabling the leading
Centurion Battalion[1] to manoeuvre into ambush positions near
the roadway. Egyptian shelling died down as darkness fell.
Cautiously the second Centurion Battalion and the remainder
of the brigade, which had been following in the tracks of the
first unit, then joined it.

Farther to the south the Sharon Ugda was having difficulty in
breaking through the Egyptian defences, and Brigadier Yoffe
was told to send his second Centurion Battalion to support
Brigadier Sharon. This unit moved southwards just before 2300.
Brigadier Yoffe's other formation, C Armoured Brigade, remained behind near Nitzana. It had been planned that it should
move through to Abu Ageila when Brigadier Sharon had broken
through in that sector. Shortly after the second Centurion
Battalion had moved off southwards, the headlights of an
Egyptian mobile force, of two armoured brigades from the
4th Armoured Division, were seen approaching Bir Lafhan from

---

[1] 'K113 Battalion had only 24 tanks.' (*Tanks of Tammuz.*)

the direction of Jebel Libni. They were moving in a dual counter-attack and reinforcement role, and as they had not left their former positions near the Central Ridge until dusk, they had not been detected by the Israeli Air Force. The first Israeli shots hit three Egyptian T-55 tanks.[1] Immediately all lights on the Egyptian vehicles were extinguished, and after a brief pause both sides started shooting at each other. Then an Egyptian fuel and ammunition truck was hit and set on fire, which lit up the scene. The forward Egyptian tanks slid away backwards into the cover of darkness. In an attempt to seek them out one Israeli tank used its searchlight, but it was hit and the tank commander killed, after which the firing died down. Thus by midnight Brigadier Yoffe's sole Centurion Battalion, with its back up against the strong Bir Lafhan position, faced two Egyptian brigades, equipped largely with T-55 tanks which had an infra-red night vision device. Both forces, neither knowing the exact strength nor the intentions of the other, warily held their fire during the hours of darkness.

THE SHARON UGDA

Farther to the south the Sharon Ugda had waited for about a fortnight at Shivta, on the Nitzana to Beersheba road, nearly 15 miles back from the frontier. Its task was to break through into the Sinai along the Central Route, but the Um Katif position near the Abu Ageila road junction blocked the way, and on its southern flank was another strong Egyptian position at Kusseima. Brigadier Sharon intended to cut through Um Katif quickly with his armoured brigade.[2]

The Um Katif defensive complex, an elongated one on a narrow tract of firmer ground and wedged between a sand-sea to the north and a low rocky massif, known as Jebel Dalfa, to the south, was about 12 miles from the Israeli border. Through it ran the main road to Jebel Libni and on to Bir Gifgafa. The main defences rested on a low feature to the south of the roadway, rising

---

[1] *Tanks of Tammuz.*

[2] 'I was convinced that I would be able to accomplish my mission in two or three hours.' Commander of M Armoured Brigade, Press Conference, Tel Aviv, 28 June 1967.

to a height of over 80 feet, known as Um Katif—hence the name given to the whole defence complex. Considering the flanks to be secured by natural obstacles, the Egyptians had prepared strong blocking positions in three lines, on the Soviet pattern, facing eastwards. Behind a protective minefield, some 300 yards in depth, were three linear trench systems, each nearly 3,000 yards in length, one immediately behind the other, with concrete emplacements and rock-constructed shelters and dug-outs. Each line was held by an infantry battalion. Some distance behind, placed in a rough rectangle, was the artillery park containing about 70 guns, a roadway leading south to Kusseima passing between the trenches and the artillery park. To the immediate south of Jebel Dalfa was the wide, dry bed of the Wadi El Arish. To the west of the artillery park was the broken Rouffa Dam, and to its west lay a camp area, lying just to the south of the Abu Ageila road junction, where one road went north to El Arish and the other (the Central Route) westwards. About one mile west of the road junction a formerly motorable track went southwards across a sand-sea and through the Daika Pass, now blocked by sand, to join the Southern Route to Kusseima. The Um Katif position was held by a reinforced infantry brigade (part of the Egyptian 2nd Infantry Division), supported by two units of T-34s and one of SU-100s—about 90 tanks in all. The tanks were spread out in depth through the position, which extended for about eight miles from east to west (being up to two miles wide in parts), close to and covering the roadway; they were disposed on the southern side. Like most Egyptian infantry brigades this one had a unit of Schmel anti-tank missiles. Brigadier Sharon was under the impression that this position was held by only one infantry battalion, which had indeed been the case up to the past two days when the majority of the Egyptian troops had been bundled into the Um Katif complex.

A camel track, just negotiable by tracked vehicles, skirted and bypassed the main Um Katif positions through the sand-sea to the north, but was blocked by a small Egyptian force consisting of an infantry company, a company of tanks (about 20 T-34s) and a dozen guns on a small feature known as Hill 181. There were other outlying positions on small features that gave good fields of fire and observation; the nearest, about two miles from the Israeli border and close to the main roadway, was known as Tarat Um Basis. Another, called Um Tarpa, lay about three miles behind it, also covering the main roadway, immediately behind which the camel track led off into the desert. A motorable track led from the Israeli border to the southern tip of the trench system, running roughly parallel to the main road and about one mile south of it. An Egyptian position blocked its terminus. In fact, practically all the roads and tracks leading in to the Um Katif position and the Abu Ageila road junction were picketed by Egyptian troops.

The Centurion Battalion, with a company of mechanized infantry, were selected to lead the charge across the rough, undulating ground between the border and Um Katif. An artillery barrage and an air strike by Fouga Magisters was put down on the main Um Katif positions commencing at 0815. At 0840 the first Israeli tanks crossed the frontier near the deserted UN Post at El Auja. They were almost immediately fired on from Tarat Um Basis, which the Israelis suspected was covered by a minefield, so the Centurions bypassed it, shelling the position as they did so. Israeli artillery kept up an intermittent fire on Tarat Um Basis until it was taken some hours later. Moving mainly to the south of the main road in open order, the Centurions approached the next position, at Um Tarpa, and came under fire from it. As this was a 'regardless of cost' operation, two companies of Centurions with a company of mechanized infantry overwhelmed the position. They immediately ran into a minefield when they attempted to avoid a large crater that had been blown in the road. The Centurions crept forward through the minefield, losing seven tanks disabled in the process.

As the Centurions were reorganizing after Um Tarpa, where Brigadier Sharon claimed his first T-34s, they came under heavy fire from the main Egyptian position, so one company of Centurions was hastily sent along the camel track to occupy the Abu Ageila road junction from that direction, while the other two Centurion companies quickly spread out in line facing westwards, taking cover in the undulating ground. Immediately the fourth Centurion company came up the Battalion moved into the assault, but under the weight of enemy fire it soon came to a halt. Seeing that this had failed, the brigade commander ordered the whole of the Centurion Battalion to change direction and move along the camel track to get quickly to the Abu Ageila road junction, while the Sherman Battalion, which had been following behind, was told to take over the frontal attack and crash through Um Katif on the main road to meet it there.

The Sherman Battalion advanced in open order, but almost immediately came under heavy fire which forced it to halt. It was now just past noon, and after four hours the Israelis had still not breached the Um Katif defences. Brigadier Sharon called for an air strike on Um Katif, which went in at 1230 and lasted for several minutes, during which an Israeli Fouga Magister was shot down by the Egyptians. The Sherman Battalion had continued the advance during the air strike, but as soon as the Israeli planes disappeared, the Egyptian guns again opened up on the advancing tanks, causing them to stop.

Meanwhile the leading Centurion company moved slowly in single file along the camel track until about 1100, when it came under fire from the Egyptian position at Hill 181. The Centurions were forced to withdraw a little way. On the southern flank, M Armoured Brigade Reconnaissance Unit had been sent on a detour to move westwards over the broken ground towards the higher parts overlooking the southern end of the trench system, and also to keep a watch on the road to Kusseima to give early warning of any reinforcements or counter-moves from that direction.

Brigadier Sharon, now realizing the true strength of the Um Katif position, was compelled to admit that his quick 'regardless of cost' plan to break through to the Abu Ageila road junction had failed. But the blocking position at Um Katif had to be broken to free the Central Route, so he decided to call up his infantry brigade and Paratroop Battalion, and he made plans for a night assault. Meanwhile the Israeli mobile guns had moved up to the Shermans and an intensive tank-gun and artillery fight broke out that lasted until about 1400, when a dust storm reduced visibility considerably. Intermittent shelling by both sides continued all the afternoon, during which the Shermans in small groups advanced to snipe at Egyptian positions and then to withdraw before creeping forward to have another shot. At about 1700 the dust storm cleared, and Egyptian shelling was resumed; it continued right into the night, when flare shells interspersed with high explosive shells kept the Shermans pinned down. The Israeli tanks continued their 'sniping and movement' tactics to tempt the enemy to open fire to reveal his positions, and also to give the impression of an impending frontal armoured attack.

Y Infantry Brigade, ordered to make a flanking assault on the trench system, left Nitzana in buses at about 1300. By 1400 it had reached Tarat Um Basis, which had just been finally reduced by the mechanized infantry of M Armoured Brigade; here the troops had to get out as the two-wheel drive vehicles could go no farther, the surface of the road from there to Um Katif being extremely poor, subject to sand drifts and with many craters. The heavily-laden infantrymen marched along to Um Tarpa and then forked off along the camel track, the intention being that they should continue along it until level with the open flanks of the trenches and then turn southwards to assault them. It took them several hours to get to their start-lines. The Centurion Battalion on the camel track, which had been forced to withdraw by the Egyptian position on Hill 181, had regrouped and moved into the assault again at about 1500, occupying it as the Egyptians evacuated. Slowly the Centurions moved forward, leaving one company to hold Hill 181, but they had not reached the Abu Ageila to El Arish road by the time darkness fell.

Brigadier Sharon decided to use the Paratroop Battalion to silence the Egyptian guns, and a squadron of 12 helicopters was allocated to lift them into action. At 1800 the paratroops were put into civilian buses and moved forward over the frontier to Tarat Um Basis. Here the men had to get out and march to Um Tarpa, where the helicopters (only six and not the promised 12) were waiting for them. Sharon planned to put them down on the Jebel Dalfa feature so that they could assault downhill, but there was a last-minute change of plan. This was partly because it had become known that the artillery park was at least one mile behind the forward trench system on a separate part of the Um Katif feature, protected to a degree by the open dry bed of the Wadi El Arish to its south and a rocky defile to its east, along which ran the road to Kusseima. This information nullified the 'assault down hill' part of the plan, so with the smaller number of helicopters available Brigadier Sharon decided, once he knew Hill 181 to be secure, that it would be better and safer for the paratroops to attack from the north out of the desert. Only about 150 paratroops could be used because of helicopter restriction and they were taken in three separate flights, the first leaving at about 1900 as daylight was failing. Brigadier Sharon was now co-ordinating the moves of his troops to their start-lines ready for an all-arms attack, and he set H-Hour to be at 2300. A company of tanks was moved to the south-east of Um Katif to cover the track leading to Kusseima, and the Reconnaissance Unit was moved further westwards around the Jebel Dalfa feature to watch the Daika Pass. By 2000 the paratroops had landed in their assembly area, about three miles to the north of the road in the sandy desert terrain, and soon were moving in four small groups towards their objective. But the Egyptians had been alerted by the helicopter movement, and at 2100 put down mortar fire on the spot where the helicopters were waiting, actually hitting the marker panels, which forced the aircraft to move some distance away for safety. Brigadier Sharon had calculated that the marching paratroops would require only two hours to reach the roadway, but sand dunes, some up to 40 feet in height, had to be traversed, and so they fell behind schedule. It was almost 2300 hours before they came in sight of the Egyptian gun positions and saw the gun flashes. However, H-Hour was put back to 2330, which enabled them to reach the roadway without being detected.

Just before the original H-Hour (2300) Brigadier Sharon was told that he could not have the aircraft strikes he was counting on to support his assault on Um Katif. Both he and Brigadier Gavish, GOC Southern Command, knew the true air situation, but they also knew that Jordan had entered the war and that troops and resources were being diverted to Jerusalem. Brigadier Gavish urged him to postpone his attack until dawn, when ample Israeli aircraft would be available to soften up the Egyptian defences, but Sharon's mind was made up. Realizing that neither the paratroops nor the infantry brigade, nor indeed the Centurion Battalion, would be in their assaulting positions in time, he merely retarded H-Hour. At 2330 Sharon put down a barrage, using all his 100 guns,[1] on to the trench system. It was reputed to have been the biggest artillery barrage ever fired by the Israelis. Fire control was placed entirely in the hands of the infantry brigade commander, and although it was due to last for 30 minutes he stopped it after only 20 minutes, feeling that the defenders had had enough and that it was the moment for his men to attack. He sent two of his battalions to deal with the first and second trenches respectively, keeping his third back in case any anti-tank precautions were necessary, but a few minutes after the trench fighting began he decided to commit it to clearing the third trench. As the Israeli infantrymen moved into the assault the Egyptian artillery opened up on them but much of the effect of the bursting shells was absorbed in the soft sand.[2] The three infantry battalions, whose leading elements carried red, blue and green lights respectively, so that other Israeli formations and the artillery could chart their progress, moved slowly along the lines of trenches.

As soon as the barrage opened the Sherman tanks crept forward to positions south of the road, ready to break through immediately the Israeli infantry reached the roadway. To the west of Um Katif, just before H-Hour, the Centurion Battalion, having emerged on to the Abu Ageila to El Arish road and over-run an Egyptian position, turned southwards and edged towards the camp area near the road junction, when it was fired on by T-34s. Soon a miniature tank battle was in progress. By midnight the battle for Um Katif had been joined, with Sharon mounting a set-piece attack, using armour, paratroops and infantry, and assaulting on three sides. The outcome was by no means a foregone conclusion, as the Israelis still did not know the exact strength or the locations of all the defensive positions.

South of Um Katif, during the First Day, the Israeli N Armoured Brigade opposite the Kusseima garrison (which consisted of a reinforced infantry brigade, supported by nearly 100 guns and 100 tanks, and a unit of Schmel anti-tank missiles)

---

[1] 'In 20 minutes some 6,000 shells fell on Um Katif.' Yael Dayan.

[2] 'Our greatest luck was the dunes which absorbed the falling shells. In the event that a shell falls even a few metres away, it is absorbed by the sand.' Commander of Y Infantry Brigade, Press Conference, Tel Aviv, 12 June 1967.

remained passive, except for a few reconnaissance vehicles that moved over the border to keep a close watch on the enemy.

Farther south still W Armoured Brigade to the southwest of Mizpe Ramon made no major move against the Egyptian positions at Kuntilla, but during the morning a small Israeli reconnaissance force crossed the border from Suiwila and occupied some wells behind and to the south of the main Egyptian positions. They remained there all day. Kuntilla was held by an infantry brigade (of the 6th Infantry Division). At about 1600 the Egyptian Reconnaissance Unit attacked the Israelis at the wells, drove them out and followed them across the border, then made several thrusts at W Armoured Brigade, causing it to withdraw some distance. The Egyptian unit withdrew at dusk, and the situation in this sector became passive. The Egyptians regard this daring raid as one of their most praiseworthy actions during the war.

COMMENTS ON THE FIRST DAY'S FIGHTING

By midnight on the First Day, after just over 15 hours' fighting, Israeli forces had broken into the Gaza Strip and overrun the Rafah defences, but they had failed to take Um Katif, the Jiradi Pass and Khan Yunis; one armoured battalion faced two Egyptian armoured brigades, and part of an Israeli armoured brigade was cut off between the Jiradi Pass and El Arish. Gaza and the northern part of the Gaza Strip remained intact in Egyptian hands, as did El Arish, Kusseima and Kuntilla. Jordan had entered the war, and the paratroop assault on El Arish had been cancelled. There had been gaps in Israeli field intelligence, due no doubt to the last-minute moves of Egyptian formations. The strengths of the defenders at Khan Yunis, Jiradi, Um Katif and Rafah had been underestimated, and the extent and locations of many positions were not known. In general, the Egyptian defences were well camouflaged, and were frequently not detected until they opened fire. They were also initially stoutly defended; the rigid linear-type of defence suited the character and training of the Egyptian soldiers very well, while their artillery shooting was quite accurate.

The Israeli policy of advancing 'regardless of cost', and their practice of attacking suddenly detected Egyptian positions with all guns firing, proved effective but expensive in lives and vehicles. The idea of giving all commanders a general directive usually worked to the Israelis' advantage, jerkily forcing the momentum along instead of allowing it to roll to a halt as it might have done on occasions. Israeli communications within formations and units were often poor, bringing the inevitable fog of war down in a cloud over parts of the battlefield. The practice of Israeli tank commanders advancing with open turrets, and having to signal manually from them, was also an expensive one. By midnight the Israeli senior officers were in an anxious mood; the initial attacks on Um Katif had failed, and the Jiradi defences had again unexpectedly rallied to block the Israelis on the Northern Route. The threat to cut off Eilat and the southern Negev remained, and there was alarm at the Israeli casualties incurred so far. Brigadier Gavish had wanted Sharon to wait until dawn before attacking Um Katif because he feared a night attack might mean heavy losses and a failure could be bad for morale. The Israeli senior commanders saw that the Egyptian first line positions at Kusseima and Kuntilla remained untouched, that the second line positions such as El Arish, Bir Lafhan and Jebel Libni had yet to be breached, and that the Egyptians in defence had many advantages, not the least being their good camouflage and artillery shooting. They also saw that the Egyptians were tactically able to hit back heavily, and indeed throughout the night an Egyptian armoured counter-attack was anticipated at any moment. On the credit side the Israelis felt that at the worst the battles for Um Katif and Jiradi might have to be temporarily halted until dawn, when Israeli aircraft in number could be brought up in close support. Also, there were armoured and infantry brigades in reserve just over the Israeli border which could be moved forward as reinforcements.

At midnight all the units of the three Ugdas which were either committed, or about to be committed to battle, were completely exhausted, stuck in the sand or stranded for lack of fuel. Moreover, administrative chaos prevailed during the hours of darkness in the Tal Ugda sector owing to the crowded single roadway. Some supply vehicles did not know where their units were. No long-range interdiction tasks were undertaken by the

Israeli Air Force in the Sinai on the First Day, which meant that the bulk of the Egyptian forces there were as yet untouched by aircraft action, and so fully inclined to believe their own false radio broadcasts as to the large number of Israeli aircraft destroyed in aerial combat. The general absence of Egyptian aircraft overhead was explained to the soldiers by their officers, who said they were engaged over Israel but would be giving ground support in the Sinai on the morrow. Egyptian morale accordingly remained fairly high.

The Second Day (Tuesday, 6 June 1967)

THE SHARON UGDA

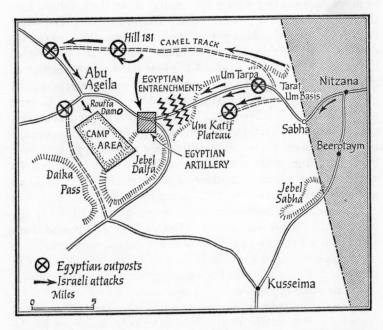

By 0001 on the Second Day the battle for the Um Katif position was fully joined, as half-an-hour previously the three battalions of Y Infantry Brigade had commenced to fight their way along the Egyptian trenches. Progress was in fits and starts, dependent upon the opposition encountered. The coloured lights carried by the soldiers enabled the Israeli artillery to see their precise positions. It took almost two hours before the southern ends of the trenches were reached. In most cases, after firing back at the attackers, the Egyptians retired to the depths of their bunkers and emplacements. Because of this and the darkness the Israelis mainly kept to the parapets and did not actually enter the trenches. Had they done so a small number, or even a single Egyptian soldier, could have held up the advance.

Behind the infantry trenches, at 0001, paratroops were fighting furiously inside the Egyptian artillery park. Half-an-hour previously they had reached the roadway; they easily penetrated the barbed wire fencing as there was no protective minefield at this point. Two of the four groups crossed the road at intervals, to move on a slightly wrong course, but when they realized this they retraced their steps to the north side of the road. The other two groups continued on the correct course, and were not detected until within 200 yards of the guns, when a burst of Egyptian small arms fire caused the first paratroop casualties in this battle. The paratroops made a rush and overran several guns, killing some of the gunners and causing others to take shelter in their bunkers. Quickly reorganizing, the paratroops made another rush towards another group of guns and succeeded in overrunning them too. By this time the alerted Egyptians were firing back from other parts of the artillery park, and the Israelis were forced to withdraw to the roadway, carrying their dead and wounded with them. As they neared the road an Egyptian convoy of about half-a-dozen vehicles approached from the west, so the paratroops fired on it from a flank as it passed them and killed all the drivers. One of the vehicles, an ammunition truck, blew up. The explosion killed two Israelis and wounded six others. A few minutes later another small Egyptian convoy, this time coming from the east, was also fired on by the paratroops and some of its vehicles set on fire. The flames illuminated the whole area, making the position extremely dangerous for the Israelis, as by now many Egyptians had emerged from their bunkers and the place was criss-crossed with small arms fire. It was 0200, and the battle for the trenches to the east was still raging. Dawn came at about 0400, so the paratroops collected their four dead and 13 wounded at a bunker they had made their temporary base. As he wanted the roadway clear for a dawn armoured pincer movement, Sharon ordered the paratroops to return to their helicopters.

By 0330, with their dead and wounded, they had all recrossed the road, and were marching painfully northwards through the sand dunes. At first light the helicopters moved towards them and picked up the wounded, but as they were wanted elsewhere (to fly fuel to Brigadier Yoffe's Centurion Battalion) the paratroops, including the two groups not committed to action, were ordered to make their way south-east, skirting Um Katif, where the battle was still raging. Utterly exhausted, they rejoined the roadway to the east of Um Katif at about 1000, where they were picked up by civilian buses.

In the west the Centurion Battalion of M Armoured Brigade, which had been exchanging shots with T-34s, broke through the Egyptian perimeter outposts at about 0100, reached the Abu Ageila road junction, blocked off the road to Jebel Libni, shot up the camp area, and began edging its way towards the Rouffa Dam. The Israelis were breaking into Um Katif from the rear, but for some time there was confused firing.

At 0200 Sharon ordered the Sherman Battalion to break through the outer defences and advance west along the road into Um Katif, by which hour the infantry battalions had reached the southern end of the Egyptian main trenches and begun working their way back again. However, there was a two-hour delay as, owing to the crowded road, the flail tanks required to clear the way through the minefield at the eastern entrance to Um Katif could not get forward. A huge crater blocked the roadway at this point, and the Shermans were cautiously edging round it when one hit a mine and blocked the route again.[1] Mechanized infantry and reconnaissance elements came forward to clear the roadway, but when it was realized that mines were the real trouble the personnel, joined by tank crews, dismounted and slowly probed their way forward on foot. In the process several half-tracks and one more Sherman were disabled.

Meanwhile the infantry again reached the roadway and made

---

[1] 'I gave the order to move through the crater. Four tanks passed and the fifth hit a mine, and blocked the road.' Commander of M Armoured Brigade, Press Conference, Tel Aviv, 28 June 1967.

contact with the waiting Shermans, which would not risk advancing until a path was cleared through the minefield. All therefore had to pause for about one hour.[1] Already the Shermans were turning their guns on to the trenches to try to neutralize the lively Egyptian fire which had been resumed. The infantry had not really cleared the trenches properly, the defenders having merely retired to the shelter of their bunkers. During this Y Infantry Brigade clearing operation 12 Israelis had been killed and another 45 wounded, but they claimed to have killed over 300 Egyptians and taken another 100 prisoner. By 0400 a path had been cleared through the minefield. The tanks of the Sherman Battalion moved forward along the road, shooting as they went and engaging the scattered T-34s. As daylight came a running battle developed with the Shermans steadily pushing their way westwards.[2] At the other end of the Um Katif position daylight enabled the Centurion Battalion, which had been ordered to move on to the road at 0230, to engage the T-34s and SU-100s blocking the western entrance. By 0500 the Israeli tanks were dominating the Rouffa Dam, the camp area and the Abu Ageila road junction. By 0600 the leading tanks of the Sherman Battalion had fought their way to the Rouffa Dam, where they made contact with the Centurion Battalion. This did not mean that the roadway was completely Israeli-controlled. In fact, the whole area swarmed with Egyptian tanks that manoeuvred about aimlessly, and with Egyptian soldiers, who either milled around in confusion or hesitantly manned their guns or positions.

With the dawn came Israeli close air support which pounded the known Egyptian positions. Although by 0600 Um Katif was still not completely Israeli-dominated, C Armoured Brigade, the other formation of the Yoffe Ugda, consisting basically of

---

[1] 'Around 0330 Motke's first tanks arrived.' Commander of Y Infantry Brigade, Press Conference, Tel Aviv, 12 June 1967.

[2] 'A tank battle started – without knowing who was shooting at whom. The time was about 0400. Each of the two tank commanders screamed that the other was shooting at him. We then decided to act the way we do in war games. I told one of them to stop firing, and the other commander was to inform me whether he was shot at and vice versa. It became clear that the enemy tanks were somehow mixed in with our tanks. We were able to destroy their tanks from as close as 10, 20 or 30 metres.' Commander of M Armoured Brigade, Press Conference, Tel Aviv, 28 June 1967.

two Centurion Battalions, began to move from Nitzana along the Central Route through the Um Katif position, where tanks and vehicles of the Sharon Ugda paused in their fighting to pull aside from the roadway to let them pass. This armoured brigade moved westwards to a rendezvous at the Jebel Libni crossroads beyond the Jebel itself. By 0800, with aircraft support, the Sharon Ugda had silenced most of the Egyptian guns and accounted for many Egyptian tanks. A number of T-34s and SU-100s had slipped away southwards into the desert.

The armoured battle over[1] and the breakthrough effected, Brigadier Sharon was ordered to leave Y Infantry Brigade behind to mop up Um Katif, and go with his M Armoured Brigade to deal with Kusseima. The Israeli infantrymen, supported by the Sharon Ugda artillery and occasional air strikes, spent the remainder of the day systematically winkling out the Egyptian defenders, many of whom fought back hard, especially during the morning. A few, but not all that many, were taken prisoner when cornered or wounded, but the majority of the infantry brigade managed to escape from Um Katif, taking many of their wounded with them. Although slightly outnumbered, the Egyptians held out well in defence. For example, the infantry battalion holding the camp area (there were four battalions in this Egyptian brigade) was not brought into action until about 0800; it resisted until noon, despite Israeli artillery fire and air strikes. During the afternoon its personnel–like others in the Um Katif position–crept away into the desert, leaving the Israelis in possession. It was about noon that General Murtagi, the Egyptian GOC in the Sinai, realized that the Egyptian Air Force had been virtually destroyed, and he ordered his troops to fall back on to the second line of defence.

At about 0800 Brigadier Sharon, with M Armoured Brigade, moved off southwards along the track to Kusseima, but his progress was slow. His men were tired, his guns needed more ammunition and his vehicles required fuel. During the tank fighting at Um Katif the Sherman Battalion claimed some 30 Egyptian tanks, and the Centurion Battalion a similar number,

---

[1] 'We counted as destroyed over 30 of their tanks. We did not count, however, other vehicles and artillery, which were destroyed in large numbers.' Commander of M Armoured Brigade, Press Conference, Tel Aviv, 28 June 1967.

which must indicate that at the very least some 30 Egyptian tanks had managed to slip away. The Israeli losses were admitted to be 19 tanks and three half-tracks.[1] The Sharon Ugda halted at about 1000 as its leading tanks were fired on from Kusseima, when still over five miles distant. The following hours were spent in reorganization and replenishment. At about 1700 Sharon was ordered to leave Kusseima (he had expected to be told to attack it in conjunction with N Armoured Brigade) and to sheer off southwards across country in the direction of the Kuraiya Passes to engage Shazli Force. He set off but had not gone very far when darkness fell and he decided to rest for the night, so that his men would be fit for battle on the morrow.

Brigadier Sharon's reduction of the Um Katif positions was well conducted, and he 'played the battle' well. The few occasions when confusion and miscalculation prevailed were attributable to the vagaries of war rather than to lack of skill and foresight. He was hampered to a degree by faulty intelligence and had constantly to throw in more troops as he came to realize just how strong the position was, until he was conducting a combined arms, set-piece attack. He was successful and in war one cannot argue with success. He had correctly calculated that there would be no counter-attack from Kusseima, and that the Israeli Air Force and the Yoffe Ugda would halt the flow of any reinforcements from the west. Although at the height of the battle practically all his troops were engaged, if he had been counterattacked his very large artillery group would have been able to hold it until the air force could be brought into the picture. In all battles many probabilities have to be examined and weighed. In this particular one Sharon's judgement proved to be skilled and shrewd.

To the south of Um Katif the garrisons at both Kusseima and Kuntilla remained passive throughout the Second Day, as did Shazli Force. Nor did any Israeli formations cross the border into the Sinai; all seemed to be watching and waiting.

THE YOFFE UGDA

From midnight to dawn on the Second Day the Centurion Battalion, of K Armoured Brigade of the Yoffe Ugda, lay in an

---

[1] Yael Dayan.

uneasy position about 3,000 yards south of the Egyptian main Bir Lafhan defences, facing the tanks of two Egyptian armoured brigades. There was hardly any firing between these two opposing forces during the hours of darkness; in fact, the Egyptian tanks had withdrawn some 3,000 yards to be out of range until they could see what they were actually up against. The other Centurion Battalion of K Armoured Brigade, which had been sent to help the Sharon Ugda, had been told that it would not be required before it reached the Abu Ageila road junction, and had slowly made its way back to join Brigadier Yoffe again, arriving just before first light.

At about 0400 the Bir Lafhan position began shelling the Israeli tanks, causing them to shuffle uneasily between the sand dunes, but both units were more concerned with the problem of refuelling. A refuelling point was established about 2,000 yards to the east and fuel was brought up in helicopters (which had just picked up the wounded paratroops at Um Katif). Other stores were dropped by aircraft. One by one the Centurion companies went there to replenish their vehicles. At daybreak the Egyptian tanks came to life and started to edge their way forward. Almost immediately they came under heavy and repeated Israeli air strikes, which tended to cause them to scatter but did not stop them advancing. A few shots were fired and by 0600 a tank shooting match had developed. On to this scene an hour later came trundling C Armoured Brigade, which had just moved through the Um Katif position while the Sharon Ugda battle was still in progress. Emerging from the western end, this brigade turned northwards at the Abu Ageila road junction and joined in the tank battle, catching some of the Egyptian tank units in the flanks. For some time the Egyptians fought back, but they were pounded both by the Israeli Air Force and Israeli Centurions.[1] At about 1000, after suffering many vehicle casualties, the Egyptians broke off the action and withdrew westwards. At 1100 the Israeli armour was ordered to move towards Jebel Libni.

---

[1] 'Twenty-eight of their tanks were in flames, the enemy crews had retreated three and a half kilometres, and then our air force went into action, and the whole area was covered by burnt vehicles.' Commander of K Armoured Brigade, Press Conference, Tel Aviv, 12 June 1967.

In this tank battle one Israeli tank battalion had held off two Egyptian armoured brigades during the night, and two Israeli armoured brigades, with air support, had defeated them. It was a decided and timely victory, to which much of the credit should go to the Fouga Magisters, as the presence of such a large force so near to both Um Katif and El Arish posed a distinct danger to the Israelis. Had these Egyptian armoured brigades, instead of timidly hanging back, advanced in the darkness to overwhelm the single Israeli tank battalion, they would have been able to hit at either the Tal Ugda or the Sharon Ugda, when the Israeli situation might have been seriously impaired.

THE TAL UGDA

At 0001, in Brigadier Tal's sector in the north, the main part of S Armoured Brigade, including the major parts of the Centurion and Patton Battalions, were concentrated near the outskirts of El Arish. They had successively broken through the Jiradi Pass, which was now blocked for the third time as the Egyptians had again returned to their guns. A company of Centurions had moved to the mouth of the Pass from Sheikh Zuweid, to be joined there by the Mechanized Infantry Battalion of S Armoured Brigade, brought forward from the Rafah area, as units of L Armoured Brigade were hopelessly stuck in the sands somewhere to the south of the Northern Route. After an hour's fighting, during which the Egyptians continually fired flares and illuminating shells, the Israelis were able to force their way into the Pass and to dominate the route through it, although many Egyptians passively remained in their defensive positions. Because of this the Mechanized Infantry Battalion was ordered to stay and hold the Jiradi Pass, which was such a vital communication. In fact, this Israeli unit spent all the Second Day mopping up in this defile and did not complete the task until dusk.

As soon as the Jiradi Pass was opened the S Armoured Brigade Command Group, with the Centurion company, moved through it to join the remainder of the brigade near El Arish, which it reached at about 0300. Supply vehicles began to follow. One tank company was positioned to block the road south from El Arish to Bir Lafhan, and another the route westwards to Kantara, thus cutting the town off completely. There was some shelling from El Arish, although it was not strongly defended, during the course of which an Israeli fuel tanker was hit and set on fire. This lit up the whole scene and forced the main body of Israeli tanks to withdraw some distance for safety. Many of the supply vehicles did not arrive until about 0500, and so the Israeli force was not ready to go into action until at least two hours after daylight. During the refuelling two Egyptian aircraft came over the supply point and machine-gunned Israelis, causing casualties.

It had been intended that L Armoured Brigade should take the El Arish airfield, to the south of the town, but as its vehicles were still stuck in the sand S Armoured Brigade was detailed to carry out this task instead. Advancing at about 0600, it began to battle against T-34 tanks, anti-aircraft and anti-tank guns for the airfield. With the assistance of air strikes the airfield was cleared of Egyptians by 0730 hours. This accomplished, S Armoured Brigade was told to carry on southwards and assault the Egyptian blocking position at Bir Lafhan, which was then shelling Brigadier Yoffe's tanks. This Egyptian position, facing southward, was composed of sets of trenches on the Soviet pattern, and was accordingly more vulnerable to assault from the north. Brigadier Tal's armoured tactics now changed from those of crashing through rigid defences with an armoured punch driven home hard at selected points, 'regardless of cost', to those of 'sniping', in which tank gunners showed their skill at long-range shooting by picking out and quickly hitting Egyptian targets. Leaving one company to block the road to Kantara, the remainder of the Centurion Battalion advanced centrally down the road, opening fire at long distances. While this long-range sniping was in progress, the Patton Battalion moved into the desert to the east to make a flanking assault. This pressure, by two Israeli prongs, caused the Egyptians to withdraw from their positions and disappear into the desert, as the Centurions closed in and charged them frontally. Assisted by several air strikes, S Armoured Brigade had by 1100 broken completely through the Bir Lafhan defences, without incurring any casualties, to make contact with Brigadier Yoffe on the other side. This had taken out the cornerstone of the Egyptian defences in this area, even though the town of El Arish had been bypassed to be dealt with later.

THE YOFFE AND TAL UGDAS

With the Egyptian armoured formations now in full retreat down the Central Route, it was decided that the Yoffe Ugda, supported by one brigade from the Tal Ugda, should advance to attack and seize Jebel Libni, one of the largest Egyptian installations in the Sinai, which had a large airfield. The remainder of the Tal Ugda was to advance along the Northern Route after El Arish had been cleared. It had been the intention to send L Armoured Brigade with Brigadier Yoffe, but as it was still some distance away in the sand, even though S Armoured Brigade was thought to deserve a rest, it was assigned to go with the Tal Ugda. After refuelling it was ready to move off. With two brigades leading–K Armoured Brigade (Yoffe Ugda) and S Armoured Brigade (Tal Ugda)–and with L Armoured Brigade (Tal Ugda) following some way behind, the Israeli armoured force moved south-west from Bir Lafhan to Abu Ageila, where it turned west on to the Central Route. After being briefly halted twice by Egyptian resistance, which was overcome by good tank shooting, the two forward brigades reached the outskirts of Jebel Libni at about 1600. Both swung into a pincer attack on to the airfield, closely supported by aircraft. Several Egyptian tanks were destroyed, while many others withdrew into the desert terrain behind the airfield, as did some of the gunners and infantrymen.[1]

The main Egyptian defensive position was firmly on a feature on the edge of the airfield between the two Israeli brigades, physically separating them, as they were on opposite sides of the airfield. During the afternoon the Israeli brigades took the airfield and camp north of the road junction, where they remained. The Egyptians had numbers of T-55s, T-54s and SU-100s which, together with their artillery, spasmodically fired at the Israeli force throughout the night, causing it to withdraw a little way. As the Tnuva trucks arrived, the hours of darkness were spent in refuelling and regrouping.

Meanwhile, on reaching the Jebel Libni crossroads, C

---

[1] 'While advancing we were able to destroy six or eight of their tanks, and four tanks at the airfield.' Commander of K Armoured Brigade, Press Conference, Tel Aviv, 12 June 1967.

Armoured Brigade (Yoffe Ugda) was detailed to move south towards Bir Hassana. At about 1200 its leading tanks were to the west of a radar position known as Abirik, which was deserted after an attack by the Israeli Air Force. However, some T-34s were scattered about the slopes of a nearly open wadi (stream bed); they opened fire on the Israelis, who became involved in a two-hour battle. Although about half a dozen T-34s were destroyed, others continued to fire, so C Armoured Brigade bypassed the position and sheered off westwards.

During the afternoon of the Second Day senior Israeli commanders received information that General Murtagi had given orders for all Egyptian troops to withdraw to the third line of defence, which rested on the Central Ridge, of which Bir Gifgafa was a key point. This caused a change of emphasis; Brigadier Tal was instructed to remain at El Arish for the time being, as the Battle for Jerusalem was causing anxiety, but to be prepared to move swiftly with his armoured brigade against Bir Gifgafa. It was decided to send only a small, light force along the Northern Route to Kantara, which for clarity can be called the Northern Force.[1] It consisted of the S Armoured Brigade Reconnaissance Unit (of 18 recoilless guns on jeeps), an AMX company (of eight tanks) and half-a-dozen self-propelled guns. The Northern Force moved off from El Arish, with headlights blazing, at about 2230.

THE GAZA STRIP

In the Gaza Strip, in the early hours of the Second Day, a paratroop battalion and a Sherman battalion were in position blocking Gaza, and most of the morning was spent in manoeuvring Israeli units into better tactical positions. Several air strikes were made on Egyptian defences near Gaza. The mopping up of Rafah had been left to a paratroop battalion. Although the resistance was not so tough there were many mines, and several paratroops were wounded during the morning.[2]

---

[1] In the Israeli official account it is referred to as Granit Force after its commander, Colonel Israel Granit.

[2] 'In the same battles 150 of their soldiers were killed.' Second-in-Command, P Paratroop Brigade, Press Conference, Tel Aviv, 28 June 1967.

As soon as the El Arish airfield had been taken, Brigadier Tal ordered the other battalion of P Paratroop Brigade, which had fought the exhausting battle for the Rafah South Position the previous day, and which was standing by to help take El Arish, to move in and seize Khan Yunis. Acting in conjunction with a battalion of X Infantry Brigade (in position near Nir Oz), the paratroops in half-tracks closed in on Khan Yunis, but soon found themselves tied down in the narrow streets and alleyways where, despite air support and heavy mortar fire, they could make little headway. Both tanks and paratroops ventured some way into Khan Yunis three or four times, but withdrew again as the resistance was tough. The brigade commander decided against making a night attack, withdrew his men and regrouped in the locality, where they rested until dawn.

When it was realized that mopping up the Gaza Strip would not be quickly achieved, it was decided to concentrate first against Gaza, so the majority of the troops available were diverted there. The Israeli attack on Gaza was made from several directions by four separate battalions and a unit of Shermans, which literally shot their way into the centre of the city.[1] By 1700 Gaza was in Israeli hands and several thousand prisoners had been taken.[2] Next the Paratroop Battalion and an infantry battalion of X Infantry Brigade, with some Shermans, turned round, joined the other Paratroop Battalion, and closed in on Khan Yunis. As darkness fell the Israelis began fighting their way into its outskirts; the movement continued throughout the night.

With the fall of El Arish the Gaza Strip had become of secondary importance, but it was obviously desirable to occupy it as soon as possible as it represented an enemy threat to the rear. When the strength of the opposition was appreciated the divided Israeli forces in the Strip were concentrated and flung first of all against Gaza. Only when Gaza had been taken was attention given to reducing Khan Yunis.

---

[1] During this fighting 14 UNEF soldiers were killed and 25 wounded when the UN building in Gaza, where they were awaiting repatriation, was hit by Israeli mortar fire.

[2] Lieutenant-General Abdul Monan Husseini, the Military Governor, formally signed the surrender document at 1020 the next day.

COMMENTS ON THE SECOND DAY'S FIGHTING

The evening of the Second Day must have been a time of great relief for the senior Israeli commanders. The day had opened on a note of acute anxiety, with the battles at Um Katif, the Jiradi Pass and El Arish unresolved. It closed on a far more confident one for them as the Egyptians had been ordered to withdraw to the Central Ridge, which meant they had virtually given up half the Sinai. Early in the day the battle for Um Katif had been won, the Jiradi Pass opened, the El Arish airfield taken and the Bir Lafhan defences breached. Just before dusk the Jebel Libni airfield had been taken and Gaza had fallen. It had been a good day for the Israelis – and a decisive one. In the Sinai the change of armoured tactics from 'regardless of cost' charges to long-range sniping had proved very effective and less costly. In particular, the Centurion gunners had showed their deadly skill. Yet although a day of successes for the Israelis, it had not been an easy one by any means, as in many instances, and certainly until noon, the Egyptians fought back and had to be forced out, which caused many Israeli casualties. This Egyptian aggressiveness had been countered largely by frequent air strikes. But as the Israelis advanced there remained plenty of resistance to be mopped up, and by dusk Egyptian snipers were active in El Arish, Jiradi, Sheikh Zuweid, Rafah and other places.

By the end of the day, with complete control of the air, many of the Israeli supply problems began to sort themselves out. Israeli information techniques were good, and designed to help win the war. For example, it was not announced until the next day (the Third Day) that the El Arish airfield had been seized by them. This was partly to confuse the Egyptian High Command and other Egyptian headquarters, and partly because the Israelis did not wish to invite retaliatory attacks; a few Egyptian aircraft were still flying and there were Egyptian bombers somewhere in the background that could not be ruled out. The Israelis quickly developed this technique, and as a matter of course delayed announcing the capture or occupation of places.

For the Egyptians the day had not dawned too blackly. The larger part of their forces in the Sinai were as yet uncommitted to battle and morale was fairly good, being bolstered up by the false reports of Radio Cairo that the Israeli Air Force had been eliminated. General Murtagi had ordered two distinct counter-attacks in which one armoured brigade was to move against Rafah and the other was to assault the Sharon Ugda at Um Katif but both were beaten back before they became effective. When the acting GOC of the 7th Infantry Division (the GOC had been wounded and evacuated) was taken prisoner at El Arish, Brigadier Tal had wanted him and other senior Egyptian officers taken prisoner at the same time to persuade the Egyptians at Bir Lafhan to surrender, but they all refused to co-operate in any way. As the day wore on the picture became blacker, as battles were lost and Israeli aircraft appeared in numbers to make air strikes and carry out interdiction tasks deep in the Sinai, over which there was almost a complete absence of Egyptian planes. That two or three Israeli planes were shot down gave the Egyptians some encouragement.

At about noon the Egyptians' situation suddenly became black indeed as General Murtagi realized, perhaps for the first time, that the official radio communiqués were false and that the Egyptian Air Force had practically been destroyed. Without supporting air cover he knew that his mobile forces would be at an immense disadvantage in the open desert. Until this moment he seems to have been of good heart, as he still had under his hand mobile formations available to be thrown into battle. Egyptian communications, never very good, were already over-strained by the end of the First Day's fighting, and by the morning of the Second Day they began to break down and fail him. By noon on the Second Day General Murtagi lost communication with a large part of his command, and so was deprived of the means to manoeuvre his troops in a battle that was still not lost at this stage. At around this time he gave the order to withdraw to his main defensive line along the Central Ridge. While this message undoubtedly got through to some formations and units, others were already out of touch and so left helplessly on their own without any 'operational directives'. They were thus left undecided whether to stand and fight or to retreat. By the end of the Second Day there was considerable confusion within the Egyptian forces in the Sinai that spread rapidly to verge almost on panic at headquarters. Already a few officers were blatantly deserting their men, and by dusk there was a patchy exodus of single vehicles moving westwards.

The Third Day (Wednesday, 7 June 1967)

THE TAL UGDA

At Jebel Libni S Armoured Brigade, of the Tal Ugda, and K Armoured Brigade, of the Yoffe Ugda, remained until dawn on opposite sides of the airfield, separated and dominated by the main Egyptian positions on the feature that lay between them. Being the nearest to the enemy, K Armoured Brigade had been subjected to a certain amount of long-range shelling from the Egyptians throughout the hours of darkness, while S Armoured Brigade was more fortunate as it was able to withdraw into the shelter of the sand dunes. The Israelis used this time to refuel and plan a dawn attack. At first light, assisted by heavy air support, both brigades assaulted together in a pincer movement. Under the intense fire and bombing the defenders soon pulled out and escaped westwards. This important step achieved, the Tal Ugda was ordered to move along the Central Route to block the Ishmailia Pass, while the Yoffe Ugda was to move south-westwards, first to Bir Hassana, and then to seize and hold the Mitla and Giddi Passes. The two Ugdas parted company.

Brigadier Tal's next objective was the Bir Hamma airfield, about 20 miles west of Jebel Libni, and he advanced with the Centurion Battalion of S Armoured Brigade leading. The Centurions arrived at Bir Hamma, which was held by an infantry brigade (of the 3rd Infantry Division), supported by a battalion of T-34s and SU-100s, and some guns. Without hesitating, assisted by an Israeli air strike, the Centurions charged the defences frontally. After firing a few shots the defenders gave up after about half-an-hour's resistance and slipped away westwards. During this small battle some black tanks were spotted by the Israelis, who took them to be new Soviet models just delivered to the Egyptians. They were about to shoot them up when the tank commanders, standing up in their turrets and signalling,

143

made them hold their fire. They were simply Israeli tanks that had been covered with soot and smoke when a fuel dump had exploded nearby. This was one of several occasions when Israeli tanks narrowly avoided shooting up other Israeli tanks. It is reckoned (but not confirmed by the Israelis) that on at least five separate occasions Israeli tanks fired on each other in the confusion of battle in the Sinai, and that at least eight Israeli tanks were disabled by fire from their own side.

Brigadier Tal's next objective was Bir Rod Salim, about 25 miles farther westwards along the Central Route. The Patton Battalion led the way. At Bir Rod Salim there was a brief fire-fight between the Pattons and Egyptian T-55s, after which the Egyptians again withdrew, leaving the Israelis in possession of considerable supplies and enabling Tal's vehicles to refuel.[1] Fuel and ammunition were also dropped by parachute, with some urgently-needed vehicle spares.

L Armoured Brigade, which had been stuck in the sands south of El Arish for so long, had joined Brigadier Tal at Jebel Libni and had followed on behind S Armoured Brigade. It now took the lead to hurry along to block the Central Route just to the west of Bir Gifgafa camp, and so cut off retreating Egyptians moving along lateral roads by way of Bir Thamada to get through the Ishmailia Pass. S Armoured Brigade, after refuelling, followed to deal with any opposition—mainly from small groups of Egyptian tanks that had taken refuge just away from the roadway—that was bypassed by the leading Israeli formation. The Central Route presented a confused picture as Israeli and Egyptian tanks frequently mingled with each other, both desperately trying to move westward. Sometimes they would recognize each other and fire, but at other times not.

The Sherman and AMX Battalions of L Armoured Brigade reached Bir Gifgafa—another sprawling complex of military installations with a large airfield—at 1530, and at once engaged a radar hill position just to the north of the road. At Bir Gifgafa there was a road junction where a lateral road joined the Central Route from the south. The Egyptian objective at this stage was

---

[1] 'We destroyed one Stalin tank, 12 T-55s and more than a battalion of armoured troop carriers with their material.' Commander of S Armoured Brigade, Press Conference, Tel Aviv, 12 June 1967.

to keep open the vital Ishmailia Pass, which was a short distance to the west of the Bir Gifgafa camp. The main defences were in front of the Ishmailia Pass. The Sherman Battalion remained to the north of the road junction, while the AMX Battalion, encircling it from the north, moved into a blocking position on the main road to hold any counter-attack from the west. While these moves were in progress the Israeli forces were attacked by Egyptian aircraft, which caused some casualties. Israeli aircraft were quickly on the scene, but in the ensuing dogfights one other Israeli plane returning from the Canal area was shot down.

At about 1700 Brigadier Tal, with elements of S Armoured Brigade, arrived at a small feature known as Jebel Kutumia, south of the roadway and about two miles to the east of Bir Gifgafa Camp, just in time to see a cloud of dust raised by an Egyptian mobile force moving northwards along the lateral road from Bir Thamada. It was elements of the 4th Armoured Division just emerging from a defile about six miles south of the Central Route and trying to get back to the west side of the Central Ridge. Brigadier Tal ordered L Armoured Brigade to hold the road junction, and detailed the Patton Battalion and one company of Centurions (all the armour he had under his hand at that particular moment as the other tanks and vehicles were refuelling a few miles back) to strike the Egyptian force in the flank. The Israeli attack took a little time to get under way, and a large part of the 4th Armoured Division elements had already emerged from the defile and were moving across country towards the Ishmailia Pass (and so avoiding Bir Gifgafa Camp and road junction) before the Israeli tanks opened fire. Then began a battle that lasted for two hours, which died down only as darkness descended—mainly for lack of fuel and ammunition. Brigadier Tal ordered his tanks to remain in their positions on the flank of the lateral road and the companies to return to refuel one by one. This had been a real tank battle, but for the Israelis it was at the best a drawn one, as they were unable to prevent the major part of this Egyptian armoured division escaping through the Ishmailia Pass. The Israelis claim to have destroyed over one dozen T-55 tanks and 50 armoured personnel carriers, and to have killed hundreds of Egyptians. This was probably true, but there were also many Israeli casualties, both of personnel and vehicles, and at least one Israeli ammunition truck blew up. During this battle there had been some intervention by Egyptian aircraft and at dusk an Egyptian armoured counter-attack forced the Patton Battalion to give ground.

The AMX Battalion had remained in its blocking position just to the west of Bir Gifgafa Camp throughout the battle, and as darkness fell it was attacked by Egyptian armour which pushed it back into Bir Gifgafa. The 4th Armoured Division was now flooding through the Ishmailia Pass. Brigadier Tal sent a Centurion company to support the AMX Battalion, and together they were able to force their way back to the original blocking position. By virtue of the changed tactical situation this AMX Battalion position had become a shielding one for the Tal Ugda, which was no longer able to do anything to prevent the escape of the Egyptian armour and vehicles.

The Third Day had been one of advance and battle for the Tal Ugda, which had begun by helping to reduce the Jebel Libni position and had followed up by successively overrunning camps and positions along the Central Route, to fight a pitched tank battle near Bir Gifgafa. As the day ended Brigadier Tal was on the defensive, with his forward AMX Battalion under some enemy pressure, but he had made a deep penetration to arrive almost at the foot of the Central Ridge, the strong Egyptian third line of defence.

THE YOFFE UGDA

After the successful combined attack with the Tal Ugda on Jebel Libni, in which opposition had suddenly collapsed, the Yoffe Ugda was ordered to move southwards to block the Mitla and Giddi Passes and so cut off both Shazli Force, still believed to be in position in the region of Wadi Kuraiya, and the Egyptian 6th Infantry Division, stretched along the Pilgrims Way. Brigadier Yoffe's K Armoured Brigade left Jebel Libni at about 0800, advancing along a lateral road and ploughing through small Egyptian camps, when fire from the Israeli tanks caused the enemy to scatter hastily without making any resistance. On this stretch of road to Bir Hassana Brigadier Yoffe's tanks occasionally became inter-mixed with those of the retreating

Egyptians.[1] Sometimes the enemy tanks in their haste to get away fired at each other as well as at the Israelis, and at other times they simply turned aside in the desert to escape.

Bir Hassana was taken by K Armoured Brigade by 1200 hours against only light opposition and was there joined by C Armoured Brigade. Now the urgent need was to advance as fast and as far as possible, and Brigadier Yoffe was ordered to make all speed he could for the Mitla Pass and to block it, so K Armoured Brigade mustered what tanks were 'runners' (they amounted to just over 20) and set off again at about 1300 towards Bir Thamada, passing through the now deserted Bir Hasana camp complex. There was hardly any opposition as all Egyptians in the region were intent on withdrawing to the Central Ridge as fast as they could.

At Bir Thamada, about 20 miles from the Mitla Pass, Yoffe halted his handful of tanks at the deserted fuel depot, where he was able to replenish his vehicles from the stock he found there before moving on again. By 1700 he had debouched into open country within sight of the eastern end of the Mitla Pass, just over a mile distant, but his momentum was running down. His Centurions were almost at the end of their tether, and despite the supply he had gained at Bir Thamada his fuel was running low. The leading Centurion formation had only nine tanks, four of which were being towed as they were out of fuel. As the Israeli Centurions came out into the open the retreating Egyptians did not fire at them as they mistook them for their own retreating tanks, both sides having Centurions.[2] This respite enabled the nine tanks to get into position without interference near the Parker Memorial (a squat, stone monument to a former British administrator), which was on a slight rise. While this was being done, more Centurions ran out of fuel and had to be towed into position. At about 1830 an Egyptian mobile column, mainly elements of the 6th Infantry Division, approached the Mitla Pass from the direction of Nakhel. The Israeli Centurions

---

[1] 'The Egyptians were panicky and entered into the middle of two of my units, which destroyed about 30 of the enemy's vehicles.' Commander of K Armoured Brigade, Press Conference, Tel Aviv, 28 June 1967.

[2] 'They too had some Centurion tanks in this area and they thought us to be Egyptians.' Commander of K Armoured Brigade, Press Conference, Tel Aviv, 28 June 1967.

opened fire, but ineffectively because of their unfavourable position. All the Egyptian vehicles got safely into the Mitla Pass, although in the fading daylight they were bombed and napalmed as they moved through it by Israeli aircraft. The Israelis then pushed several abandoned enemy tanks right into the mouth of the Pass, thus narrowing down and channelling the entrance. This task had just been accomplished as darkness fell (at about 1900) when a small group of about 20 Egyptian vehicles approached. The Israelis fired, and this time only one succeeded in getting into the Pass, the others being destroyed, damaged or dispersed.

A few more of K Armoured Brigade's tanks and vehicles caught up with the leading elements, and the fuel problem became acute. An Egyptian tanker was captured and its contents used, and fuel was sent up in cans by half-tracks from Bir Thamada as soon as it was dark, but this barely kept the Centurions running. With so few of K Armoured Brigade's tanks left capable of action, the situation was such that Brigadier Yoffe decided to change over his two brigades, at night and in the middle of an action.[1] He had little option as the leading brigade had so few 'runners' that it was hardly capable of holding the mouth of the Pass, let alone meeting and holding any Egyptian attacks, while C Armoured Brigade was in a much healthier and stronger state. As the day ended this complicated manoeuvre was well under way, with the Centurions of C Armoured Brigade moving forward to the eastern entrance of the Mitla Pass while the depleted tanks of K Armoured Brigade were withdrawing. Many of their tanks and vehicles were towed, owing to lack of fuel or mechanical breakdowns, to a small abandoned Egyptian camp known as Bir At Dama, about 15 miles to the north, to reorganize, refuel and carry out repairs.

After helping the Tal Ugda to eliminate the Egyptian defences at Jebel Libni early in the day, the Yoffe Ugda moved nearly 80 miles, fighting a brief engagement at Bir Hassana, but re-

---

[1] 'They were at the end of their power, they had been fighting for 72 hours or more non-stop. So I had to do something in the middle of a battle, something which is not usually done, trying to put a brigade in to take over the job of another brigade, and at the same time keep the tanks still firing, and the boys did it, and did not fire at each other.' Brigadier Yoffe, Press Conference, Tel Aviv, 12 June 1967.

covered sufficiently to reach Bir Thamada and eventually the mouth of the Mitla Pass at the end of its tether, where it engaged elements of the Egyptian 6th Infantry Division hurrying westwards. While the two brigades in the Yoffe Ugda were changing over under cover of darkness, many Egyptian vehicles were slipping through the still open Giddi Pass, about 20 miles to the north.

THE SHARON UGDA

At dawn on the Third Day the Sharon Ugda (now reduced mainly to M Armoured Brigade), which had rested for the night south of Um Katif near the Kusseima to Bir Hassana road–that is, the Southern Route–was refreshed and ready for further action. It had been detailed to move south to seek the Shazli Force, but as Kusseima was about to be assaulted by N Armoured Brigade, it was told to wait for the time being in case it was necessary to attack from the rear. Kusseima, formerly the HQ of the Egyptian 2nd Infantry Division, was defended by an infantry brigade with supporting tanks and guns, the defences being set out on the usual three-tiered Soviet pattern facing east. At dawn the Israeli N Armoured Brigade, consisting of a Sherman, an AMX and a mechanized infantry battalion, left Beerotaym and moved into Little Sabha, the Egyptian border post, about 10 miles from Kusseima. They found it deserted. The mechanized infantry battalion, with the AMX tanks, moved slowly towards Kusseima, carefully picking a way through the minefields, while the Sherman Battalion made a detour to the west. During this period successive air strikes were made on the Kusseima defences from dawn onwards. There was no answering fire and aerial reports indicated that the positions were deserted. At about 1000 both prongs of N Armoured Brigade closed in on Kusseima to find that the complete garrison had decamped during the night, while N Armoured Brigade had watched and the Sharon Ugda had slept.[1]

Once it was realized that Kusseima was empty the Sharon

---

[1] The Egyptian brigade had buried most of its guns and equipment in the sand nearby. To the Israeli troops moving cautiously in because of anticipated mines and booby traps, it seemed as though the whole brigade had moved out taking their guns, tanks and vehicles with them. It was not until 7 July 1967 that Israeli

Ugda was ordered to continue on southwards to engage the Shazli Force. It was now a test of endurance of both men and vehicles as they moved over loose sand, along rough camel tracks and across rocky outcrops. During the late afternoon some of Sharon's tanks were fired on at long range by elements of Yoffe's C Armoured Brigade, which was pursuing a somewhat parallel course and which had zigzagged a little too far eastwards. At least two of the Sharon Ugda tanks were disabled before the problem of identification was sorted out by Israeli aircraft. Progress along the vague twisting camel tracks was slow and time became important. As darkness fell M Armoured Brigade switched its headlights full on and continued on in three separate columns. At about midnight an Israeli jeep was blown up as the leading vehicles reached the outer edge of a brigade position (of the Egyptian 6th Infantry Division) near Jebel Karim, about 20 miles to the north-east of Nakhel. An Egyptian patrol fired on the Israeli tanks, but the return fire damaged an Egyptian vehicle so the patrol withdrew. Teetering on the edge of an unknown minefield, Sharon decided to halt, to refuel, to rest and wait for daylight. He did not know that as soon as it grew dark the last elements of Shazli Force, rapidly pulling out from their positions near the Wadi Kuraiya, started to move westwards towards Bir Thamada, going behind (to the north) of the Sharon Ugda, aiming for the Giddi Pass. The main body had decamped the previous evening.

To summarize the day for the Sharon Ugda, after pausing in the early morning to see if it would be required to help take Kusseima, it then marched south-westwards, to make for Nakhel on the Pilgrims Way and block it. Its task had been to cut off the retreating Egyptians, but so far it had failed, as the Kusseima garrison had crept past while it slept in the early hours of the morning, and now, while it was halted by a minefield, the last of the Shazli Force was likewise slipping away behind its back. It seemed that Brigadier Sharon was more expert at positional battles than mobile desert warfare.

---

search squads found near Kusseima, partly revealed by the shifting sand, 12 Stalin tanks and scores of trucks. It was several weeks later that a full search was made, this time to discover intact the full complement of the 30 T-34 tanks of the brigade, with other guns, vehicles and equipment.

To the south of Kusseima W Armoured Brigade had crossed the frontier at dawn and advanced towards Kuntilla, but it halted when it came within artillery range and contented itself with a watching role for the remainder of the Third Day. Its primary task remained that of protecting Eilat from Shazli Force, and it was held ready until the situation became clearer.

SHARM EL SHEIKH

The Egyptian positions guarding the Straits of Tiran had not been forgotten by the Israelis, and although their deception plans were pointed at them the Israelis' real priorities were elsewhere. They intended to take the Sharm El Sheikh complex, which was held by about 1,600 Egyptian troops, in an airborne operation early on the Third Day; after a bombardment to commence at 0500, paratroops were to be dropped to seize the airfield and clear the defensive positions. At dawn aerial reconnaissance indicated that Sharm El Sheikh was being evacuated, that few defenders remained and that a number of vehicles had already made good progress along the coastal track that led to El Tur. This information was relayed to the three Israeli MTBs lurking in the Gulf of Akaba nearby ready to take part in the assault. At about 0430 they moved into Sharm El Sheikh, where some of the sailors landed, to find that the two main gun positions and the concrete observation platform were indeed deserted. The sailors hoisted the Israeli national flag above the observation platform. They also noted that while there seemed to be a few Egyptian soldiers in the vicinity of the airfield and camp, they were apparently preparing to evacuate. Anticipating that an aerial bombardment was due to commence soon, the sailors put to sea again and relayed the information back to the main operations room at GHQ. The air strike and paratroop drop were cancelled. Instead, a single Noratlas, carrying Israeli paratroops, landed on the runway at about 0515, followed within a few minutes by two others. Israeli soldiers quickly spread out, occupying the gun and other positions and clearing the airfield. They met resistance, which was soon overcome, at one point only, when a platoon of Egyptians fired at them and then set fire to the fuel tanks. The Israelis took about 80 prisoners and counted nearly 20 Egyptian dead. Ras Nasrani was occupied by sailors from the Israeli MTBs and found to be deserted. The key to Eilat was now in Israeli hands.

When the last UNEF personnel had evacuated Sharm El Sheikh on 23 May they had put the desalination plant out of action. As the Egyptian garrison was successively increased in size, so it was faced with an acute water problem. There was no civilian population. Water had to be brought over daily in Egyptian ships, right up to and including the First Day of the war.[1] However, after a timid foray part way up the Gulf of Akaba on the night of the Second Day, the Egyptian warships pulled out and moved over to Hurghada, on the Gulf of Suez, and to other small Egyptian ports on the Red Sea, thus leaving Sharm El Sheikh waterless, as it had no wells worthy of the name. Water had been severely rationed, and this decided the Egyptian commander to evacuate the major part of his garrison and to leave only one infantry company behind. Accordingly, about midnight on the Second Day, he moved off with all the vehicles he had, crammed full of soldiers, along the coastal track that led to El Tur. Other soldiers were told to make their way over the mountains towards the St Catherine Monastery track, where they would be picked up.

During the afternoon of the Third Day a detachment of paratroops was taken by helicopter from Sharm El Sheikh, across the tip of the Sinai Peninsula, to El Tur, the small oil centre, which it occupied without difficulty. Some of the paratroops were then flown by helicopter further northwards along the coast of the Gulf of Suez, to the other oil centre at Abu Durba, which was also in Israeli hands by dusk.

THE NORTHERN FORCE

In the north, during the early hours of the morning of the Third Day of the war, the Northern Force rushed along the Northern Route with headlights full on. Aircraft reconnaissance had shown that there were no large bodies of Egyptian troops along this route but only a few small camps and supply depots.

---

[1] The Israelis also had to bring water in by ship for some time for their occupation troops.

In fact, by this time the majority of the Egyptian soldiers had either abandoned them and were in vehicles heading west, or were about to leave. A few shots were fired at the advancing Israelis from time to time, but when the Egyptians saw the tanks, half-tracks and jeeps bearing down on them, they hastily got out of the way. At least once during the day the Northern Force was attacked by Egyptian aircraft. By dusk it had reached Romani, the Egyptians withdrawing from the camp there as the Israelis came in sight. The Israeli problems were those of fuel and rest, rather than stiff opposition, and drums of fuel were dropped by aircraft.

THE EL ARISH AREA

At dawn on the Third Day of the war Y Infantry Brigade, which had spent the previous day mopping up the Um Katif positions, was put in civilian buses and sent to El Arish, which had been bypassed and ignored by the advancing Israeli forces. The day was spent in bringing the town under control, dealing with snipers and rounding up prisoners, who now began to give themselves up in large numbers.[1] During the afternoon one battalion was sent to take over the Jiradi Pass from the Mechanized Infantry Battalion of S Armoured Brigade, to allow that unit to rejoin its brigade. Another detachment was sent to carry out a sniper-clearing operation in Sheikh Zuweid.

THE GAZA STRIP

In the Gaza Strip two battalions of P Paratroop Brigade, two battalions of X Infantry Brigade and the Sherman Battalion closed in towards the centre of Khan Yunis from all sides in the darkness of the early hours of the Third Day, heavy artillery and mortar fire signalling the start of the assault. The paratroops moved in from the seaward side and the other units from inland. Held by a brigade of the 20th Palestinian Division, it was the only remaining town in the Gaza Strip left in Arab hands. The

---

[1] 'We started clearing up the town, a task which lasted for a long time. Several of my good officers were killed here.' Commander of Y Infantry Brigade, Press Conference, Tel Aviv, 12 June 1967.

Palestinians fought back hard, and many only surrendered when daylight brought the threat of renewed aerial bombardment. Many of the small positions fought on until actually overrun by half-tracks, and although the Israelis reached the centre of the town by 0900 fighting continued until about noon.[1] The rest of the day was spent in winkling out snipers, rounding up prisoners and imposing military government on the whole of the Gaza Strip, where resistance had suddenly collapsed everywhere. At about noon the commander of P Paratroop Brigade, with one of his battalions in half-tracks and jeeps, set off along the Northern Route to join the Northern Force.

COMMENTS ON THE THIRD DAY'S FIGHTING

By dusk on the Third Day the Israelis had reached the foot of the Central Ridge, the third line of Egyptian defences. Everywhere east of this feature Egyptian forces were withdrawing, Kusseima had been evacuated the previous night, as had most of the Shazli Force, while the remainder was in the process of sneaking past the Sharon Ugda and the 6th Infantry Division was rushing along the Pilgrims Way towards the Mitla Pass. Egyptian communications had completely broken down and there was utter confusion and complete lack of co-ordination; no one knew quite what to do or what anyone else was doing. The order to withdraw had percolated to most units, whose only aim was to reach the passes in the Central Ridge, which they believed were held by their own troops, when they thought they would be safe. For information officers listened on their transistor sets to conflicting Israeli and Egyptian news bulletins.

Throughout the day the Israeli Air Force had machine-gunned, bombed and dropped napalm on Egyptian vehicles, which were extremely vulnerable to air attack in the open desert or on the crowded, narrow roadways. Everywhere Egyptians were abandoning their vehicles, partly because of the Israeli air attacks but mainly because they had run out of fuel, and taking

---

[1] 'The Palestinians opposed with strong resistance, they mined all the roads in the town and sniped from windows of the buildings. They built strong positions alongside the roads and fought from them.' Second-in-Command of P Paratroop Brigade, Press Conference, Tel Aviv, 28 June 1967.

to the desert in the hope of making their way back to the Canal region. Israeli advances and Egyptian retreats were often merged into one another, and tanks and vehicles of both sides sometimes mingled together. Recognition was frequently difficult as, for example, both had Centurions, AMXs and Pattons.[1]

The Israelis had now been fighting hard for three full days, and the strain was telling. The men were exhausted and the vehicles were reaching the absolute limit of their mechanical endurance. Breakdowns were frequent, and several units had more 'non-runners' than 'runners'. Fuel supply remained an acute problem, and many Israeli tanks and vehicles had to be left behind for this reason.

Most of the Egyptians were not looking for trouble, but in several instances some fighting spirit remained. There were flashes of aggression, such as the counter-attack against the Tal Ugda near the Ishmailia Pass, and the hard defence near the Abirik radar position that forced C Armoured Brigade to deviate from its route, while in the Gaza Strip the Palestinians fought back hard until bombarded into submission. In the tank clashes on this day it became apparent that a T-55 could take all that a Patton could give, while the Centurion could take anything that any tanks the Egyptians had could give. There were also a few daring and surprising sorties by Egyptian aircraft which caused Israeli casualties, especially at refuelling points. Radio Cairo admitted that its forces had withdrawn from their advanced positions and were fighting 'in second line positions due to continuous and heavy air attacks in which foreign aircraft were taking part'. Towards evening the picture of the Sinai was one of crowded roadways littered with destroyed and abandoned vehicles, with many bottlenecks which slowed down both those advancing and those in retreat. Numerous prisoners had been taken and a lot of others had given themselves up, but many Egyptian soldiers were in the desert still hoping to find their way westwards.

---

[1] 'Wheel sharply off the road, and then shoot up every tank that remains on the road,' was an order given by one Israeli commander. (*The Sandstorm.*)

The Fourth Day (Thursday, 8 June 1967)

THE NORTHERN FORCE

After resting and refuelling at Romani, less than 40 miles from Kantara, the Northern Force set off at dawn. So far its advance had not been opposed, but now the Israelis began to meet increasing resistance. From dawn onwards there was hard and unexpected opposition from the Egyptian Air Force which made attacks on the Northern Force throughout the morning.[1] At about 0800 the Israelis ran head on into an Egyptian blocking position on the road, held by a unit of para-commandos in armoured personnel carriers supported by about 20 T-55 tanks, which made a counter-attack on the Northern Force and brought it to an abrupt halt. A series of charges, combined with excellent shooting by the gunners with the recoilless guns, caused the Egyptians to fall back, but it was 1000 before the Israelis were ready to move forward again. In this fight some T-55 tanks had bogged down in the salt marsh on either side of the roadway when trying to manoeuvre against the Israelis, as had a couple of Israeli jeeps.

Next the Northern Force encountered a strong Egyptian position only about 12 miles from Kantara, and it was still halted when the commander of P Paratroop Brigade arrived with a battalion of paratroops in half-tracks and a company of Pattons. He at once flung the Pattons into the attack. The Egyptians allowed the Pattons to pass through their positions and then they blocked the way again when the cut off Pattons came under fire from Schmel anti-tank guided missiles. Although several Pattons were hit, none was disabled. Then the reconnaissance element tried unsuccessfully to break through the Egyptian position and had to fall back after suffering casualties of both personnel and jeeps. The AMX tanks tried to make an outflanking movement through the sand to the south of the road, but several stuck fast and the whole group became cut off from the remainder of the Northern Force, as was the Patton company.

---

[1] The Egyptians say they flew 32 sorties in all.

By this time the Israeli Air Force had come into action against
the attacking Egyptian planes, shooting some down and driving
the others off. More air support was called for. At 1230, covered
by an air strike, the commander of P Paratroop Brigade launched
his battalion in half-tracks on a narrow front into the assault.
Almost immediately he was wounded and had to be evacuated,
which caused the attack to falter. More air strikes were made
on the Egyptian position, and at about 1500, when the paratroops
launched another assault, the Egyptians withdrew. For the past
two hours Israeli aircraft had been systematically destroying
the Egyptian tanks and vehicles one by one. The Northern
Force spent the remainder of the afternoon in pulling tanks and
vehicles out of the loose sand and the salt marsh, and it was not
until 1700 that it was able to resume the advance. At about 1800,
when only about four miles from Kantara, the Northern Force
was suddenly attacked by a few Egyptian tanks supported by
paratroops in armoured personnel carriers, and a fight developed.
The Israeli troops rallied and counter-attacked, assisted by the
tanks and recoilless guns. After about one hour's fighting the
Egyptian resistance died down as darkness fell, and the Israelis
were able to press on towards Kantara, which they entered at
about 2000—the first Israeli soldiers to reach the Suez Canal in
this war.

Leaving two companies of paratroops and the Patton company
in Kantara, which was deserted, the remainder of the Northern
Force moved southwards along the Canal bank until it ran up
against opposition near the El Firdan Bridge, a swing-type
railway bridge, which the Egyptians were holding to get as many
as possible of their tanks across to the west bank. The Israelis
remained watching all through the night, and with air support
mounted a dawn attack on the Fourth Day (Friday, 9 June)
which overwhelmed the bridgehead defences. The Northern
Force stayed near the El Firdan Bridge and at Kantara, but at
both places came under artillery, anti-aircraft and anti-tank fire
from across the Canal. Some Schmel anti-tank guided missiles
were fired at the Israelis from the west bank. At 0900 a detachment from the Tal Ugda, which had reached the Canal opposite
Ishmailia and was moving north along the east bank, made
contact with the Northern Force.

THE TAL UGDA

On the Central Route, near Bir Gifgafa Camp, the Tal Ugda was in a rather difficult and embarrassing position, as it was unable to prevent a large number of Egyptian vehicles slipping through the Ishmailia Pass. The AMX Battalion, of L Armoured Brigade, together with a Centurion company, was holding a position just to the west of Bir Gifgafa Camp and exchanging shots with Egyptian tanks. This fire-fight continued until about 0200, when the Egyptians mounted an attack on the AMX Battalion—probably the only deliberate armoured attack they made during this war. The AMXs came under heavy fire from the T-55s, and although supported by Centurions they had to manoeuvre to avoid being knocked out. After a number of AMXs had been hit, and the Israelis had suffered other casualties when one of their trucks loaded with mortar bombs blew up, the AMX Battalion broke contact at about 0300 and withdrew some two miles. The Egyptians did not follow up, and so missed an opportunity to hit the Tal Ugda hard. Egyptian firing died down and after about an hour, just before dawn broke, the AMXs crept forward again and got into a good tactical position not far from the one they had been driven from.

During the night S Armoured Brigade had been pulled back to refuel and rest. This took some time as the road was choked with supply vehicles, and when the brigade was due to move forward again parts of the roadway had to be cleared with bull-dozers. Just before dawn S Armoured Brigade moved up close behind the AMX Battalion (of L Armoured Brigade), ready to force its way through the Ishmailia Pass which, it was realized, was strongly defended. The Sherman Battalion was still holding the road junction. The other unit of L Armoured Brigade, the Mechanized Infantry Battalion, was still on its way from the Jiradi Pass. During the night the Egyptians had reinforced their Ishmailia Pass defences, and as the Israeli Centurion Battalion moved forward at daylight its leading tanks were halted. The Egyptian defences were far stronger than they had anticipated. This Egyptian position extended to about five miles in depth, being made up of a series of defended localities supported by about 100 tanks placed on either side of the roadway, where they were shielded from frontal fire by high sand dunes. These narrow inward-facing defences were protected on the flanks and rear by loose sand, which the Egyptians considered to be impassable. The Israelis slowly and methodically attacked this series of defensive positions, dealing with each individually as they came to it. The Centurions, which could withstand the fire of the Egyptian T-55s and T-54s, advanced three abreast down the roadway, assaulting frontally, while the quicker and lighter Pattons came in through the loose sand to shoot up the defences from the rear. Each single attack was heavily supported by Israeli aircraft, which was able to signal the exact locations of each Egyptian tank and also to attack it with napalm. This hard battle continued throughout the morning and well into the afternoon,[1] during which time at least 40 Egyptian tanks were destroyed for the loss of only two Israeli tanks. The day had been won by quick and accurate shooting by the Israeli Centurion gunners and the Israeli Air Force.

Towards dusk Egyptian vehicles bunched together, frantically trying to force their way through the Ishmailia Pass, and the last of the T-55s withdrew from the defensive positions, thus giving the Israeli Air Force a good target. Napalm was dropped on to the crammed mass of vehicles, setting many alight. As daylight faded all semblance of Egyptian defence collapsed, as the survivors struggled desperately to escape westwards. The scene was fitfully lit by the many burning vehicles. While this battle had been in progress, units of L Armoured Brigade had mopped up all resistance in the Bir Gifgafa Camp and airfield.

The Israelis were anxious now to reach the Canal and seize the crossings so the Centurions moved right into the mouth of the Pass and dragged or pushed wrecked and disabled vehicles to one side, to enable the Patton Battalion to race through it. With headlights full on the Pattons cleared the Pass and made their way along the Central Route to the Canal. There was now

---

[1] 'It took us six hours to cover five kilometres – but we managed to destroy some 40 enemy tanks along this stretch.' Brigadier Tal, Press Conference, Tel Aviv, 12 June 1967.

'I covered these seven kilometres in six hours, but at the end of this time everything behind me was on fire: the tanks, the armoured troop carriers, the vehicles, and their brigade was completely destroyed.' Commander of S Armoured Brigade, Press Conference, Tel Aviv, 12 June 1967.

little opposition, except for two brushes, in one of which the Israelis destroyed some Katyusha rocket vehicles. The only serious resistance was encountered about two miles from the Canal at a track intersection, when four Egyptian tanks and an infantry company were able to halt the Israelis briefly. The leading Pattons neared the Suez Canal at about 0030 (on the Fourth Day, Friday, 9 June), and as they did so the Egyptians on the bank signalled to them with torches, thinking they were their own tanks hurrying to get across the pontoon bridge before it was too late. The Tal Ugda had arrived opposite Ishmailia. At dawn, as mentioned, Brigadier Tal sent his reconnaissance unit along the east bank, which made contact with the Israeli Northern Force at El Firdan Bridge at about 0900.

THE YOFFE UGDA

By dawn on the Fourth Day Brigadier Yoffe had completed his complicated move of changing over his two brigades. He had C Armoured Brigade at the eastern end of the Mitla Pass, and the somewhat dog-tired and depleted K Armoured Brigade in the area of the Bir Thamada road junction about 15 miles northeast of the Mitla Pass. Brigadier Yoffe received information that the Egyptians were mounting a counter-attack, which had commenced at dawn, from the southern end of the Suez Canal, and which was aimed at the Mitla Pass. Leaving only one Centurion company at the eastern end, which in the course of the morning successfully beat off a few desperate attempts by groups of Egyptian tanks and vehicles to break through, he moved with the remainder of the battalion through the choked pass itself as quickly as he could. The single roadway was littered with destroyed, damaged and burnt-out vehicles, twisted guns and other débris of war, which had to be dragged or pushed off the roadway before the Israeli tanks could pass. It was noon before the Israeli Centurions reached the western end of the 15-mile-long Mitla Pass to hold it against the Egyptian counter-attack. However, this was not necessary, as Israeli aircraft had already caught and destroyed most of the Egyptian assaulting force in open country long before it reached the Mitla Pass, thus turning this final Egyptian offensive into a retreat by noon.

The other Centurion Battalion of C Armoured Brigade had been ordered to move from the eastern end of the Mitla Pass along a rough track to the south-west which led to Ras Sudar on the Gulf of Suez. (A Centurion Battalion of the Sharon Ugda moved forward to take its place to seal off the Pass, and relieved the other Centurion company which eventually made its way to the western end to join its battalion.) Just after dawn a company of paratroops, from the detachment landed by helicopter at Abu Durba, had been put down by helicopter at Ras Sudar, where they hit up against a strong Egyptian position which the Israelis had been unable to overcome. Brigadier Yoffe's Centurions arrived at Ras Sudar at about 1230 and a combined armoured and infantry assault was made on the Egyptian defences, in which over 100 Egyptian prisoners were taken. The remainder of the defenders slipped away into the desert. At Ras Sudar the Egyptians had held out for some hours, and for a while the Israeli paratroops had a real battle on their hands.

At noon K Armoured Brigade, having recovered somewhat and collected in more of its tanks, was ordered to move and block the nearby Giddi Pass, where it at once ran into a group of about 30 T-55s and T-54s which were holding it. The brigade acquitted itself with credit. Having detached sub-units to cover certain approaches, at 0900 about 16 tanks moved into the Pass and forced their way through, and although Egyptian aircraft flew over and attacked the Israelis, they stood their ground and shot back. Israeli aircraft came on the scene and drove off the Egyptian planes. Then they attacked the Egyptian armoured vehicles with cannon fire and napalm, but it was almost dusk before K Armoured Brigade had captured and cleared the Giddi Pass and routed the Egyptians.

At 1900 the Israeli commanders heard that the Egyptians were about to ask for a cease-fire. Determined to reach the Suez Canal before this happened, they gave the order to race there. Accordingly all the Centurions of the Yoffe Ugda that were still 'runners' were told to move across the some 30 miles of open desert to the Canal as fast as they could. By 0230 (on the Fifth Day, 9 June) Brigadier Yoffe had tank detachments on the east bank in three places, and was also in a good position at Ras

Sudar to close in quickly and seize Port Tewfik when daylight came.[1]

THE SHARON UGDA

When dawn broke on the Fourth Day Brigadier Sharon's M Armoured Brigade, which had been halted on the edge of a minefield protecting the Egyptian Jebel Karim position, saw before it many abandoned vehicles which included 18 Stalin tanks, 30 T-34s, six Centurions and some SU-100s, all intact and ready for battle. Only a few soldiers remained with the brigade commander who, the previous day, on receiving orders to withdraw, had put all his men on trucks and taken them towards the Suez Canal. He had, however, bumped up against the Israeli Centurions holding the eastern end of the Mitla Pass, his troops and vehicles had been scattered by Israeli tank and aircraft action, and many had left their vehicles and fled into the desert. He had returned to his abandoned tanks at Jebel Karim, where he was captured.

Brigadier Sharon, ordered to move towards Nakhel, about 20 miles away, found the going very difficult. When still some six miles distant, at 1200, he heard that the other brigade from the 6th Infantry Division, which had been holding Kuntilla, was rushing westwards along the Pilgrims Way. By this time Nakhel, at an important road junction which had wells and had been an important 'ancient oasis stop' for camel caravans, was largely deserted by Egyptian troops.

Earlier in the day Israeli aircraft had continually attacked the Egyptian positions at Kuntilla, but when they appeared to be empty the waiting and watching W Armoured Brigade advanced towards them, to find that they were in fact deserted.[2] The Egyptian brigade had moved out during darkness, so the Israeli armour took up the chase along the Pilgrims Way. By 1400 the

---

[1] 'So this [my] division, in just less than four days, finished something like 157 tanks—counted—and reached three points on the Canal.' Brigadier Yoffe, Press Conference, Tel Aviv, 12 June 1967.

[2] On 7 July 1967 Israeli search squads found the vehicles of the venturesome Egyptian reconnaissance unit partly buried in the sand. They consisted of seven BTR-40s and BTR-152s, seven ASU-57s and PT-76s and five Soviet scout cars, mostly mounting Schmel anti-tank missiles.

Israelis were approaching Thamed, where there were some fortifications and reports of T-34 tanks, so an air strike was requested. It hit only stragglers, and the Israeli armour passed quickly through this staging post. The retreating Egyptians were several miles ahead, and were reaching Nakhel, where Sharon was deploying his units to deal with them. He sent his Sherman Battalion to block the Pilgrims Way just to the east of Nakhel, and used both his Centurion and Mechanized Infantry Battalions to attack the withdrawing Egyptian brigade in the flank. Several air strikes were made on the moving vehicles. In desperation the Egyptians tried to fight their way through the Nakhel ambush, using their tanks and guns, but after an hour they were beaten back. Many of their vehicles had been destroyed and troops were abandoning them to seek refuge in the desert from aerial attack. But many pockets of resistance remained in and around Nakhel, and the Sharon Ugda, assisted by air strikes, spent the afternoon clearing the camps and surrounding area. This fighting continued until about 1700. Meanwhile, Sharon had been ordered to send his Centurion Battalion to the Mitla Pass. In the evening, just before dusk, he was joined by such forward elements of W Armoured Brigade as had been able to force their way through the destroyed and abandoned vehicles and guns choking the defiles between Thamed and Nakhel. It was later estimated by the Israelis that there were over 150 such vehicles, mostly victims of Israeli Air Force attacks, in this 30-mile stretch. As darkness fell the Nakhel area became quieter.

COMMENTS ON THE FOURTH DAY'S FIGHTING

The Fourth Day had been one of general collapse of the Egyptian forces in the Sinai, but there were notable exceptions, such as the last-ditch counter-attacks against the Northern Force and towards the Mitla Pass, the dogged defence of the Ishmailia and Giddi Passes, and the prickly resistance at Nakhel and Ras Sudar. Despite Israeli efforts on land and in the air, the Egyptians had momentarily held the Israelis at bay while they ferried some 100 of their best tanks back across the Canal into Egypt proper, but by the end of the day it was all over – Israeli air power had proved too much. Credit should be given to many Egyptian formations and units who had remained more or less intact and, isolated and without orders or accurate information, attempted to fight back against such odds. The Israelis estimate that over 1,000 tanks of both sides took part in the final battles for the passes in the Central Ridge, making it the biggest tank struggle since World War II and one of the largest in history. During the day communiqués were issued by the Egyptians stating that their troops were fighting fierce battles against the Israelis (which was true) and that Israeli ground forces were supported by foreign air forces (which was not true). An Egyptian delegate informed the UN Security Council that his Government would accept a cease-fire if the Israelis would; although the Israelis agreed in principle, they were determined to reach the Suez Canal first, and they ignored the cease-fire until they had done so. It was supposed to become operative as from 2000 on the Fourth Day, as ordered by the UN, which had no means of enforcing such a decree. In fact, it did not really become effective until 0230, or later on the Fifth Day (Friday, 9 June). The cease-fire was opportune for the Israelis as their soldiers and vehicles had reached the limit of their endurance, and it was only by a superhuman effort that they were able to force a small number of their vehicles to the east bank of the Canal. An ever-increasing number of vehicles had to be left where they had stopped, because of lack of fuel or mechanical break-down. The fighting units that reached the Canal did so with only about 30 per cent, or less in some instances, of their vehicles. On the Fifth Day, when foreign correspondents were being triumphantly shown the east bank in Israeli possession, this proportion had risen considerably; many vehicles were refuelled, patched up and sent forward to join their units, so that a good impression of strength and endurance would be presented to the world's television and news cameras. No foreign pressmen were allowed to accompany the Israeli formations fighting in the Sinai—only selected Israeli nationals, who fed the news back to Tel Aviv where it was censored or rewritten for world consumption.

COMMENTS ON THE SINAI FIGHTING

The war in the Sinai theatre was over. In four days the Israeli forces had defeated those of the Egyptians and subdued the whole of the Sinai Peninsula from the Negev to the Suez Canal, and from the Mediterranean to Sharm El Sheikh. In terms of men, tanks, guns and equipment on land, the Israelis were roughly half the strength of the Egyptians. How then was this swift victory accomplished? It should clearly be recognized that the Israeli key to success was their complete mastery of the air, which gave their land forces virtual relief from enemy aerial harassment. Had this not been so the quick result could not have been achieved. On land the Israeli success was due to material concentration of force at the vital points and speed in exploitation.

It should be noted that on the First and Second Days Egyptian soldiers in many places fought extremely well, as was admitted by the Israelis[1] and witnessed by the silent fact that some 1,500 Egyptians were killed in the battles to break through the Rafah defences. It was only on the Second Day, much to the relief of Israeli commanders fighting in the Sinai, that the Israeli Air Force was able to give massive ground support to the attackers, carry out interdiction tasks, machine-gun, rocket and bomb Egyptian tanks and vehicles—which were vulnerable to air attack in the open desert—and to drop napalm on vehicles and positions. The Egyptian camouflage was good and their artillery shooting[2] excellent but, with one small exception near Kuntilla, they were out of their depth when it came to mobile warfare. The Egyptians consider their most praiseworthy actions to have been the battles against the Northern Force, the reconnaissance unit action near Kuntilla and the defence of Khan Yunis.

On the Second Day General Murtagi realized that the Egyptian Air Force had been knocked out and that his lengthy lines of communication were completely exposed, so he gave the order

---

[1] 'Yes, I would say the Egyptian is a good soldier, a disciplined soldier, but I think the commanders were very poor.' Brigadier Sharon, Press Conference, Tel Aviv, 12 June 1967.

[2] 'They [the Egyptians] are very good when everything is very simple; they are well organized and they are very good at shooting.' Brigadier Sharon, Press Conference, Tel Aviv, 12th June 1967.

to withdraw from the first line of defence in north-east Sinai. It is thought that he intended the other intermediate positions, such as El Arish, Jiradi, Bir Lafhan and Jebel Libni, to be delaying ones, and that he planned to stand firm regardless of the air situation along the Central Ridge and counter-attack into central Sinai from there. This was sound strategy which might have worked had he been able to put it into practice, but on the Second Day the Egyptian communication system broke down, and it can only be guessed how many formations or units received this order. What is known is that all Egyptians forward of the Central Ridge were left without positive orders from their GOC from the evening of the Second Day onwards. The fog of war descended on them in a dense cloud, and they neither knew what to do nor what others were doing. Communication is the most vital of all factors in the cohesion of any military force, of whatever size; without it the force can degenerate into little more than an uncomprehending herd that can be frightened, driven, scattered or killed. Lack of a general tactical directive to be followed in an emergency, such as the Israelis had, was a fatal omission. On the Third Day and night, when the heavy aerial onslaught caused units involuntarily to withdraw and the general withdrawal to turn into a rout, a general directive would have been most valuable. Although towards the end it became every man for himself, and some Egyptian officers deserted their troops, it is unfair to condemn Egyptian officers and soldiers thoughtlessly and generally. Many formations, such as Shazli Force, the 6th Infantry Division and part of the 4th Armoured Division, were never engaged in battle until they were sucked up in the desperate retreat which nullified their fighting capability completely. The comment must be that had the Israelis not destroyed the Egyptian Air Force (in the Sinai theatre at least) they would most probably have been halted at the foot of the Central Ridge, exhausted and battered, instead of reaching the Suez Canal, as they did.

The Egyptian disadvantages revealed in this fighting, apart from the poor communications, were a too rigid defensive doctrine with positions facing a fixed direction only and flanks and rear exposed, too great a reliance on the 'impassability' of terrain, no appreciation of mobile desert warfare, and lack of initiative in blocking routes and laying ambushes to cut off and deal with Israeli forces, which for periods were short of fuel and extremely vulnerable to such tactics in a deep penetration role. There was no 'scorched earth' policy, and supply and fuel dumps, tanks, guns, vehicles and equipment were left to fall intact into Israeli hands. Another interesting fact is that as there was a general shortage of maps for the Egyptians the surrounding desert expanses were literally unknown wildernesses to them.[1] During the Second and Third Days, when Israeli aerial attacks were heavy, many Egyptians left their vehicles and positions to escape the bombs, bullets and napalm, and took to the desert hoping to find relief from attack and shelter and water at tiny oases, wells or Bedu encampments. In this they were frequently disappointed. Without maps, and away from known roads or tracks, they became lost and many fell victims to the sun, heat and thirst.

The number of Egyptian casualties is still subject to some speculation. The first Egyptian figures, published on 30 June 1967, stated that 5,000 soldiers had been killed in action. Later, on 18 November 1967, Nasser himself admitted that 10,000 soldiers and 1,500 officers (and 40 pilots) had been 'lost', that 5,000 soldiers and 500 officers had been captured, and that 80 per cent of the UAR's army equipment in the Sinai had been lost too. In late June (1967) *Al Ahram* reported that hospitals in and around Cairo were full of wounded, three-quarters of whom suffered from napalm burns. The Israelis never admitted using napalm, but they never denied it either.

Only a few Egyptian prisoners were taken on the First Day, and not many more on the Second, but from the Third Day onwards they began to give themselves up in increasing numbers, thus providing an embarrassing problem for the Israelis, who were still busily fighting the battle. The prisoners were usually disarmed and kept in large groups by the roadside under a light guard, often a slightly wounded Israeli soldier. On the Fourth Day, when hordes, short of food and water, surrendered, the policy was simply to disarm them and tell them to make their own way westward to the Canal. Most of them did this, the large

---

[1] Some of the Egyptian maps captured by the Israelis had markings on them in Russian, which could hardly have helped.

majority eventually managing to get back to Egypt. A few were shot by their own troops, some on the Fourth Day when in panic they attempted to rush across the bridges in mass while the Egyptians were frantically working to get as many T-55s and other modern tanks over to the west bank, and others when they tried to cross in makeshift boats during the hours of darkness and were mistaken for assaulting Israelis. Once they reached the Canal the Israelis set up a ferry service to ship Egyptian prisoners to the other side, and Israeli trucks ran a shuttle service collecting Egyptian soldiers in from the desert to send them home. Egyptian officers were usually flown back to camps in Israel for interrogation. At the end of the war the Israelis announced that they held just over 3,000 Egyptian prisoners. Many senior Egyptian officers captured had attended instruction courses in the Soviet Union. Under questioning they affirmed that their Soviet advisers had advised them to construct strong defences in three successive supporting lines facing 'the front' and to ignore the flanks; thus the concept of rigid defence was forced on them. They also put much of the blame for defeat on to Field-Marshal Amer (this was long before his 'suicide'), saying that he had been appointed Commander-in-Chief of the Armed Forces only because he was President Nasser's friend, that he was not up to the job, and that he let himself be over-influenced by the Soviet Military Mission.

As regards material, the Egyptian army in the Sinai lost most of its equipment—it was a débâcle. Out of about 900 tanks, over 500 were destroyed in battle and another 300 abandoned intact. These figures indicate that about 100 managed to escape back to Egypt,[1] but practically all the guns and most other vehicles were lost. The Israelis claimed to have taken 400 field guns, 50 self-propelled guns, 30 155-mm guns and about 10,000 trucks and other vehicles. Many items of Soviet equipment captured, such as the T-55 and the SU-57(2)s, were of intense interest to Western countries, as was the one large missile site, with nine SAM-2s ready for launching, complete with guidance control mechanism and instructions, taken intact between the Mitla Pass and the Canal. It is also of interest to note the remarkably few instances

---

[1] Israeli figures are still classified, so this is the best estimate possible.

of use of the Schmel and its relative ineffectualness, which gives
cause for reflection to those who predict that the anti-tank missile
will exterminate tanks in any major war of the future.

Egyptian morale has been generally adversely commented
upon by the world press. While certainly never as high as that
of the Israelis, it was fairly stable at the beginning, and in
patches remained reasonably good, although in general after the
Second Day it sank fast. However, some units that had not
received the order to withdraw fought on until they were overwhelmed or had expended their ammunition, fuel or water. The
less well-equipped 20th Palestinian Division, which had Egyptian
officers, fought on bravely until it was finally smothered by
Israeli air attacks and bombardment.

The Israeli campaign, mounted with 'regardless of cost'
assaults, developed in three phases. The first was the initial
breakthrough in the north-east and centre, the second the
penetration in depth, and the third the rush for the passes in the
Central Ridge to contain the withdrawing Egyptians. A fourth, or
impromptu, phase was the hasty scramble to reach the Canal
before, and after, the cease-fire. The reasons for the Israeli
victory are several, the most important being the freedom of the
air. Others include the concentration of force at the impact area,
so that the ratio of strength was always in Israeli favour, the fact
that commanders at most levels were given tactical directives
and allowed a large measure of initiative in how they accomplished their mission, high morale, a high standard of training,
good organization and a vital incentive–they dared not lose.
Their communications, although not perfect, were far better
than those of the Egyptians. Control of the air enabled commanders to liaise by helicopter and see for themselves. These
advantages more than made up for any shortcomings. Israeli
commanders were always well forward with their men. The
practice of tank commanders advancing into battle with open
turrets gave them improved vision at vital moments and enabled
them to signal each other manually when intercommunication
failed, as it did on occasions, but it was a dangerous one. The
Israeli armour was forced to adopt the 'regardless of cost' tactics
for the initial breakthrough, but they were modified as soon as
Israeli forces probed forward in deep penetration, leaving any

mopping up to be done by follow-up units. For example, Um Katif, Rafah, Jiradi and El Arish were alive with resistance and snipers many hours after the main breakthrough. The Israeli armoured columns were able to carry out this deep penetration phase successfully as their formations were largely self-contained, the supply-carrying Tnuva trucks tagging on behind with three days' fuel and supplies although at times there was administrative chaos on the single narrow roadways.

The Israelis felt the pinch of supplies during the Fourth Day, as most of their Tnuva trucks were two-wheel drive civilian vehicles, which had difficulty in keeping up and broke down. These trucks were generally regarded by Israeli commanders as a drag on operations. My guess is that future plans may substitute military four-wheel drive vehicles which may be 'moth-balled' when not mobilized. In the armoured advances many Israeli tanks fell out for lack of fuel and because of break-downs, but all were soon back in action again—the Israelis admitted the loss of only 61 tanks in the Sinai fighting. In the final rush for the Canal only the fittest made it, but those that fell out or dropped back were quickly put right and sent forward on the Fifth Day, when foreign journalists were allowed for the first time to visit the Sinai and see the forward positions. The Israelis did not count damaged tanks as lost if they could be repaired, an advantage the Egyptians lacked.

The essential Israeli policy of 'regardless of cost' took its toll in casualties and caused deep anxiety until the initial break-through was completed. Although it was known that the Egyptian Air Force had been eliminated, the Israeli commanders also knew that an initial failure would have meant withdrawal, reorganization and re-assaulting. Egyptian morale would have gained and Israeli morale suffered, especially as contrary to cal-culations Jordan had entered the war and the fight for Jerusalem had begun, which might siphon off reserves and material from the Southern Command. Official Israeli casualties for the Sinai fighting were given as 275 killed and 800 wounded.[1] Three Air Force pilots, shot down in dog-fights, were taken prisoner.

The Soviet tanks were technically superior to those of the

---

[1] The Sharon Ugda had 58 killed and 182 wounded according to Yael Dayan.

Israelis, but they were designed to fight on the plains of Europe, while the tanks possessed by Israel had been modified to fight in the Sinai desert. The British Centurion[1] seems to have come out best in the Sinai fighting, being able to take all that the T-55, Egypt's most modern and powerful tank, could give it. Israeli tank gunners were of a much higher standard and better trained than their Egyptian opposite numbers, able on the average to fire off at least two shots to their opponent's one in battle. This terrific advantage swung the balance on several vital occasions, but the Egyptian anti-tank and field gunners were good, often causing Israeli tanks to sheer away from them. The ancient but well-maintained Super Sherman of World War II vintage functioned surprisingly well, and even though many fell out because of mechanical trouble, they were soon patched up again.

Israeli deception plans contributed to victory. The announcement of the capture of places was usually delayed to confuse Egyptian forces and to give them a false picture of how the fighting was going. Cautious and modest Israeli communiqués gave the impression that Israeli forces were still in eastern Sinai, when they were actually approaching the Suez Canal. Periodically, to confuse and mislead Egyptian commanders, false messages were given in Arabic, with an Egyptian accent, over radio sets captured in the field. The conclusion must be that the Israeli campaign into the Sinai in 1967 was brilliantly conceived and boldly executed.

---

[1] Four British Chieftain tanks were in Israeli hands for evaluation purposes, but none was committed to action. They were seen after the war in the compound of the British Embassy at Tel Aviv.

CHAPTER 6

The Jordanian Front

Unlike the Egyptian forces, those of Jordan still bore an un-mistakable British stamp; they relied completely on voluntary service, the soldiers enlisting for various periods. Their total strength[1] amounted to about 58,000 of whom some 56,000 were in the army,[2] which was on the British pattern, the 'teeth' being formed into seven infantry and two armoured brigades. The two armoured brigades, the 40th and the 60th, each had two armoured battalions, each with about 40 Patton tanks. A mechanized infantry brigade was equipped with US M-113 armoured person-nel carriers. The technical arms and services, such as the signals and engineers–consisting largely of West Bank personnel (who amounted to almost 20 per cent of the Army's total strength), as did two of the infantry brigades–tended to be disaffected, and Hussein's main strength lay in the loyalty of his armoured and other infantry brigades, which were manned predominantly by desert Bedu. About one-third of the Army consisted of mercen-ary Bedu from the adjacent deserts of Syria, Iraq and Saudi Arabia. The Commander-in-Chief was General Habes Majali, a Beduin, who had been trained at Sandhurst and who had held the position since 1957, when he was instrumental in saving King Hussein from assassination.

In March 1965 Hussein abolished his Ministry of Defence. He scattered its responsibilities and duties among other ministries and departments to avoid any one person or group gaining sole control over the armed forces, or any substantial part of them. This enabled him to concentrate power over them in his own hands. At the same time he disbanded the 10,000 strong Pales-tinian National Guard, which had been formed as a part-time

---

[1] The tiny Jordanian Navy consisted of about 100 personnel who manned a few small craft and landing craft on the Gulf of Akaba.

[2] Sometimes referred to as the Jordan Arab Army.

home guard for villages on the West Bank; it had, however, developed into a somewhat surly organization, potentially hostile to the King. Only very few of the discharged National Guardsmen were taken into the regular army, which caused discontented muttering on the West Bank. As incidents increased and the border situation with Israel worsened, in November 1966 Hussein announced that he would introduce conscription, increase his army, fortify the frontier villages and arm civilians living in them. Little or nothing came of these promises, which were merely a verbal sop to West Bank nationalists. Hussein did not trust the people of the West Bank with arms, and had no intention of giving them any if he could help it.

Over £60 million, more than half the country's budget, was spent on defence, and the Jordanian army was well equipped for its size, having nearly 200 tanks, chiefly Pattons (M-47s and M-48s) and Centurions, and about 200 guns.[1] America had supplied over 250 armoured personnel carrers (mainly M-113s, which were in use with the armoured brigades), some recoilless guns, and the US M-2 carbine, which was replacing the British rifle. Jordan also had some British armoured cars and reconnaissance vehicles. The bulk of the artillery consisted of British 25-pounder field guns and 17-pounder anti-tank guns, although there were also some 155-mm ones (Long Toms). A large proportion of the arms and equipment, especially radar, guns and ammunition, had been obtained from Britain, but there had been a recent infusion of American material.[2]

Morale was good and the state of training high in the Bedu formations but somewhat less so in mixed or 'West Bank' units. In general the reputation of the Jordanian army, the successor of the old Arab Legion, was high as it had fought well at times. Consequently it was viewed with some respect by the Israelis and a corresponding degree of envy by several Arab states.

---

[1] 'The Israelis claim that Jordan deployed 270 tanks [armoured vehicles?] and 150 field guns during the war.' (*Six Day War*.)

'We had 176 Pattons and some other light armoured vehicles.' King Hussein, (*Sunday Telegraph*, 15 September 1968).

[2] The value of the American military equipment was reported to be about $5 million, which was about equal to the amount of other economic assistance given to Jordan by America that year.

THE JORDANIAN DISPOSITIONS

Apart from two infantry brigades on the East Bank of the Jordan, all the other formations were positioned on the West Bank, one in north Samaria, one opposite Kalkilya, one north of the

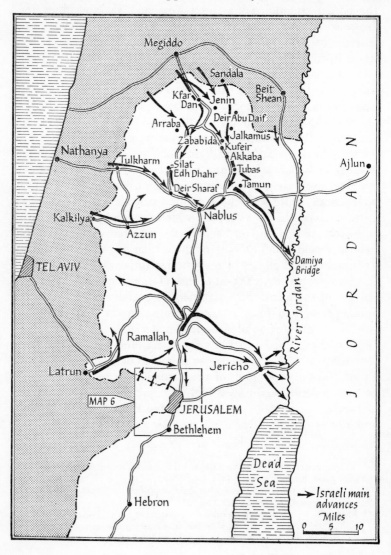

Latrun Salient, one in Jerusalem and one in the Hebron Hills, while the two armoured brigades lay back, the 40th near the Damiya Bridge and the 60th near Jericho. The 12th Independent Armoured Battalion was in Samaria in support of the infantry and the 10th Independent Armoured Battalion was in the Hebron area with a similar role. The infantry brigades, in static defences, covered the most obvious Israeli attack routes, and the defensive plan was to try to hold any assault near the frontier while the armour swiftly moved up to beat it back. Hussein, General Riad and his Egyptian staff, and Major-General Amer Khammash, the Jordanian Chief-of-Staff, all realized that the Jordanian army was too small to guard adequately a 350 mile frontier, as it lacked a second line of defence and had insufficient air cover. They realized that Jordan could not resist a concentrated Israeli attack for more than 48 hours. Such an attack was never thought to be a real danger, however, as it was anticipated—despite previous Arab bad faith—that as Israel would have to fight on several fronts at once only a comparatively small proportion of its armed forces would be directed against Jordan.

King Hussein has since declared that he had no offensive plans, but this is not quite accurate. Vague plans existed to penetrate into Israel near Nathanya, at its narrow waist opposite Tulkharm, with armour and infantry to cut the country in half, and also to encircle and strangle New Jerusalem; but these were envisaged as part of a combined Arab operation in which the Syrians and Iraqis would sweep into Haifa and the Egyptians surge northwards to Tel Aviv, but no details had been worked out or agreed upon. More to the point, the Jordanians had planned limited offensives to improve the local tactical position in certain sectors, to be executed as opportunity presented itself. These included taking the former Government House (now the headquarters of the UN Truce Supervisory Organization), Ramat Rahel and the Israeli Mount Scopus enclave in the Jerusalem area, Bir Main and Kibbutz Shalavim in the Latrun area, and the northern part of the Gilboa Hill feature, in the north.

General Riad,[1] as the overall commander on the Jordanian

---

[1] General Riad had been Deputy to General Ali Amer, Chief of Staff, of the United Arab Command.

Front, saw the military weaknesses of the Jordanian army and of Jordan itself. He had arrived in Jordan on 1 June, and on the evening of 4 June he held a conference at which Hussein, Egyptian staff officers and senior Jordanian officers were present. The conference agreed that with so few troops a large-scale offensive was initially out of the question, certainly until the promised Iraqi and Saudi Arabian formations arrived, so it was decided to hold the existing defensive lines and positions. General Riad intended to put the expected four Iraqi brigades, one of which was to be armoured, into the northern part of the West Bank opposite Nathanya, both to draw off Israeli pressure from the south and to be ready to advance to cut Israel in half. He planned to use the Saudi Arabian brigades in the Hebron Hills, in the Jerusalem area, and also perhaps to bolster up the Latrun Salient defences. General Riad still felt that the northern part of the West Bank and the Jordan Valley would be particularly vulnerable to Israeli penetration thrusts, and he is reported to have suggested that Hussein should ask Syria for some brigades to cover this part of Jordan.[1] The King sent his request to Syria, but received no answer.[2] It was agreed at this conference that should it come to war, the initial task of the Jordanians would be quickly to neutralize Israeli airfields by aerial and artillery bombardment, and then to exploit as opportunity occurred, particularly in the Jerusalem sector.

THE ISRAELI DISPOSITIONS

On the Israeli side of the Jordanian frontier the northern part came under the Northern Command and the southern part under the Central Command. Hussein had stood aside in 1956 and now, despite the recent pact with Nasser, it was hoped that in the event of hostilities he might confine himself to a brief show of force by firing artillery and small arms but taking little other aggressive action. The Jordanian plan to encircle and

---

[1] King Hussein, *Sunday Telegraph*, 15 September 1968.

[2] General Riad said 'The Syrian Front can easily be held by a third of the Syrian forces. As I see it, the Syrians can carry out their assignment with only five of their 15 brigades. I suggest you ask them immediately to send their ten reserve brigades to bolster our front.' (*My 'War' with Israel*, King Hussein.)

besiege New Jerusalem, as had been done in 1948, was no longer a serious threat as now five separate roads led into the city, whereas formerly there had been just one tenuous one. However, the Israelis did take seriously the fact that Jordanian guns could shell far into Israel right up to the outskirts of Tel Aviv. The Israeli General Staff had several contingency plans. One was for a general offensive against Jordan with the object of completely seizing the West Bank and pushing Hussein back beyond the River Jordan; like other Israeli offensive plans, this was expected to be put into operation only when circumstances and the political climate were appropriate. Like the Jordanians, the Israelis had several plans for limited offensives to gain local tactical advantages along the frontier, such as against the Latrun Salient (sometimes referred to as the 'dagger pointing to the heart of Tel Aviv'), of linking up with the Mount Scopus enclave and seizing certain strategical positions in and around Jerusalem, and of taking and neutralizing such danger points as Tulkharm, Kalkilya, and even Jenin.

If the Jordanians attacked in the Jerusalem sector, or if the Israelis were ordered to make local gains there, the plan was initially to use J Infantry Brigade, a reserve brigade whose personnel all lived in the Jerusalem area and which consisted of three infantry battalions and a unit of Sherman tanks. If it was required to link up with the Mount Scopus enclave, an armoured brigade would be made available, but as yet it was not intended to send any extra forces to Jerusalem, as this course might be misconstrued by the Jordanians, whom the Israelis did not want to alarm. As the local commander was told he would have to hold and deal with any local attacks with his own resources, he prepared as well as he could—civilians, including school children, were mustered to construct emplacements and shelters, fill sandbags and dig trenches, while soldiers strengthened the outer defences by laying more mines and erecting more barbed wire.

The Israelis took particular care not to provoke Hussein. On 1 June they agreed to postpone the routine relief of the Israeli garrison on Mount Scopus, as the Jordanians said they could not guarantee its security as it passed through their territory owing to the hostile attitude of the inhabitants. The Mount Scopus enclave was a left-over from the 1948 War, as at the time of the cease-fire the Hebrew University buildings there were occupied by a beleaguered Israeli army detachment. The area was declared a demilitarized zone by the UN[1] as were certain other stretches of territory along the frontiers. The Israeli garrison was allowed to remain and was relieved at fortnightly intervals under UN supervision and protection. Although it should, strictly speaking, have been manned by policemen with only small arms, it in fact consisted of 120 Israeli soldiers. Moshe Dayan had also suggested that several small routine troop movements and training exercises, due to take place in and around Jerusalem, should be cancelled so as not to appear to offer provocation.

THE IRAQI FORCES

Although the Iraqi forces were not involved in the actual ground fighting against the Israelis, a little should be known about them to complete the background to this war. President Abdul Rahman Aref governed Iraq by decree, and was subject only to the pressures of the National Council of the Revolutionary Command. On 10 May he had re-shuffled his Cabinet and himself had taken on the additional post of Premier. The Baathists had been eclipsed and banned, the only permitted political party being the Arab Socialist Union. Comprising about 169,240 square miles and having a population of about 8·26 million, the country's economy was based on agriculture and oil, the production of the latter having risen steadily to about 65 million tons annually. The Soviet Union had provided some assistance and machinery to help nationalize the land, and much of the military equipment.

Iraq had about 82,000 men under arms, about 70,000 of whom were in the army, there being a two-year period of selective conscription in force. The army was basically organized into five divisions, one of which was armoured. Although Iraq was reported to possess about 600 tanks, mainly T-54s and T-34s with a few British Centurions, it was reckoned that only about 400 were 'runners' owing to poor maintenance and overwork.

---

[1] Some of the buildings on Mount Scopus were occupied by UN personnel.

Iraq had received five batteries of SAM-2s, which were not yet operative. A para-military force of about 10,000, and a mechanized brigade of security troops were permanently based in Baghdad. The Iraqi army had been fighting the Kurdish insurrection in the nothern parts of the country for over six years, and a high proportion of both officers and soldiers had experience of active service. It was widely alleged that the army had a vested interest in keeping the Kurdish War alive, and was deliberately nullifying all attempts to negotiate a cease-fire. Abdul Rahman Buzzaz, the first civilian Premier for some time, attempted in September 1965 to come to terms with the Kurds, but was ousted from office before he could implement a cease-fire agreement. Morale in the armed forces was improving, but had not really recovered from the frequent purges made by President Kassem; it was estimated that during his four and a half years in power he executed, imprisoned or removed over 2,000 officers—a large slice from an officer corps of about 8,000.

Iraq has no common frontier with Israel. The major part of its army faced northwards against the Kurds, but in company with other Arab states it was loudly anti-Israeli and, having never signed any armistice agreement with Israel, intended to take part in any joint Arab attack on Israel. Its relations with adjacent Arab neighbours were mercurial, and its leaders alternately quarrelled or made friends with those of Jordan, Syria and Egypt. At first President Aref intended to send troops to support the Syrian (but not the Jordanian) military effort against Israel, and had in fact dispatched a brigade into Syria. However, after the 30 May agreement he changed his mind, withdrew his brigade from Syria, suddenly became friendly with Hussein, and agreed to send a whole division into Jordan.

THE SAUDI ARABIAN FORCES

A brief mention should also be made of the Saudi Arabian forces. Ruled despotically by King Faisal, oil-rich Saudi Arabia comprises an area of about 927,000 square miles, the greater part of which is barren desert, with a population estimated at about 6 million—no formal census has ever been taken. The defence forces, consisting of volunteers, were about 36,000 strong, of whom about 30,000 were in the army, which was basically formed into five truck-borne infantry brigades and a small armoured formation. Arms and equipment included 100 tanks (mainly American M-24s), American trucks, British field guns, Vigilant anti-tank missiles and a Thunderbird air defence system, the latter primarily for defence against UAR aircraft operating from the Yemen. A para-military force of about 20,000, known as the White Army, was used to maintain internal security; in a way it was a political counter-balance to the regular army.

The ruling Saud family were traditional enemies of the Hashemites (of whom King Hussein was one) and over the years no love had been lost between Jordan and Saudi Arabia, although on the other hand border friction was almost non-existent. Since 1962 the Saudi Arabians had been fighting Nasser by proxy in the Yemen; it was only because of this that King Saud, and later his brother, King Faisal, who ousted him in November 1964, made spasmodic contact with King Hussein, offering support and giving him sums of money. Like all other Arab leaders, King Faisal gave strong lip-service to Arab unity against Israel, and he was certainly interested in having a token force take part in any war against that country. The snag was that his army was small—very small for the size of his domain—and faced dangerous threats from the UAR Expeditionary Force in the Yemen and the hostile ambitions of the Republican Yemenis. However, in the latter part of May 1967 he sent three of his five infantry brigades northwards, intending that they should enter Jordan to help King Hussein, but as Hussein's 30 May agreement with Nasser displeased him he ordered his troops to halt at Tabuk, a small oasis town in the north-west of Saudi Arabia, about 30 miles from the Jordanian border. Despite Hussein's pleadings to King Faisal, who was in Britain at the time, he would not allow the Saudi Arabian brigades to move any further northwards.

The First Day (Monday, 5 June 1967)

In Amman, it will be remembered, General Riad received at about 0900 the signal from Field-Marshal Amer ordering him to commence hostilities. At 0930 Hussein made his impassioned speech to his nation, but owing to the false message planted by Israeli counter-intelligence, it was not until about 1100 that the Jordanian artillery began to open up on its pre-selected targets in Israel. This bombardment, with the 155-mm 'Long Toms', continued throughout the day, into the night and during the following day; in fact, until the guns were silenced by the Israelis. The shelling came from various points along the Jordanian frontier; places hit included Tirat Zvi and Beit Shean in the upper Jordan Valley in the north, Sandala and army positions on the northern part of the Mount Gilboa feature to the north of Jenin, Ramat David, near an airfield in the Jezreel Valley, Kfar Sava and Kfar Sirkin on the Sharon Plain, Ramat Aviv and the outskirts of Tel Aviv, and some suburbs of New Jerusalem, including the village of Castel, at the foot of Mount Castel, where an Israeli field headquarters was established.[1]

Once Israel had launched its aerial strike on Egyptian airfields and ordered its troops to take the offensive in the Sinai, certain moves were made to persuade Jordan to remain neutral. Premier Eshkol sent a message to Hussein through General Odd Bull, the UN Commander, who was at Government House, to the effect that the Israelis would not initiate hostilities against Jordan, but adding that Israel would react 'with all our might' if Jordan attacked. The UN Commander passed it to Hussein, who did not receive it until after 1100, just after his aircraft had left to bomb Israel. He is alleged to have remarked: 'They started the battle. Well, they are receiving our reply by air.'[2] Eshkol followed this up by broadcasting a similar statement over the radio,[3] obviously designed for a wider Jordanian consumption,[4] but King Hussein's mind was made up.

In Jerusalem an uneasy quiet during the morning was at first broken only by the occasional shot or burst of small arms fire from the Jordanian side, but at about 1100 some mortar bombs fell on Israeli territory and Israeli outposts replied with bazooka

---

[1] Other places the Israelis claim were also hit included Eyal, Ramat Hakovesh, and Yad Hannah. (*Six Day War.*)

[2] *My 'War' with Israel.*

[3] Israel had no television at this time.

[4] Over the radio Premier Eshkol announced that he 'would not attack any country which did not first launch an attack against us. But any aggressor can be sure of being met by the full weight of Israeli arms.' (*Six Day War.*)

fire. The small arms fire increased. The Israelis replied in kind but not with the same intensity, as they felt that Hussein had to put on some sort of face-saving show. Israeli casualties in these spates of firing were few as most people sought refuge in their sandbagged emplacements, shelters or stone houses and remained there for the next three days. The streets of New Jerusalem were empty of soldiers and military vehicles. At 1145 Ramat Rahel, the southern outpost of New Jerusalem, came under artillery fire, and at about the same time shells and mortar bombs burst on Mount Scopus.[1] Israeli territory had been bombed by Jordanian aircraft, and the Israeli attitude hardened. The General Staff had given the order to smash Hussein's air force. Already the UN Commander had asked for a cease-fire, a request to which the Israelis had agreed, but which the Jordanians rejected.

Hussein next decided to make a local gain by occupying Government House, which was in demilitarized territory, and an infantry battalion was detailed for the task. This was a serious step as it brought him into direct conflict with the United Nations. At 1200 General Odd Bull again asked for a cease-fire, and this was again agreed to by the Israelis, but no reply came from the Jordanians, whose troops at that moment were moving into the demilitarized zone. An hour later two Jordanian companies had, as Radio Amman announced,[2] taken possession of the small wooded area to the immediate north of Government House, in which some 100 UN personnel had gathered. Completely misled by false reports that an Egyptian armoured column had entered the Negev, General Riad decided to send the 60th Armoured Brigade from Jericho south by way of Hebron to assault the Israeli armoured centre at Beersheba and then to go on to meet the advancing Egyptian column. Before this Jordanian formation commenced to move at about 1300, the order was countermanded and, instead, the formation was redirected towards Jerusalem and the Ramallah Ridge. General Riad then ordered the 40th Armoured Brigade to move from the

---

[1] At 1245 Radio Amman announced that Mount Scopus had been occupied by the Jordanians. This was completely false.

[2] The Jordanian occupation of Government House had already been prematurely announced by Radio Cairo at 1030.

Damiya Bridge area to Jericho, to replace the 60th Armoured Brigade and to be in a more advantageous position to support a limited offensive in the Jerusalem sector. This formation also began moving at about 1300. Considering that the Jordanians had received no reply from their request to the Syrians to send reinforcements to Jordan, this latter move was most surprising and unsound.

THE NARKISS UGDA

Brigadier Narkiss, GOC Central Command, was already in Jerusalem watching the ugly situation developing, and as it worsened he began assembling his battle group, which for convenience can be called the Narkiss Ugda, of which he took command, although he commanded his brigades directly from his Command HQ and not from a field Ugda HQ. This Ugda eventually comprised three reserve brigades, which were J Infantry Brigade, H Armoured Brigade, and Q Paratroop Brigade, the latter consisting of one regular and two reserve paratroop battalions, with no armour and few half-tracks. Also under Brigadier Narkiss's command were two other formations, L Infantry Brigade from near Latrun and S Infantry Brigade from the Sharon Plain. Shortly after Jordanian troops entered the Government House area, H Armoured Brigade, already assembled at Ramle at 1300, began moving towards Jerusalem on three separate routes, one battalion on each. Just previously, at 1230, he had heard that the Jordanians were entering the Government House compound, and he was told to drive them out. He gave the task to J Infantry Brigade, the only formation under his hand at the time. At 1430, just as Israeli troops were crossing the armistice line, General Odd Bull once more asked for a cease-fire, but this time he was ignored by both sides. Two Israeli infantry companies, with six Shermans in support, moved east towards that position. A half-hour fight ensued in which the Israelis lost eight dead as they forced the Jordanians, who were just about to move towards the adjacent experimental farm from which the Israelis had emerged, from the small wood shielding Government House. A shell from a Sherman gun blasted open the gate to the actual compound, and by 1500 the whole position was in Israeli hands, the Jordanians escaping in the direction of Abu Tur eastwards. About 18 dead Jordanian soldiers were counted in the covering wood. An Israeli convoy of trucks was sent up and General Odd Bull and his UN personnel were evacuated into Israel, although they asked to be repatriated through Jordan. Later that day the Israeli flag flew from the mast at Government House. In the compound were many vehicles, both UN and Jordanian, most of them damaged and some of them on fire.

Meanwhile reports reached Brigadier Narkiss of armoured movement in Samaria.[1] These concerned the Jordanian 40th Armoured Brigade, which was beginning its journey to Jericho, but he naturally thought its destination might be Jerusalem. He reasoned that if it could get on to the Ramallah Ridge or plateau, the elongated feature that lay between Ramallah and Jerusalem, it could either hit him in the flank or encircle him. This meant he would have to use H Armoured Brigade to seize the Ramallah Ridge to forestall such a move, instead of having it available for an advance to Mount Scopus. Narkiss asked for another formation, and was allocated Q Paratroop Brigade, then waiting on the airfield at Aqir to take part that evening in an assault on El Arish. The El Arish project was cancelled when Jordan entered the war. At 1400 Narkiss was allocated one paratroop battalion, half-an-hour later another one, and then the whole brigade, which suddenly had to condition itself to a completely different role – that of fighting in a built-up area instead of an airborne assault in desert terrain. However, the switch was not completely 'off the cuff' as this brigade had been ear-marked to fight in Jerusalem as its secondary role, and its commander had spent some time there the previous week on reconnaissance. Narkiss intended to use the paratroops to assault the Police School, Ammunition Hill and other strong points that blocked the way to Mount Scopus. Once Mount Scopus had been taken it was hoped to be able to exploit the situation and eventually break through into the Old City. It was some time before the brigade was ready, and it was not until 1900 that it finally set off in civilian buses for Jerusalem.

---

[1] It will be convenient to refer to the northern part of the West Bank as Samaria.

From 1500 onwards several Israeli aircraft made rocket and cannon attacks on the Jordanian 40th Armoured Brigade as it moved southwards, and these continued even when it was ascertained that its destination was Jericho and not Jerusalem. It arrived at Jericho at 1700 and the vehicles quickly dispersed into the surrounding broken country to avoid the attention of Israeli aircraft—the column had already lost two Pattons and ten other vehicles in the course of the hazardous journey. By 1600 H Armoured Brigade was nearing Jerusalem, and Narkiss briefed its commander, who had arrived ahead of his tanks. Narkiss, who had repeatedly and unsuccessfully asked permission to assault Latrun, Abdul Aziz Hill and other positions, had been held on a very tight rein by Moshe Dayan and General Rabin, both of whom were reluctant to stir up hostile Jordanian activity until the Sinai fighting had been more satisfactorily resolved. Now he was given a limited go-ahead by the General Staff, as it was felt that the opportunity was presenting itself to make important, but limited, gains by battle. H Armoured brigade was ordered to seize the Ramallah Ridge, which looked down on and dominated parts of New Jerusalem and the eastern end of the Jerusalem Corridor. The three battalions were to go straight into battle on their individual axes to take their objectives without pausing. Other smaller ridges tentacled out from the main one; in particular three of these reached southwards, each having Jordanian positions on their northern, and higher, parts, and Israeli positions on their southern extremities. It was along these three north-south minor ridges that the Israeli tanks were to attack the main Ramallah Ridge. The westernmost one had Maale Hahamisha (a kibbutz and sanatorium), Abu Gosh on its southern end, all in Israeli territory; northwards, in Jordanian territory, there was Radar Hill, a former British concrete strong point, with Biddu, a fortified village just behind it on the main ridge. The centre minor ridge had on it the village of Castel and Beit Meir in the Israeli portion, and Abdul Aziz Hill, just over the Jordanian border. On the eastern minor ridge the village of Beit Iksa, with Beit Kika on a spur, lay just within the Jordanian portion. The three strong Jordanian positions were Radar Hill, Abdul Aziz Hill and Beit Iksa.

At 1700 the three columns of H Armoured Brigade crashed

through the wire obstacles at the border and started their three-pronged offensive. Until darkness set in they probed their way upwards and forwards. The Jordanian positions were protected by mines, and as the brigade had no 'flail tanks' the soldiers had to walk in front to detect them. In this initial advance over 40 Israelis were wounded, but only half-a-dozen tanks were lost. The first Jordanian post to fall, at 1720, was Abdul Aziz Hill, which was heavily shelled by the Israelis, who then charged in their half-tracks through a smoke screen up the fairly gentle slopes of the upper hill to overrun the position. They then took, successively, Radar Hill, Beit Iksa and Beit Kika. Many concrete bunkers were encountered, and a Sherman tank was detailed to deal with each one separately as it was detected; this was done with flat-trajectory fire at point-blank ranges. By 1900 H Armoured Brigade had fought its way along the three minor ridges to reach the southern edge of the main Ramallah Ridge, where it halted. During the hours of darkness its mechanized infantry element carefully probed forward, removing mines and marking out safety lanes. The main ridge, which contained the Jordanian road running west to Latrun, was flatter, less rugged and more open, being really a small plateau and therefore better for armoured movement and fighting.

Meanwhile, Narkiss decided to cut the Jordanian road south from Jerusalem to Bethlehem. He ordered the battalion of J Infantry Brigade to continue along the southern spur on which Government House stood (as did also Ramat Rahel) to Sur Bahir, a Jordanian village on the same feature. For convenience this can be known as the Sur Bahir Ridge, two of whose features constituted the main defences – 'Sausage Hill', south of Government House, and 'Bell Hill', east of Ramat Rahel. At 1800 the Israelis moved forward. In the advance two Shermans were lost, one by sliding down a ravine and the other by anti-tank fire. Three Jordanian soldiers suddenly emerged from a shelter, killing three Israelis and wounding the battalion commander (he had already been wounded in the initial charge to clear the wood near Government House but he had remained with his unit). This time he was evacuated. 'Sausage Hill' was taken just after 1800. The village of Sur Bahir was entered by the Israelis at about 2000, but a Jordanian counter-attack drove them out again an hour later, and 'Bell Hill' had been taken by about 2020. After an exchange of fire the Israelis fell back some distance, as they were in an exposed position, but the firing did not die down until about 2300. This limited offensive had failed in its objective, which had been to take and hold the Sur Bahir Ridge and thus sever the Jerusalem to Bethlehem road. The Jordanians were able to continue to use this road, their only land means of communication southwards to Hebron during darkness.

Q Paratroop Brigade was expected to arrive in Jerusalem just before midnight. Narkiss planned to use it to attack the Police School and the Sheikh Jarrah district. The battalion commanders had been rushed to Jerusalem during the afternoon for reconnaissance and briefing, and personnel of the resident J Infantry Brigade, familiar with the ground, were attached to them to help. A Brigade Command Post was established and in the twilight boundaries were allocated and landmarks located. Narkiss wanted to launch an assault under cover of darkness as he felt this would give a better chance of getting through the built-up areas without too many casualties, but now that the Israelis had command of the air General Rabin and the General Staff advocated a daylight attack, to be closely and heavily supported by aircraft and artillery. Narkiss thought that air strikes might not be able to give close enough support, or be accurate enough in a fast-moving house-to-house battle, and there was considerable discussion over this. He had his way and began to prepare for an assault at 0200 (on the Second Day, 6 June).

THE LATRUN BATTLE

To the west the battle for Latrun was beginning. Latrun was on a Jordanian salient sticking right into Israel, only 20 miles from Tel Aviv and some 15 from New Jerusalem. At the head of a series of defiles, it had been the gateway to Jerusalem in 1948, when the Israelis failed repeatedly to capture it so they had to realign the roadway to bypass Latrun. During the afternoon on the First Day, Jordanian guns from positions at Latrun began to shell the nearby kibbutz of Nahson. By evening the Israeli L Infantry Brigade, which had a unit of Shermans, started to force its way along the disused road that ran through the narrow defile of Shar Hagai,[1] just inside Jordanian-held territory. The tank unit engaged the Latrun Police Post, while the remainder of the brigade advanced from the north-east towards it, elements peeling off to take the huge fortress-like monastery and the Arab villages of Imwas and Yala. When darkness fell these advances halted until dawn.

THE PELED UGDA

In the Israeli Northern Command a force was assembled which can be known as the Peled Ugda. It consisted of O Armoured Brigade and E Infantry Brigade, all from Northern Command, and also some infantry units from Central Command. Commanded by Brigadier Elad Peled, Director of the National Defence College, its primary purpose was to deal with any hostile moves made by the Syrians in the north. The order to take action against Jordan instead was received by GOC Northern Command at about noon, when his troops were still dispersed in their assembly areas, and it took nearly five hours to get them moving on to their respective axes. Clearly, this move had not been expected, but once under way the Israelis quickly swung into action. The plan was that the armoured brigade should cut into Jordanian territory, encircle and attack Jenin from the south, block the roads between Jenin and Nablus, and also exploit down to the Damiya Bridge over the River Jordan. Jordanian artillery had been shelling Ramat David, where the Israelis had an air base, from positions just to the west of Jenin.[2] Jenin lay on the southernmost edge of the extreme part of the Jezreel Valley, about 11 miles from the Afula-Megiddo cross-roads. It was surrounded by hills on three sides—the north, the west and the south—and the obvious and easier approach was up the valley from the north-east. This sector was held by the 25th (Khalid Ibn El Walid) Infantry Brigade, supported by an armoured company of about 15 Pattons of 12th Independent Armoured Battalion.

---

[1] The Arab name was Bab el Wad (Gate to the Valley).
[2] Jenin had been taken by the 2nd (Carmeli) Brigade in 1948, which had been driven out again by the Iraqis. An Israeli attempt to recapture it had been repulsed with loss.

As a diversion a battalion from E Infantry Brigade moved from Beit Shean, in the upper Jordan Valley, through Tirat Zvi. Crossing the border at about 1600, it advanced southwards along a track parallel to, and on the west side of the River Jordan. Overcoming the tiny frontier post, the Israeli infantry moved about 10 miles and halted as darkness fell. During this limited advance only scattered shots were fired by either side. The intention was to make the Jordanians think that the main objective was a complete encircling movement of Samaria, the first stage being to seize the Damiya Bridge.

In two separate columns, O Armoured Brigade crossed the frontier at 1700. The main column, consisting of an armoured battalion of Shermans, a mechanized infantry battalion (less one company) and a reconnaissance unit, moved from Megiddo (in Israel). The leading tanks crashed through the tiny border post at Moshav Ramon, catching the defenders completely by surprise and enabling the leading vehicles to get through without a shot being fired at them. Suddenly realizing what was happening, the Jordanians quickly recovered and opened fire at the mechanized infantry following in half-tracks. Next the Jordanian artillery opened up and halted the attackers for about half-an-hour. The Israeli tanks then moved along a motorable track towards Yamun and Kfar Dan, two villages to the north-west of Jenin. By 1930 the Shermans had entered these two places, meeting hardly any resistance. A battery of 'Long Toms' was taken near Yamun. The mechanized infantry, having dealt with the border post, caught up with the main body, which reformed and began to move south-eastwards to get into the hills shielding Jenin from the south, a movement that was continued in darkness. As the Israelis crossed the main Jenin to Nablus road at a point where it ran through the Dotan Valley (a long shallow depression in the shape of an arc to the south of Jenin) they came across a Patton tank that had been set on fire by an air strike. Several fields were ablaze too.

Also at 1700 the other column of O Armoured Brigade, which consisted of an armoured battalion and a company of mechanized infantry, crossed the Jordanian border in the region of Ara (in Israel). Overrunning the small Jordanian post, it made its way south-east along a small road towards the village of Yabad.

When darkness fell the Israeli tanks, which were about four miles from the village, halted for the night.

JORDANIAN PROBLEMS

Back in the Jordanian camp there were problems. The Iraqi brigade (8th Motorized Brigade) and the Palestinian battalion had set off that morning making for Mafraq, but in the afternoon had been detected and attacked by the Israeli Air Force. Dozens of vehicles had been destroyed and set on fire and many casualties had been inflicted. At about 1900 the forward elements reached Mafraq, and under cover of darkness other vehicles limped in. Shocked and battered, the troops were in no condition to take up positions in the Jordan Valley as General Riad had planned. The next day the Iraqi brigade made an effort to make for Jerash and Irbid, but it was harassed from the air, and in fact never went into action against the Israelis.[1]

The Syrians failed General Riad too. At about 1900 he received a signal from them that they could not help because they had no air cover. This was a grave set-back to General Riad, who had just received news of the Israeli penetrations and feints into Samaria. At 1915[2] he sent a signal to General Fawzi, the Egyptian Chief of Staff, explaining what was happening and asking for Syrian and Iraqi air support. Riad saw his mistake, and belatedly tried to rectify it by ordering the 40th Armoured Brigade, which was settling down in positions around Jericho, to move back to the Damiya Bridge area. This formation got under way at about 2130. As it moved through the night it was again detected by the Israeli Air Force which made several attacks on the lengthy column but only set a few vehicles on fire.

COMMENTS ON THE FIRST DAY'S FIGHTING

On the Jordanian side things had not gone well. The tiny air force had been destroyed, leaving the army without air cover.

---

[1] Three other Iraqi brigades were on their way to Jordan. They arrived near the frontier on the Second Day, where they were held back by President Aref when he realized how serious the situation was.

[2] *Sunday Telegraph*, 15 September 1968.

The Iraqi brigade and the Palestinian battalion had been knocked out of the fight, the Syrians had declined to send help, the one armoured brigade was frantically retracing its steps, and reports were coming through of Israeli penetrations into Samaria. Israeli communiqués were cautious in the extreme; for example, the attack on the Iraqis was not mentioned at all. Although the Jordanian Front had a low priority on the First Day, in the Jerusalem sector preparations were being made to launch an attack to reach Mount Scopus, and the Israelis were assaulting the Ramallah Ridge.

The Israeli moves against Samaria were limited, with the apparent intention of mainly silencing Jordanian artillery. The Peled Ugda had been caught rather unprepared and Brigadier Peled praised his Ugda for the speed it moved into action.[1] The Israeli General Staff did not want to fight on two fronts at once, and there was some argument as to how much emphasis should be given to the Jordanian Front.

In New Jerusalem efforts were made to keep up normal appearances, and the Israeli Knesset (Parliament) met as usual in the evening, although spasmodic mortar fire was coming down in the vicinity of the Knesset building. One of the items on the agenda was to swear in Moshe Dayan as Minister of Defence, but although he attended briefly to give the good news of the results of the air strike, he was not formally sworn in until after the war.

The Second Day (Tuesday, 6 June 1967)

THE NARKISS UGDA

By 0001 the three columns of H Armoured Brigade had reached the first main crest of the Ramallah Ridge, the mechanized infantry having slowly and painfully cleared safety-lanes through the minefields for the tanks to pass along. The western and central columns converged as their minor ridges met and joined

---

[1] 'The ability to improvise at all levels from Army commanders down to the commander of brigades, the battalions, the companies, and down to the platoon, facing targets and assignments for which they were not always prepared.' Brigadier Peled, Press Conference, Tel Aviv, 17 June 1967.

the main one, and they fought a second breakthrough battle near Biddu, commencing at 0200, which lasted half-an-hour. Firing at Jordanian emplacements at short ranges, the Israeli Shermans overcame the defences and took the village. These two armoured battalions then turned east, and moved along a road to Nebi Samuel.[1]

The easternmost battalion of H Armoured Brigade, which the previous evening had divided into two parts to take Beit Iksa and Beit Kika respectively, edged slowly forward through the minefields, also making for Nebi Samuel on the main plateau on the main road. Aided by flares, the Israeli armour made a pincer movement on Nebi Samuel, which was entered at about 0330.[2] The whole brigade then continued on eastwards along the road, and as dawn broke it overran the key village of Beit Hanina, which was in a defile. Continuing eastwards at about 0600 H Armoured Brigade reached the main Jerusalem to Ramallah road at a road-junction near the feature known as Tel El Ful,[3] where it deployed into a blocking position.

To the south were a series of Jordanian positions held by a battalion of the Jordanian 29th Infantry Brigade, mainly based on features known as Shafat, French Hill and the defile of Givat Hamivtar, on either side of the road from Ramallah—the main defences covering Jerusalem from the north. One Israeli armoured battalion was detailed to break through these positions to link up with Mount Scopus. It was deploying to assault Shafat, the first defensive position to the west of the road, when it was suddenly warned that a battalion of Jordanian Pattons was approaching Tel El Ful. Israeli tanks reached the Ramallah road only just as a battalion of the 60th Armoured Brigade arrived from Jericho. This battalion had been detailed to hold Tel El Ful, which dominated the Ramallah road in this area. The Israeli battalion was just able to change direction and get into ambush positions when the Pattons were upon it. A violent

---

[1] Traditionally the place of burial of the Prophet Samuel, Christian pilgrims called it the Hill of Joy as from it they caught their first sight of the Holy City. An Israeli attempt to take it in 1948 had been beaten off with loss.

[2] 'Nebi Samuel fell in an easy fight.' Commander of H Armoured Brigade, Press Conference, Tel Aviv, 16 June 1967.

[3] The Biblical Givat Shaul—the Arabic name applies to the village surrounding the Tel.

close-range tank battle ensued, in which both sides lost tanks. After a while the Israelis were forced to withdraw a short distance. As their fuel was extremely low, the Pattons did not follow, but withdrew a little way. The Israeli tanks again formed up and made another assault, but were beaten back by the Pattons for the loss of three tanks. Eventually the Israelis forced the Jordanians to retreat and to abandon about a dozen Pattons which were out of fuel and another half-dozen which had been disabled by Israeli action.[1] It was about 1000 before the Israelis were in undisputed possession of Tel El Ful.

Next an Israeli armoured company was detailed to attack Shafat, which fell fairly quickly. Then two armoured companies moved straight in to assault the defile of Givat Hamivtar, immediately to its south, on the slopes of which were several entrenched positions with anti-tank weapons. Twice the Israeli armour was beaten back, but Givat Hamivtar fell at about 1100. Israeli casualties were evacuated from the battlefield by helicopter. The whole Israeli armoured battalion quickly regrouped and turned towards French Hill on the east side of the road, immediately north of Mount Scopus, which also had entrenched positions and anti-tank weapons on the slopes. (By 1200 the southern part of French Hill had been occupied by paratroops from Q Paratroop Brigade, which had already reached Mount Scopus.) At 1430 the Israeli tanks were hit by Jordanian anti-tank fire as they formed up in the valley to the north-west near the main road to assault French Hill. The Israeli battalion was scattered and driven back, losing five tanks. Assaulting again at 1530, supported by heavy mortar fire from the paratroops who had reached the top of French Hill, the Israelis found that the Jordanians had evacuated their positions on the slopes. By 1700 the vital northern defensive arc shielding Jerusalem from the north, from Mount Scopus to Tel El Ful, was in Israeli hands. Tanks and men had been lost in the fighting.

---

[1] 'There were about 30 Pattons on the heights. Six or seven were destroyed while 13 escaped to Jericho.' Commander of H Armoured Brigade, Press Conference, Tel Aviv, 16 June 1967.

THE LATRUN BATTLE

To the west, near Latrun, L Infantry Brigade resumed the advance at dawn and quickly succeeded in taking a vital road junction and adjacent villages. Most of the Jordanian garrison had withdrawn, and only a few wounded remained to be taken prisoner, but over 20 dead were found in the positions. This accomplished, the whole of the Latrun salient was next cleared and an armoured advanced guard moved eastwards along the Ramallah Ridge to reach the Ramallah road junction at 0845, when it ran into a Jordanian road block, which was only taken after considerable opposition. During the afternoon L Infantry Brigade reconnaissance unit advanced southwards along the Ramallah road to occupy the Aratot (Kalandiya) airfield.[1]

The remainder of L Infantry Brigade with its Sherman tanks, all under command of Brigadier Narkiss, moved eastwards along the road from Latrun. After overrunning the village of Beit Horon, situated at a track junction, it continued on, to join at the Ramallah road junction the main body of H Armoured Brigade, which had been ordered to hold that position until the battle being fought by one of its armoured battalions to the south was satisfactorily resolved.

Once the Israeli armoured unit had cleared the Mount Scopus position, the order was given for the other two battalions of H Armoured Brigade to advance northwards along the road to seize Ramallah. The leading tanks moved off at about 1600. L Infantry Brigade was told to remain and hold the road junction. Arriving at the southern outskirts at about 1830, Israeli tanks approached Ramallah at speed and, with all guns firing, rushed through the town and back again several times. There was some Arab resistance at first but after about three-quarters of an hour of these tactics, just after darkness fell, the town became quiet. The Israelis withdrew their tanks from the centre, one unit getting into a blocking position on the road just to the north of Ramallah, and the other in position just to the south in a similar role. During the hours of darkness Ramallah remained quiet, as did the Israeli tanks, which did not want to give away their

---

[1] Later renamed the Jerusalem Airport.

exact positions as they did not know the objectives of the Jordanian armoured moves that were in progress.

THE BATTLE FOR JERUSALEM

To the south the vital battle for Jerusalem was being mounted. By 0001 all three battalions of Q Paratroop Brigade had arrived and were being briefed. The Israeli sector was now under almost continuous mortar and artillery fire from Jordanian positions to the east. Brigadier Narkiss had won his argument – he had been backed by his battalion commanders. It was to be a night attack, to commence at 0200. In fact, H-Hour had to be put back 20 minutes to allow the troops to get to their start-lines. The three battalions were each given objective and routes, and each was allocated one company of Shermans from the armoured unit of J Infantry Brigade. The general directive was to seize the Mount Scopus Ridge, from which the Israelis would be able to look down on the Old City.

The Jordanian defences, manned by units of the 27th Infantry Brigade, consisted of concrete and stone bunkers and emplacements, usually connected by a trench system. They lay slightly back from the Armistice Line, behind which were a number of strong positions. In front of the first line of defences was a stretch of open land, varying in width from just a few yards up to about 300 yards, which was liberally planted with mines and on which were erected barbed wire fences and obstacles. First of all the Shermans moved forward to get into positions to give covering fire to the assaulting infantry, but the noise of their engines and tracks was heard by the Jordanians, who opened up all along the front with all the weapons they had, and the Israelis took casualties even before they made contact with the enemy.[1] A lot of bangalore torpedoes and explosive charges were used in crossing the open ground, but the Israelis suffered many casualties in breaching this outer belt of mines and barbed wire, and once they had done so they were plunged into desperate hand-to-hand fighting in trenches and bunkers, which in many instances lasted

---

[1] 'This is what happened to scores of our fellows.' Commander of Q Paratroop Brigade, Press Conference, Tel Aviv, 15 June 1967.

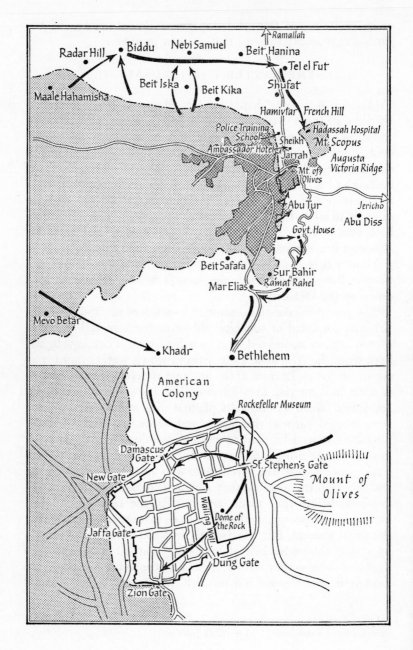

until 0700. This was followed by house-to-house fighting, when they had to deal with snipers, grenades and booby traps, as retreating Jordanian soldiers took refuge in buildings and fought back. Several houses had to be cleared more than once. In this, the biggest and fiercest infantry battle of the war, there were many acts of heroism on both sides, and casualties were particularly heavy.

The first paratroop battalion, the northernmost one, split into four separate company columns. Two of them made a pincer movement on to Ammunition Hill, perhaps the strongest of all the Jordanian defensive positions, which was to the north-east of the Police School. It was held by about 200 defenders, and a five-hour battle ensued–generally acknowledged by both sides to be the fiercest engagement in the whole war. The Israelis eventually emerged battered but triumphant, for the cost of over 50 killed and three times as many wounded, while at least 106 dead Jordanian soldiers were counted on Ammunition Hill and practically all the other defenders were wounded.

The third company column of paratroops made straight for the Police School,[1] a large fortress-type building of concrete, which together with the Mandelbaum Gate area dominated the Sheikh Jarrah district. The Police School was taken by the Israelis by 0345. This small column then became involved in house-to-house fighting in the Sheikh Jarrah district, where it was able to assist the fourth company column, which had been plunged right into this built-up area from the start.

The second paratroop battalion, crossing the border just to the north of the Mandelbaum Gate[2] in two columns, forced its way through a district known as the American Colony, another area full of strongly constructed buildings. The third paratroop battalion moved to its start-line near the Mandelbaum Gate, but did not cross the Armistice Line until dawn. From 0220 until about 0415, when dawn broke, the paratroops fought practically on their own with infantry weapons, forcing their way through fence after fence of barbed wire obstacles, as in the

---

[1] It had been used by UNRWA.

[2] This was the name for the single UN-controlled entrance and exit between Jordan and Israel. Merely wooden structures blocking a street, it took its name from an adjacent deserted house once inhabited by a person called Mandelbaum.

darkness and confusion it was not possible to give calculated and accurate artillery or aerial support. However, a certain amount of mortar and artillery fire, directed from Mount Castel, was put down on Jordanian positions, mainly following radio requests from soldiers actually fighting. As every single building was well known to the Israelis and had been carefully plotted, this fire had some value, especially to harass the Jordanians in the background and to interdict supplies and reinforcements. Two searchlights, mounted on the tall Histradut Building in New Jerusalem, were used in three instances to direct interdiction air strikes. The Jordanians tried hard but unsuccessfully to douse these lights with fire. When daylight came the Sherman tanks rushed forward, moving up closer to where the paratroops were fighting, to bring their guns into action at pointblank range to blast buildings that contained defenders or snipers. The tank crews were local soldiers who knew the area and the strong points to shoot at. The Israelis hoisted their national flags on the tops of buildings as they advanced, which gave their aircraft and artillery a good indication of their forward positions. Covered routes were blasted through houses to enable ammunition, which was being used at a great rate, to be pushed forward and for casualties to be taken to the rear.

By 0600 the company paratroop columns in the north, after a two-hour-long battle, managed to seize the Ambassador Hotel, a strong building that dominated the roads in that part of the city. From there Shermans and half-tracks made the first land contact with the Israeli enclave on Mount Scopus. Generally, by 0700, all the Jordanian main positions had been overrun, and everywhere the paratroops were fighting from house to house. By about 1000 they had forced their way as far east as a narrow depression known as the Wadi El Joz, by which time their ammunition was becoming exhausted and their momentum ran down. The men were weary, and an urgent tactical regrouping was essential in case of a Jordanian counter-attack. After having fought through Sheikh Jarrah, elements of the second paratroop battalion nearly reached the Rockefeller Museum, a large building close to the north-east corner of the Old City. In short, they had deviated slightly south.

The third paratroop battalion, which had been held up near the

Mandelbaum Gate, crossed the Armistice Line at dawn. Its company of Sherman tanks which blasted a way through the Jordanian defences, had been ordered to move southwards through the American Colony towards the Old City, and then to turn east just before reaching the Damascus Gate (in the centre of the northern wall) to clear an area just opposite Herod's Gate,[1] close to the Rockefeller Museum. At this stage the Israelis planned to break into the Old City by way of Herod's Gate. The paratroops succeeded in almost reaching the Damascus Gate, but were less successful in their street fighting when they attempted to move eastwards, and their momentum ran down before they reached their objective. By 1000 the areas penetrated by the Israelis fell quiet, and the lull was broken only by the occasional grenade explosion or sniper's shot. All the Arabs, soldiers and civilians, had hastily evacuated eastwards, leaving the streets and houses deserted. About 200 Jordanian soldiers, mostly wounded, became prisoners, but the rest had withdrawn successfully. The Israelis badly needed a breathing space to rest and replenish, and as there was a deceptive hour of calm between 1000 and 1100 they thought they were going to get it–but this was not to be.

At about 1100 Jordanian reaction set in. Soldiers lined the high walls of the Old City and sniped at anyone who moved, and observers directed mortar and artillery fire on to any vehicle in sight. The Israelis were in parts pinned down in their positions. The slightest movement brought down Jordanian fire, which made reorganization and supply very difficult. They were also dominated by the higher ridge to the east, just south of Mount Scopus, on which stood the Augusta Victoria Hospital, which overlooked Sheikh Jarrah and the American Colony districts. Brigadier Narkiss was anxious to assault the Old City. The General Staff, however, had doubts and recommended that the potentially dangerous high ground to the north and east of the Old City (that is, the Augusta Victoria Ridge, the Mount of Olives and the Et Tur feature, the latter controlling the road

---

[1] There were seven gates to the Old City: the Zion, Jaffa, St Stephen's, Damascus, Dung, Herod's and the New Gate. There was an eighth, the Golden Gate. The last-named is sealed and (according to tradition) is to be opened only for the Messiah to pass through.

from Jerusalem to Jericho) should be taken first. Narkiss was given permission to attack the Augusta Victoria Ridge, and for this task he detailed the paratroop battalion, with its Sherman company, that had reached the Rockefeller Museum. The assault commenced at 1300, with the Shermans giving fire support from static positions, but as soon as the jeeps and half-tracks came out into the open, half-a-dozen of them were destroyed within as many minutes by Jordanian anti-tank guns on the objective, and a shower of mortar bombs from the Old City also caused casualties. Sheltering as they were behind buildings, the Shermans were unable to give effective supporting fire to the attackers. One Sherman was disabled by a direct hit. Two air strikes were made on the Augusta Victoria Ridge, but they did not silence the Jordanian guns, so after an hour this abortive attack was called off. Narkiss intended to wait until dark and then mount a night assault to seize the ridge.

All the Sherman companies had suffered loss in the fighting. Because of the renewed Jordanian shelling they were taking time to reorganize and prepare for further action, so it was decided to use two companies of H Armoured Brigade, which were already on Mount Scopus, to advance and to fire at the Augusta Victoria Ridge from a flank to support the attack. However, the General Staff was becoming impatient, and under its urging Narkiss agreed to advance the time of his attack to 1800. The same battalion of paratroops, with its Sherman company, was employed, and the assault was preceded by an air strike on the Augusta Victoria Ridge. The Shermans led the way with their guns firing, but the result was the same, this time because the tanks missed a turning near the Rockefeller Museum and continued on to become exposed to anti-tank fire from the walls of the Old City. Within minutes three Shermans and five other vehicles were disabled by Jordanian anti-tank guns. Narkiss had to call this assault off too. A disastrous defeat at this juncture would have been a severe Israeli setback, both materially and in morale. Already casualties and vehicle losses were causing alarm, so he planned another assault, with H-Hour at 2300, which would give him time to prepare and co-ordinate it.

At 2200 the Israelis in Jerusalem heard the sounds of tank movement from the direction of Jericho. It was in fact the main part of the second battalion of the 6oth Armoured Brigade moving towards Jericho after having received the order to withdraw. This movement was interpreted by Narkiss and the General Staff as preparation for a Jordanian counter-attack so the Israelis made ready to repel it, cancelling their projected night assault on the Augusta Victoria Ridge.

To the south of Jerusalem, on the Second Day, a battalion of J Infantry Brigade, with a company of Shermans, launched an operation beginning at dawn. It succeeded in clearing the greater part of the Sur Bahir Feature, but failed to occupy the whole of it and so was unable to block completely the road from Jerusalem to Bethlehem. At noon a second battalion from this brigade, also with a company of Shermans, moved across the Armistice Line where it cut through the district of Abu Tur, which lay between Government House and Mount Zion. The western part of Abu Tur was in Israeli territory but the eastern part was held by the Jordanians. After crashing through the outer defences, the Israelis soon became bogged down in hard house-to-house fighting. By about 1900 they had cleared a small area near the Pool of Siloam, but as darkness fell they came under increased mortar fire from the old city. The battalion commander was killed and other casualties taken, so the unit withdrew to Abu Tur.

THE PELED UGDA

Looking to the north to Samaria where the battle for Jenin was developing, at 0001 the main column of O Armoured Brigade, consisting of a tank battalion, most of the mechanized infantry battalion and the reconnaissance unit, was moving in a circular motion to get into position to attack the Jordanian defences to the south of the town. Coming from the north-east this force overran the village of Birkin about 0200 when it established a firm base, from which the main body then moved down the Dotan Valley, south of the Jordanian defences which were on the northern ridge. These positions were good ones, having a field of fire of over 3,000 yards, being held by a battalion of the 25th Infantry Brigade, supported by a company of about 15 Pattons. It is not clear why the Israelis chose this point to attack, which was not a good one. Perhaps as it was not the easiest approach they expected to gain an element of surprise and a swift victory.

Whatever the true reason, commencing at 0300, without air support, the Israeli tanks moved forward into the attack, only to be beaten to a halt within minutes by the waiting Pattons, which made good use of cover in the olive groves. A second assault had been made as much with the intention of rescuing wounded tank crews and disabled tanks as breaking through and it was stopped just as dawn broke, so the Israelis tried a ruse. Their tanks slowly withdrew down the valley the way they had come, giving the impression they were breaking off the action and abandoning their disabled vehicles. Under the impression they were withdrawing, the Pattons broke cover and coming right out into the open gave chase—a fatal mistake, as just as they did so they became involved in a tank battle in which at least eight Pattons were disabled, but the remainder rallied and reformed. Again they attempted to pursue the Israeli armour, which kept up the ruse by slowly retreating still farther, until the last of the Pattons had been put out of action. This hard-fought tank battle, in which the Pattons initially gained the upper hand, was decided in favour of the Israelis.

Then the tanks and mechanized infantry of O Armoured Brigade formed up to assault the main Jordanian defences, which had anti-tank weapons, on the rim of the valley. Several initial advances made by Israeli sub-units were repulsed, but gradually the Israelis worked their way close enough to charge and over-whelm the positions. This was not accomplished until after 0700, as the Jordanians had remained in their positions and fought back. Leaving the mechanized infantry to mop up, the Israeli armour rushed through these defences towards Jenin, making a pincer movement on the town with A Infantry Brigade, which had moved southwards over the border during the early hours of the morning. Together these two formations closed in on Jenin, which resisted strongly. House-to-house fighting continued for some time. A battle was fought for the police post, a Teggart Fortress,[1] but when this was beaten into submission by

---

[1] About 40 strong posts to house police detachments had been built in Palestine at strategic points during the time of the Arab revolts. They were known as Teggart Fortresses, after an Inspector-General of Police.

the guns of the Shermans white flags began to appear at windows, and by 0730 Jenin[1] was in Israeli hands.

As soon as Jenin was taken the Commander of O Armoured Brigade received a report that about 60 Jordanian Pattons were advancing towards him on the Tubas Loop Road from the south-east. They were two battalions of the 40th Armoured Brigade returning to their former positions after their useless and sense-less journey to Jericho. Jenin and Nablus were separated by huge, rocky massifs known as Mount Eval and Jebel Hureish. The main road from Ramallah had to deviate to the west to reach Jenin. On the other side of this mountain mass was another road from Nablus to Jenin, which for convenience and clarity can be called the Tubas Loop Road, as it ran through that town. Nablus, about 42 miles north of Jerusalem, is wedged in a narrow plain between Mount Gerizim (Shechem in Hebrew), the Holy Mountain of the Samaritans, to the south, and Mount Eval to the north. The two roads met in the Doton Valley, just south of Jenin.

O Armoured Brigade, ordered to move south to meet the Jordanian tanks, had to retrace its steps through Jenin and go out along the road by which it had entered. The inhabitants supposed that the Israelis were withdrawing, so they roused themselves to bring many bazookas and small arms into action. This outbreak of firing was not quelled until 1300 by A Infantry Brigade, which remained in Jenin. This meant that the Jenin road was closed for this period to Israeli supply echelons, which complicated matters for O Armoured Brigade. Meanwhile the Israeli armour moved south to the road junction in the Dotan Valley, arriving there at about 1100. As the Israelis entered the Dotan Valley proper they saw Jordanian Pattons blocking the Tubas Loop Road at Kabatiya. After firing a few shots the Pattons deployed into the hills on the southern side of the Valley, known as the Kabatiya Hills, into positions they had formerly occupied. This Jordanian armoured battalion had only reached Kabatiya about one hour before the Israelis reached the Dotan Valley road junction. The second battalion of this Jor-danian formation was about 15 miles behind it, also on the

---

[1] O Armoured Brigade commander was wounded at Jenin during the fight for the Police Post but remained at duty.

Tubas Loop Road. The Israelis followed up and ran into an ambush, losing some 30 vehicles, including 17 Shermans. They then withdrew, formed up and charged again with a similar unfortunate result. The second assault had been made as much with the intention of rescuing wounded crews and disabled tanks as with breaking through. Both forces were extremely tired and wanted their tank crews to rest. Additionally, both were short of fuel. In the late afternoon two air strikes were made on the Jordanian positions to give the Israelis a chance to salvage some of their abandoned vehicles. This attempt was not very successful and drew fire from the Pattons, so it was discontinued. In the failing light the aircraft could not identify targets and so a proposed night attack was postponed until the following morning, while both sides edged into better positions, the Israelis being at a serious tactical disadvantage on one side of the valley with the Jordanians in the Kabatiya Hills overlooking them on the other.

On the western side of Samaria, the second column of O Armoured Brigade, consisting mainly of one armoured battalion and a company of mechanized infantry, which had arrived near Yabad, moved against an adjacent fortified feature known as Hill 334, taking it by 0100 after a tough fight. The village was cleared at dawn. This column then moved eastwards to the main Jenin to Nablus road, to turn southwards along it until it bumped up against a Jordanian defensive position at Arraba, which was supported by a company of Pattons. A tank fight developed, and three times the Israeli armour charged forward, only to be beaten to a halt by the Pattons. In this tank fighting several Israeli vehicles were hit, and three Shermans were disabled.

The third formation of the Peled Ugda now comes into the picture. U Armoured Brigade, moving south from Sandala, crossed the border at dawn to the west of Mount Gilboa (the massif that was partly in Israeli and partly in Jordanian territory), and proceeded along a rough track that led to the village of Deir Abu Daif. The intention was to advance to Tubas, and then go along the Tubas Loop Road to assault Nablus. All went well until the Israelis ran against a Jordanian blocking position on the wooded slopes of the Deir Abu Daif feature. The defenders, who had anti-tank weapons, held their fire right until the last moment, and in the first salvo halted the Israeli tanks. Withdrawing a little to reform, the Israelis brought down an air strike and artillery fire on to the Jordanian positions, while they assaulted from a flank. At the second attempt they broke through. As they continued probing forward over rocky terrain they next encountered lesser opposition at the two villages of Jalkamus and Tilfit, arriving at the latter place at about 1015. Soon the Israelis were on the high ground overlooking the Tubas Loop Road from the north-east and could see below them the adjacent villages of Kufeir and Zababida, which were actually on the loop road itself. The leading tanks were moving down on to the roadway when, at about 1015, they saw Jordanian Pattons moving into Kufeir from the south. They were the tanks of the 40th Armoured Brigade. The main body had halted at Akkaba, a village about six miles farther south on the loop road. Just one company of Pattons had been detailed to return to Kufeir, which had 'dragon's teeth' anti-tank defences across the roadway. A long-range tank duel broke out, the Pattons being in good prepared positions and the Israeli Centurions deploying out in the open to assault this road block. Three Israeli tanks were hit by Patton gunfire, which caused the Israelis to withdraw a short distance. Three Israeli air strikes on Kufeir caused little damage to the Pattons, but compelled them to move their positions. Both sides remained watching each other, and as darkness fell U Armoured Brigade withdrew still farther away from Kufeir.

On the western side of Samaria, on the Second Day, elements of S Infantry Brigade from Kfar Sava, with a company of Shermans from Central Command, crossed the Jordanian border at about 1200. Supported by artillery fire, this force had successfully occupied Kalkilya by 1400. A battery of 'Long Toms' was taken to the east of the town. Kalkilya, about 20 miles from Nablus, overlooked the Israeli Haifa to Lydda railway line and had sheltered Arab terrorists who infiltrated into Israel. The town was almost empty of people when seized and houses were looted by Israeli soldiers, much of their contents being destroyed. Many buildings were blown up and a few Arabs were arrested. Leaving one company behind in Kalkilya, the remainder of this column moved along the road to Nablus in the late afternoon and halted at about 1700 near Azzun, about 10 miles distant.

JORDANIAN PROBLEMS

Daylight had brought further Israeli interdiction air raids and attacks on the Jordanian 60th Armoured Brigade, just east of Jerusalem. At about 0530, when he realized that the Syrians would not help and that the promised extra Iraqi brigades had not yet entered Jordan, General Riad offered Hussein two choices: either to ask for a cease-fire or to withdraw from the West Bank. Hussein was reluctant at this stage to concede that such dire alternatives were necessary. He obviously hoped to be able to hold on a little longer and so be in a more favourable position should a cease-fire be imposed. At about 0545 the King had his famous conversation with Nasser about foreign intervention. At about noon General Riad was in contact with Field-Marshal Amer, who agreed with Riad that the Jordanian forces should withdraw to the East Bank. Still Hussein hesitated, vaguely suspecting an Arab intrigue to get him to abandon the West Bank, which he might never recover. He did not know how well his armoured brigades were doing, or appreciate the disadvantages and fears of the Israelis in the Jerusalem sector. The Radio Cairo communiqués were falsely optimistic, and he believed them. It was not until about 1400[1] that Hussein, despite the Egyptian war bulletins, realized that he was facing defeat. During the afternoon and evening he considered asking for a cease-fire. At about 2200, apparently without consulting the King, General Riad ordered a general withdrawal of all Jordanian forces to the East Bank. The order was transmitted to all formations, and several units were actually moving back, when about half-an-hour later the UN called for a cease-fire (which, incidentally, both sides ignored). The commander of the 40th Armoured Brigade ordered one of his two armoured battalions to conduct a fighting withdrawal towards Nablus rather than join in the eastern retreat. Thus it appeared more advantageous for the Jordanian forces to remain where they were, at least for the time being. The order to withdraw was countermanded, and Jordanian soldiers told to return to the positions they had just been instructed to evacuate. Confusion resulted, and in several

---

[1] *Sunday Telegraph*, 22 September 1968.

instances the Jordanians had to fight to get back to their former positions; in other cases the counter-order did not reach units until far too late, as happened in the Jerusalem sector, whence two battalions left before midnight.

COMMENTS ON THE SECOND DAY'S FIGHTING

Not knowing that the Jordanian soldiers had been ordered to withdraw, at the end of the Second Day's fighting the Israelis on the Jordanian front were understandably anxious. In the Jerusalem sector they were anticipating a counter-attack, and in parts of Samaria their armoured thrusts had been stopped. In the Jordanian camp the war on land had gone against them, and there was defeatism at General Riad's GHQ at Amman, although some Jordanian forces were still in strong positions—that is, until they were ordered to withdraw.

To summarize: after heavy fighting the Israelis had successfully assaulted and taken the area to the north of the Old City of Jerusalem, linked up with Mount Scopus and cleared the northern defences as far as Ramallah. But during the afternoon and evening the attacking Israelis twice failed to seize the Augusta Victoria Ridge, and a night attack on it was cancelled as it was thought the Jordanians were about to launch a counter-attack. To the south the Sur Bahir feature had yet to be completely occupied and the road from Bethlehem was still open to the Jordanians, while the area near the Pool of Siloam had to be evacuated again at dusk. The Old City stood firm, seemingly impregnable behind its huge stone walls, as did the remoter Augusta Victoria Ridge, the Mount of Olives and the Et Tur feature.

In the Judean foothills the Latrun Salient had been early and easily taken. This was a great prestige prize, as it held bitter memories of failures in the 1948 War. Jenin had fallen after a hard fight, and another prestige gain had been Kalkilya, but the two main armoured thrusts of the Peled Ugda were both halted. Some of the Israeli armoured units in Samaria had been outgunned by the Pattons. The Israelis had penetrated at other points into Jordanian territory, but were made thoughtful by the Jordanian defence of such positions as Ammunition Hill and the Jordanian armoured fighting ability south of Jenin.

The Third Day (Wednesday, 7 June 1967)

The early hours of the Third Day were confusing to the Jordanian commanders and soldiers. At 0150 Hussein[1] and General Riad issued further orders to stand fast and hold on to their positions. These were followed, at 0230, by orders to obey the UN call for a cease-fire, provided the Israelis did the same. Generally until this moment communications within the Jordanian Army had been quite good, but now they began to falter. The soldiers' morale had generally remained fairly good, and there were few reports of panic or a breakdown of discipline.

THE NARKISS UGDA

In Jerusalem, Q Paratroop Brigade and its supporting tanks waited for the Jordanian attack which did not come. At daybreak Israeli aircraft saw that no attack was being mounted, but that, on the contrary, troops and vehicles were moving away from Jerusalem. When the Israeli General Staff received this information they ordered the offensive to be resumed; assaults were to be made on the heights to the north and east of the Old City as quickly as possible. At 0800 heavy artillery fire was put down on the Augusta Victoria Ridge and other positions in the vicinity, while the attackers formed up. A heavy air strike followed, and at 0830, under an artillery barrage, the battalion of paratroops moved eastwards across the start-line, which was the Rockefeller Museum and the Wadi El Joz. This time the Shermans led the way, firing as they went, with jeeps with recoilless rifles following, while behind them came paratroops in half-tracks. Some of the half-tracks had belonged to the J Infantry Brigade and were specially given to the paratroops for this action; others had been brought up from the plains.

At the same time another battalion of paratroops that had, with supporting Shermans, made its way to the Mount Scopus feature, assaulted southwards along a narrow ridge in half-tracks on to the Augusta Victoria Ridge, jumping off in the wake of an Israeli air strike. This unit suffered casualties but drove the

---

[1] *Sunday Telegraph*, 22 September 1967.

Jordanian soldiers downhill. The third paratroop battalion remained in the American colony close to the Old City wall, while mortar fire was directed on to the walls themselves to keep the defenders' heads down. The main Israeli assaulting force from the Wadi El Joz reached its part of the Augusta Victoria Ridge without incident to find it deserted, the Jordanians having left before dawn.

Once this strategic feature had been gained, this battalion of paratroops exploited south to take the Et Tur district and the Mount of Olives. They met only scattered opposition, as the main body of the defenders had also withdrawn before dawn. Israeli troops now blocked the road from Jerusalem to Jericho at Et Tur. The remainder of the paratroops, together with the Sherman's, on the Augusta Victoria Ridge turned about and reformed, as the brigade commander had suddenly decided that the moment was opportune to charge downhill to try to breach the Old City from the east. A 10-minute artillery barrage was put down on the Moslem Quarter, immediately adjacent to St Stephens Gate. The third battalion, still sheltering near the Rockefeller Museum, was ordered to break through at Herod's Gate on the north wall, but as this proved too strong it continued on round the north-east corner, making for St Stephen's Gate.

At 0930 the Israeli assault on the Old City began. The Shermans moved down the Jericho road, almost in close order, with their guns firing, followed by paratroops in half-tracks and jeeps charging across the broken ground on either side of the roadway, while mortar fire was put down on the Old City and recoilless guns blasted the ramparts. St Stephen's Gate[1] had a fortress-like appearance; a narrow aperture admitted only one vehicle at a time, and it was approached by a 'roadway' over the 'moat', the footwalk of which was flanked by 12-feet-high stone outer walls. A burnt-out bus lay on one side of the 60-yard approach road, and along the other side were three or four abandoned cars with shrapnel scars on the bodywork. A shell from the gun of a Sherman blew open St Stephen's Gate. Seeing this the Brigade commander, himself riding in a half-track, emerged from the

---

[1] Known to the Israelis as the 'Lion Gate', from the 'four lions' on its portals— the emblem of the Mameluke Sultan, Beybars.

group of hesitating tanks and charged through the gateway, knocking down the damaged gate. He immediately turned left (or south) to make for the Temple Mount, the dominant feature in the south-east of the Old City. Hastily dismounting from their vehicles, the Israelis rushed through the St Stephen's Gate after him. Soldiers from a Jordanian Army post behind the Aqsa Mosque fired at the Israelis who were advancing on foot along the 150-yard roadway which, lined with olive and pine trees, led to the Temple Mount. Outside the Old City wall one company of paratroops detached itself from the main assaulting force and moved off southwards into the Kedron Valley to encircle the Old City from the south and to block escape routes, but they were too late. By the time they got into position the remaining Jordanian battalion had left the Old City.

The Israelis had no details of the Old City's defences. It had originally been held by a battalion of the 3rd Infantry Brigade. When Jordanian troops were ordered to withdraw just before midnight (on the Second Day), a large part of this unit had already left before the counter-order was received, so that at dawn it was garrisoned by only part of a battalion. At 0900 an order was given to withdraw (by whom it is not certain), which was obeyed by some Jordanian soldiers who left by the Dung Gate. Others remained at their posts–exactly how many is not known, as both sides decline to give estimates. They could have been only about one or two companies, perhaps 100 to 300 soldiers. Also the Israelis had to reckon with the possibility of armed resistance from the civilian population.

Once inside the Old City the Israeli paratroops entered a warren of twisting narrow streets and alleys, some cut into the rock itself, and the three units pushed their way forward in three general directions. In the north, after being held briefly by sniping from the Stork Tower (a dominating structure in the north-east corner), one battalion moved through the Moslem Quarter and then the Christian Quarter, to reach the Damascus Gate, in the north wall, and then the New Gate at the north-west corner. The second battalion moved due eastwards across the centre to arrive eventually at the Jaffa Gate on the west side. The other unit moved south to the Aqsa Mosque and then to the

Wailing Wall[1] which it reached at about 1015, before moving on through the demolished Jewish Quarter to arrive at the Zion Gate at the southwest corner.

At 1030 the Arab Governor of East Jerusalem, accompanied by the religious head, met the Israeli Brigade Commander. The Governor gave an undertaking that there would be no more resistance, and explained that the last Jordanian troops had already left. Opposition suddenly ceased, except for some isolated sniping.[2] Israeli soldiers spread out to occupy physically and search the whole of the Old City. Some inhabitants had been killed or wounded during the fighting. Loud-speakers summoned the survivors to come out from their homes and surrender. At 1100 the Chief Army Rabbi visited the Wailing Wall and ceremoniously blew his 'shofar' (a ram's horn), an act that was a great morale raiser in Israel and one that called for rejoicing, as after so many centuries Jerusalem was once more under Jewish domination—something few Israelis would have believed would happen in their lifetime.

The door of the Aqsa Mosque was blown open by a bazooka shell and some slight damage was done to the roof by grenade splinters, as there was fighting in the forecourt between the Israeli paratroops and Jordanian soldiers. The Aqsa Mosque had been used as an ammunition store. The only other damage done to any of the 'Holy Places' was the destruction of the roof of the Benedictine Monastery of the Dormition on Mount Zion outside the wall (within Israeli territory).

During the afternoon a battalion of paratroops, with two companies of Shermans, moved out to Et Tur. Then they spread out southwards and eastwards to occupy the strategic heights

---

[1] Traditionally the only surviving masonry from the Temple of King Solomon. The gold-topped Dome of the Rock, within the same enclosure as the Aqsa Mosque, was built on the traditional site of this Jewish Temple. It had been barred to Jews since 1948, when the Arab Legion occupied the Old City. Since AD 135 Jews were forbidden to visit the sites of former temples, being only allowed as far as the remains of the Herodean West Wall. There they prayed for a return to favour in the sight of God and wept over the lost glories of Israel. The place became known as the 'Wall of Tears' or the 'Wailing Wall'.

[2] 'There was really no more resistance inside the City although we lost four of our men, and two of our officers were hit during the fighting for the wall, when charging up to a house and climbing up to the roof.' Commander of Q Paratroop Brigade, Press Conference, Tel Aviv, 15 June 1967.

covering Jerusalem from the east, including Eizariya and Abu Diss, two villages on small commanding features about three miles to the south-east of the Old City. Meanwhile at 0900, one battalion of J Infantry Brigade, supported by Shermans, again advanced through the Mount Zion district, this time making direct for the Dung Gate. Movement was slow through the built-up sector, and the Shermans, unable to manoeuvre, fell behind. This unit eventually reached the Dung Gate by 1200, and then spread out to clear the area between the Pool of Siloam and Mount Ophel. There was hardly any resistance as the Jordanian soldiers had managed to escape.

During the morning the remainder of J Infantry Brigade stayed in position on the Sur Bahir feature, ready to block any counter-move, or to be available to help in the prestige Jerusalem battle for the Old City. Once the Old City had been secured, it was ordered to exploit southwards along the main road as rapidly as possible. Starting at about noon, it quickly completed the occupation of the Sur Bahir feature, making contact with Ramat Rahel, the southernmost Israeli bastion of New Jerusalem. Then one battalion moved towards Mar Elias, a Jordanian position opposite Ramat Rahel, which was occupied by 1400. One company then moved north-west to seize Beit Safafa, an Arab village on the very edge of Israeli territory, which was also occupied later in the afternoon.

The other battalion, with all available Shermans, moved southwards along the road to Bethlehem, which was entered at about 1500. Jordanian forces had left both Bethlehem and Hebron before noon. The only opposition was a few shots fired by snipers. Leaving a detachment in Bethlehem, this Israeli column moved south to Hebron, which was occupied without difficulty. After a brief pause to enable other elements of the brigade to catch up, this column split into two parts, one of which reached Samu in the south, and the other Dhahiriya, the border village on the way to Beersheba. During the afternoon a small Israeli infantry column from Mevo Betar, in the Jerusalem Corridor, moved into the hills to the south-east to occupy Hasan, an Arab village which overlooked Israeli territory.

To the north of Jerusalem, at dawn on the Third Day, the battalion of H Armoured Brigade, at the southern end of

Ramallah, swept into the town, making a show of force and occupying it with little difficulty. The Ramallah radio station was taken over and quickly brought into use by the Israelis to put out misleading broadcasts to the Arabs.[1] The battalion that had remained just north of Ramallah throughout the night moved northwards with air support along the road to Nablus, through a series of valleys and passes. It encountered no serious opposition and eventually reached that town shortly after it had been taken by other units of the Peled Ugda. Suspected Jordanian positions were attacked on the way by Israeli aircraft. At one village, while going north from Ramallah, the Israeli troops were greeted by the Mukhtar (Headman), who handed over to them an Egyptian commando, complete with Soviet rifle, who had sought his help. This armoured battalion, together with H Brigade Command Group and reconnaissance unit, moved north-east to join up with the Peled Ugda.

L Infantry Brigade with its Sherman tanks, that had taken Latrun before joining H Armoured Brigade near Ramallah, also moved through that town, deliberately making a show of force as soon as it had been subdued. It branched off to the north-west to occupy the triangle formed by Nablus, Kalkilya and Ramallah. Moving along narrow, rough tracks, and given close support by the Israeli Air Force, it had little difficulty in penetrating this region during the course of the day.

The other two battalions of H Armoured Brigade turned eastwards and moved along almost parallel roads winding down into the Jordan Valley. Reconnaissance vehicles went ahead of the main columns, and were fired upon by Pattons from Jericho when they came within range. The Israeli tanks deployed, and with air support closed in on the city in a pincer movement during the afternoon. Repeating their tactics at Ramallah, one unit of Shermans burst into Jericho and rushed through the streets several times firing their guns. By 1930 the Commander of the brigade reported that Jericho was in Israeli hands.

---

[1] Situated over 2,600 feet above sea level, the Ramallah radio station had been constructed in 1935 by the British and latterly used by the Jordanians.

THE PELED UGDA

In the north, in Samaria, units of the Peled Ugda concentrated to seize Nablus, and during the day several tank engagements were fought. The previous evening U Armoured Brigade had come up against Jordanian positions on the Tubas Loop Road near Kufeir, and had had to withdraw slightly when a battalion of Pattons of the Jordanian 40th Armoured Brigade opened fire on them. After refuelling the Israeli brigade returned to the attack at 0100. First it put down a heavy barrage on the Jordanian positions, which caused casualties to the tank crews who were sleeping in the open near their vehicles. Despite this the Jordanian tanks quickly moved into action against the Israelis, who were trying to burst their way through the blocking defences at Kufeir held by soldiers of the 25th Infantry Brigade. The fighting went on until dawn, with unconventional use of navigation lights and searchlights, opposing tanks often being within feet of each other. Kufeir was eventually overwhelmed. As dawn broke, at about 0415, a combined air and tank assault was made on the main Jordanian positions, which succeeded and enabled the Israelis to enter the village of Akkaba. Jordanian troops now hastily scattered and withdrew as daylight allowed Israeli aircraft to pick off the Pattons individually. After Akkaba had been occupied, the Israelis reformed and moved down the road to enter Tubas, which had no static defences and was almost deserted.

Next, U Armoured Brigade, which had lost not a single armoured fighting vehicle in the three hours' fighting,[1] continued on southwards on the road to Nablus, halting when it reached a junction where a road went off south-east to the Damiya Bridge over the River Jordan. One armoured battalion was sent in this direction into the Jordan Valley, which reached the Damiya Bridge at about 0930. The Israeli tanks lay back from the river for a short distance, allowing the hordes of refugees, and withdrawing Jordanian soldiers, to move over it

---

[1] Later some 35 Pattons were counted on the battlefield, of which 16 had been hit by anti-tank fire and the remainder disabled by air action. The 12th Independent Armoured Battalion lost all its vehicles, while the 40th Armoured Brigade brought only five tanks back to the East Bank.

unimpeded to the East Bank. All the Arabs were on foot by this time, as Israeli aircraft attacked all Arab identified vehicles by rocket and cannon fire and napalm. The remainder of U Armoured Brigade was ordered to take Nablus, and the reconnaissance unit, mainly on jeeps, was sent along the road to test out the town's defences. It returned with the information that there did not seem to be any defences facing north, so the Israelis quickly but cautiously moved southwards, passing safely through a dangerous defile about 0930. Practically in close order, the Israeli tanks moved along the road into Nablus, arriving there an hour later. On the outskirts the townspeople came out from their houses to cheer them, thinking they were Iraqis they had been expecting for days who had at last arrived by way of the Damiya Bridge. As the Israelis had made no mention in their war communiqués of attacking and scattering the Iraqi brigade in Jordan, there was no reason for them to think otherwise as this phalanx of tanks calmly approached their town.

On their part the Israelis too were surprised by this unexpected welcome, but assumed the Arabs were surrendering. The Israelis halted just inside the town and the cheering townspeople came towards them. An Israeli officer dismounted from his tank and attempted to take a rifle from an Arab, who resisted. There was a deadly pause as the true situation suddenly dawned on both Israelis and Arabs. The Israelis immediately opened fire, and the townspeople disappeared into the shelter of their stone houses. Israeli tanks quickly moved through the town, and spent some time physically occupying it, there being several pockets of resistance. The surrender document was signed at 1800 by the Arab mayor, who then toured the streets with a loud-speaker ordering the Arabs to cease-fire. About 1100 there had been a clash to the west of Nablus, between Israeli and an Arab armoured battalion retreating from Arraba through Sabastiya. Jordanian Pattons were withdrawing to Nablus and did not know the Israelis were already in possession, and in the fighting Israeli AMXs succeeded in knocking out ten Pattons firing at close range while an Israeli air strike claimed 15 more.[1]

---

[1] The Jordanians claim there was a large tank fight and Jordanian counter-attack to the south of Nablus on the afternoon of the Third Day—but there seems to be little foundation in this. It is denied by the Israelis.

In these two actions, at Kufeir and Akkaba, the Israeli Air Force had played a significant part in destroying or disabling at least 60 Pattons, thus enabling the Israeli ground forces to advance successfully. In the late afternoon most of the units of U Armoured Brigade dispersed to the east of Nablus to refuel, rest and reorganize where they spent the night.

Meanwhile the other Israeli formation in Samaria, the major part of O Armoured Brigade, was at 0001 in an unfavourable position in the Dotan Valley to the south of Jenin, being overlooked by a battalion of Jordanian Pattons on the Kabatiya Hills, near the road junction with the main Jenin to Nablus road on the Tubas Loop Road. The Israelis remained on the opposite side of the valley which formed a sort of no man's land between the opposing forces. They rested, refuelled, and prepared to launch a dawn attack in conjunction with air strikes. An artillery barrage was put down on the Jordanian positions from 0400 until 0415, and then at daylight an Israeli air strike was made. At 0445 the Israeli tanks commenced their first armoured assault, but no resistance was met, the Jordanian tanks breaking off the action immediately.

Reforming, O Armoured Brigade moved along the road in the direction of Tubas, following in the tracks of U Armoured Brigade. Two companies deviated to take the motorable track that ran down into the Jordan Valley. They arrived at the Damiya Bridge at about 1000, only to find that a unit of O Armoured Brigade had got there first. The other part of O Armoured Brigade, consisting of an armoured battalion and a company of mechanized infantry, which had entered Samaria from the north-west and halted for the night near the village of Arraba on the main road from Nablus to Jenin, moved off southwards at dawn. All went well until about 0800. Then it hit up against blocking Jordanian defences at the village of Silat Edh Dhahr, which controlled approaches from the west and north—a good tactical position on the rim of the steeper slopes of the mountain massif that lies just to the north of Nablus. The main defences were based on a police post, a Teggart Fortress, which had a good field of fire and was held by a company of infantry, supported by a company of 12 Pattons. The Jordanian gunners held their fire until the Israeli tanks were at close range. Their first salvoes damaged two, causing the Israeli armour to stop. The Jordanians then retreated to the vicinity of Sabastiya and again opened fire at long range. Air strikes were called down on to the Pattons, which were all eventually destroyed or disabled, and after a short fight the police post and nearby trenches were overcome. Reforming, this part of O Armoured Brigade continued southwards along the road. It halted at Sabastiya at about 1030, when one of its battalions moved over towards the Tubas Loop Road. Thirteen disabled or abandoned tanks were found in the region of Sabastiya and another 15 undamaged Pattons were counted in the defile just west of Nablus.

The main part of S Infantry Brigade with its unit of Sherman tanks, which had entered Jordanian territory, taken Kalkilya the previous day and which had halted for the night at Azzun, made slow progress towards the Tubas Loop Road although it encountered hardly any opposition. Eventually it arrived there at about noon.

At dawn the other infantry battalion of S Infantry Brigade, with a company of Shermans, crossed the border and closed in on Tulkharm, which surrendered after a brief fight put up by a handful of Palestinians, its Jordanian garrison having left some hours before. Most of the inhabitants had also fled. The Israelis remained in Tulkharm for some time, and buildings were looted and destroyed. Like Kalkilya, Tulkharm had sheltered Arab terrorists and been a stepping-off point for their forays into Israel, so it is not surprising that the place was roughly handled. It was not until late afternoon that this small force made contact with O Armoured Brigade on the Tubas Loop Road.

COMMENTS ON THE THIRD DAY'S FIGHTING

During the Third Day of the war on the Jordanian Front, Israeli fortunes changed dramatically from uneasy uncertainty at dawn to triumphant achievement by dusk. By the end of the day practically the whole of the West Bank was in Israeli hands, the Jordanian armour had been destroyed and remnants of the Jordanian Army were frantically salvaging themselves and such equipment as they could, intermingling with panic-stricken refugees flooding across the River Jordan.

In Samaria, although Jenin had fallen, Israeli armour had been held up at 0001 at Kufeir on the Tubas Loop Road and in the Dotan Valley. The column that had taken Kalkilya had only reached Azzun. Later, another Israeli column was held up at Silat Edh Deir on the Nablus to Jenin road. The armoured units of the Peled Ugda were opposed by two battalions and three companies of Pattons, about 90 tanks in all, which in some instances were in superior tactical positions. In some engagements it was the Israeli Air Force and not the Shermans that destroyed, disabled or drove back the Pattons and enabled the Israeli ground forces to advance. Credit must be given to the Jordanian armoured units for fighting so well and so courageously, as in so many places they were 'sitting ducks' to the Israeli pilots. By midday most of the Narkiss Ugda units were assembling near the Tubas Loop Road, ready to spread out to occupy physically the whole of the West Bank. Ramallah had been occupied at dawn and the Damiya Bridge over the River Jordan reached by 0930 hours. By dusk both Nablus and Jericho were in Israeli hands.

By noon on the West Bank hundreds of Arabs, mainly refugees from camps near Nablus and Jericho, were fleeing eastwards to escape the advancing Israelis. Jordanian Army units had either been eliminated, had disintegrated or were trying to obey belated orders to move quickly across the Jordan with whatever equipment they could take with them. Hussein was anxious to salvage anything he could for the defence of the East Bank, but as Israeli aircraft attacked every Arab vehicle that moved on the roads he was not very successful. His only moderately successful salvage operation was to get a few tanks, guns, trucks and vehicles over the Allenby and Abdullah Bridges during the night before the Israelis actually reached, blew up and dislocated them.

In the Jerusalem sector the picture was the same. The Israelis started the day in apprehension of a counter-attack but their fortunes changed rapidly. A bold dash across the open enabled them to enter the Old City by St Stephens Gate. They were opposed only by a depleted garrison in the act of withdrawing, and the whole of the Old City was in Israeli hands by noon. The fact that the major part of the Jordanian defending brigade in the Jerusalem sector had already left during the early hours of the Third Day contributed greatly to the Israeli success. The very nature of the caves, stone buildings, underground and semi-underground alleyways and stout stone walls of the Old City, for example, would have made it a formidable place to take by storm if held by a resolute enemy – which on the First and Second Days the Jordanians had been.

At about noon all Jordanian soldiers still in contact with their HQs were ordered to make their own way back to the East Bank as best they could. Organized resistance began to die down, as everywhere the Arab mukhtars and mayors were making contact and actively collaborating with Israeli commanders. The Hebron region had given in with hardly a vestige of a struggle, and the vehicles of an armoured company were abandoned not far from Hebron. The spasmodic sniping prevalent in some places during the day died down by evening. It was on this, the Third Day of the war, that the Syrians relented and sent an infantry brigade into Jordan; it reached Suweilah, about five miles from the Syrian border, where it remained. It spent the next day in reconnaissance and in the evening refused to take up the positions given to it by General Riad.[1] The following day (Friday, 9) the brigade returned to Syria, without ever being in action against the Israelis.

The Fourth Day (*Thursday, 8 June 1967*)

There was hardly any fighting on the Fourth Day against the Jordanians, who were frantically preparing to hold the East Bank against possible Israeli invasion. Detachments of Israeli armour fanned out at dawn along the bank of the River Jordan. In a few instances they had to winkle out isolated snipers, but that was about all. The capture of Jericho was not announced until the Fifth Day, two days after it had been taken. The main problem was handling and channelling the hordes of fearful refugees, who were allowed to move over the bridges across the River Jordan without hindrance; only Jordanian soldiers were disarmed and searched. Only about 500 prisoners were taken,

---

[1] King Hussein, *My 'War' with Israel.*

many of whom were wounded. Most of the other soldiers hid their weapons and uniforms and joined in with the streams of refugees. During the morning Hussein informed U Thant, Secretary-General of the UN, that he would accept a cease-fire, which only really became effective in the afternoon. By which time the Israelis had made good their occupation of every part of the West Bank, where the inhabitants who remained actively collaborated with them. The Israeli victory over Jordan was complete.

COMMENTS ON THE JORDANIAN FIGHTING

In three days Hussein had lost the West Bank, the richest part of his kingdom, but it had not been wrested from him without a hard fight, as is witnessed by the fact that the Jordanian military dead and missing numbered 6,094 out of a probable 50,000 soldiers who were on the West Bank during this period. An unknown number of the 'missing' eventually turned up. The number of Jordanian wounded has never been officially given, but if one takes the usually accepted ratio in war of five wounded to one killed, probably every other Jordanian soldier on the West Bank became a casualty of some sort, which leaves no doubt that the Jordanians fought well and hard. Their courage deserved better fortune. During the Second and Third Days' fighting in Samaria the Jordanians suffered over 3,000 known casualties, and another 2,000 in the breakthrough battles into the northern suburbs of Jerusalem on the Second Day. A point of interest was that units manned by 'Palestinians', which had been regarded as disaffected and restless, fought as well as the desert Bedu, who formed the bulk of the Jordanian Army.

The Jordanian Army had been beaten by the combined efforts of the Israeli Air Force and the Israeli ground forces of whom about equal numbers were engaged in action against them on the West Bank. It is highly probable that without the Israeli Air Force the Israelis might not have made such extensive territorial gains as they did and that they would have incurred many more casualties. In all something like 800 sorties were flown against Jordanian ground forces. While the Jordanians like to tell of Israeli pilots missing their targets, or hitting their own troops through miscalculation or poor identification, the sheer frequency of the sorties and the deadly density of their attacking weapons more than made up for any minor shortcomings. There had been hardly any Israeli close air support until the late afternoon of the Second Day, but thereafter Israeli air strikes effectively blocked narrow passes to restrict Jordanian vehicular movement, and destroyed or damaged most Jordanian vehicles on the roads. Thus they prevented ammunition and supplies reaching tanks and troops in the forward areas; many Pattons, for example, had to be abandoned for lack of fuel. On the whole the reliability of the Pattons in this fighting was good, very few failing for mechanical reasons alone. The Israelis themselves fielded about 250 tanks and armoured vehicles on the West Bank, of which about 100 may have suffered destruction, damage, breakdowns or fuel shortage. The Jordanians probably lost about 150 Pattons and 25 Centurions–practically all they had–and well over half their armoured personnel carriers.

The Israelis claim to have captured over 150 field guns, so that it would seem that hardly a quarter of the Jordanian Army's 200 field and anti-tank guns could have got back to the East Bank, the others being abandoned when ammunition was expended or they were destroyed by Israeli aircraft. A large number of the 'lost' guns belonged to the two infantry brigades holding the rim of the high ground behind the frontier between Latrun and Tulkharm, which were hardly involved in any ground action at all. Their casualties were comparatively light, and most of the personnel succeeded in reaching the East Bank by mingling with the refugees, but they had to abandon all their guns, trucks and other equipment, including a few Pattons.

While the conduct of Jordanian units that saw action calls for nothing but praise, the handling of the Jordanian forces in battle by General Riad is far less praiseworthy. Lacking the inspired boldness and confidence of successful commanders, he was cautious and pessimistic, and even before he knew the true adverse situation he advocated withdrawing to the East Bank. In mitigation it must be admitted that for the first 30 hours at least he was seriously misled by false Egyptian communiqués and deceived into expecting the arrival of Iraqi and other Arab reinforcements. This is some excuse for the long and senseless marching and counter-marching of the two Jordanian armoured brigades, which caused them to use up valuable and irreplaceable fuel. Had they remained in their initial positions they would have been fresh and alert, and they might have knocked out more Israeli tanks before succumbing to the Israeli Air Force.

General Riad must have had serious misgivings from the start, judging by the advice he gave to King Hussein, early on the morning of the Second Day, to ask for a cease-fire or else to withdraw to the East Bank.[1] Hussein has since been generous in his comments on General Riad's conduct of this war.[2] Describing him as a professional soldier and a capable officer, the King said that it would have been difficult for Riad to have done better as he did not know the ground, the troops or the true situation. This view was obviously voiced for public consumption in the interests of Arab unity but it was hardly an accurate military assessment. Jordanian politicians and senior officers have said that Riad was too obstinate to listen to Jordanian advice, that he confided in no one, that he relied entirely upon his own Egyptian staff officers for information, and that once he had made up his mind he forced his orders through despite many objections by Jordanian commanders. As Deputy Chief of Staff to the Unified Arab High Command he had been in Jordan on many occasions, and it could hardly be said that he did not know the ground or the Jordanian forces. (General Riad stayed on in Jordan for a few days to co-ordinate the Syrian, Iraqi and Saudi Arabian forces that were in, or came into, Jordan, and then returned to Egypt to become Chief of Staff to the Armed Forces.)

Credit for courage, calmness and determination should go to Hussein for resisting General Riad's defeatist suggestions, and for keeping his head and fighting on until his forces were clearly and decisively beaten. When, at midday on the Second Day, Nasser sent him a signal agreeing with Riad that the Jordanian forces should withdraw to the East Bank, Hussein replied that he would hang on. Much later that night he received the personal message from Nasser informing him for the first time that the

---

[1] 'If we don't take a decision within 24 hours you can say farewell to your army and the country of Jordan.' (*Sunday Telegraph*, 22 September 1968.)

[2] *Sunday Telegraph*, 22 September 1968.

Egyptian Air Force had been destroyed. Fully occupied with the political direction of the war though he was, King Hussein spent much time visiting his troops, encouraging them and seeing for himself the disastrous effects of the Israeli air strikes. The Commander-in-Chief, General Majali, seems to have been blamed for the defeat to such a degree that the King had to dismiss him from that post; however, he was retained as 'Military Adviser to the King', which kept him in an influential position.

Jordan did not have a strong efficient General Staff—as did Israel, and Egypt too to some extent—which could have been a counter to General Riad and resisted some of his less sound orders. The political nature of Hussein's position as autocratic ruler did not allow him to trust such a body to give continuing personal loyalty; indeed, he kept his throne by ensuring that no one person or group gained too much military power. His Arab allies were no help to him. The Iraqi brigade had been battered on the First Day, and the other promised brigades hovered at the frontier, only entering Jordan when hostilities ceased. The Saudi Arabian brigade crept only slowly into Jordan, and had hardly reached Maan by the time of the cease-fire. The Syrian brigade, which entered Jordan on the Third Day, refused to obey General Riad's orders, and returned on the Fifth Day.

The seizure of the West Bank was something the Israelis had not counted upon, but while it would be wrong to say that they were entirely unprepared, there was some initial lack of anticipation. The Israeli General Staff did not want to have to fight on two fronts at once, and on the morning of the First Day Brigadier Narkiss was refused permission to make local gains. After the Jordanian Air Force had been destroyed, there was a change of policy, and he was told to make tactical gains. Generally the Israeli operations against Jordan, that were begun cautiously on the First Day, developed their momentum on the Second and were fully in their stride on the Third. The first big battle was the breakthrough by Q Paratroop Brigade into the Jordanian-held northern suburbs of Jerusalem in the early hours of the Second Day, followed by repulses when it attempted to exploit to the Augusta Victoria Ridge. In Samaria on the Second Day an attempt was made to turn the Israeli feints into deep penetration tactics, which were not very successful. Israeli armoured tactics and leadership tended to vary. At times the commanders were bold and successful, and at others hesitant. The Third Day was one of changed fortunes for the Israelis, and by nightfall the whole of the West Bank was as good as in their hands. Israeli losses on the Jordanian Front were given as 107 killed and 322 wounded, with an additional 195 killed and 1,131 wounded in the Jerusalem battles, making a total of 302 killed and 1,453 wounded.

Lack of Arab security certainly helped the Israelis. Communications between Arab political leaders (often made by radio-telephone in clear) and between headquarters and formations were tapped by the Israelis. There were, however, a few blanks in the Israeli's information, such as lack of knowledge of the defences of the Old City and of the evacuation of the Augusta Victoria Ridge.

A final comment can be made on guerrilla activity. As far as is known the Israelis did not send any guerrillas or saboteurs (with the exception of the naval commandos) behind the Arab lines. Both Egypt and Jordan did, but they had little success. The two small Egyptian commando units that had arrived in Jordan on the eve of the war[1] amounted to about 120 men each, and they were to work with Jordanian commandos (believed to number less than 40) to sabotage airfields in Israel. One unit (33rd Battalion) was given the tasks of destroying the airfields or bases at Lydda, Ramle and Aqir, and the other (53rd Battalion) those at Kfar Sirkin, Hertzlia and Ein Shammer; they were to slip over the frontier on the night of the First Day. The first unit and that part of the second detailed to deal with Ein Shammer succeeded in crossing the border, but the remainder failed to do so. On the Second Day a party of these commandos was detected in the act of laying mines near Ramle, barely 10 miles from Tel Aviv. Another group was caught near Shar Hagai, and another close to the Lydda airport. The commandos were sheltered and helped by 'Palestinian Arabs' and operated in

---

[1] 'On Saturday afternoon, 3 June, eleven troop transports of the United Arab Republic arrived with parts of two battalions of Egyptian commandos (the 33rd and the 53rd). On Sunday afternoon, 4 June, I welcomed the rest of the Egyptian detachment at the Amman airport.' (King Hussein, *My 'War' with Israel.*)

regions inhabited by them. From the Third Day, when an Israeli victory was obvious, several were handed over to the Israeli Army by local mukhtars. The Israelis kept silent about the saboteurs' activities to prevent internal alarm, and it is hard to assess what success they had—certainly several Israelis lost their lives or were wounded by these operations. As regards numbers, about 40 were captured and perhaps another 40 were shot in the act. If it is accepted that they numbered about 240 Egyptians, the remainder may have succeeded in getting back to Arab-held territory. The 40 Jordanian commandos may perhaps be accounted for in similar proportions.

CHAPTER 7

The Syrian Front

Once the vital key to the Fertile Crescent and a former French possession, with an area of 71,772 square miles and a population of 5·3 million, Syria had since independence been practically continuously involved in political turmoil. After the dissolution of the short-lived United Arab Republic in September 1961, power passed to the Baathists and the army, but there was constant friction as they, and other power-seeking cliques that included minorities such as the Druze and Alawites, jostled each other. The *coup* of February 1966 had brought three political generals to control of the country. They were Nureddin Atassi, the President, Hafid al Assad, the Defence Minister, and Saleh Jadid, the leader of the Syrian Baathist Party, the last-named being regarded as the 'strong man' of the trio.

Based primarily on an agrarian economy, Syria also had natural resources that included phosphates and oil. It was hoped that oil production, which had not yet begun, would eventually amount to 4·5 million tons a year. Nationalization of the major part of commerce and industry in the state had caused businessmen and technicians to leave and the economy to stagnate. The country heaved and surged with political undercurrents, and the jails were full of political prisoners.

ARMED FORCES

For some years the Soviet Union had sparingly doled out small quantities of obsolete arms and military equipment to the Syrian armed forces, but when Syria signed the defence pact with Egypt in November 1966 this flow of military supplies increased and Soviet instructors appeared. Modern tanks, guns and vehicles were dispatched, and work commenced on 10 sites for SAM-2 missiles. In round figures the number of tanks (mainly T-34s and T-54s) possessed by Syria rose from 300 in 1960 to 550 and the number of armoured personnel carriers during that period increased from under 200 to over 500. These impressive figures tended to be neutralized by the reputed poor maintenance in the Syrian forces; despite the presence of Soviet instructors, it was doubtful whether at any given moment more than two-thirds of the vehicles were 'runners'. Much the same ratio of non-serviceability could be applied to most types of weapons and equipment. This was probably also largely true of the Syrian artillery, considered to be the most efficient part of the army, which possessed over 1,200 guns, including 133-mm field guns, howitzers, mortars, some Katyusha rockets mounted on vehicles, and about 200 Soviet anti-aircraft guns.

Selective conscription operated in Syria. The standing strength of the armed forces was about 65,000, with approximately 40,000 trained reservists available. The army strength was about 60,000, it being formed into nine brigades: two armoured, two mechanized infantry and five infantry. There were at least six reserve infantry brigades which had been mobilized, but they were far less well equipped than their regular counterparts. There was also an armed gendarmerie of about 8,000 men.

The Syrian army was able to boast of several tiny successes against the then poorly-organized, poorly-armed and desperately struggling Israelis in 1948. Weight of numbers and arms was then heavily in their favour, but despite the façade of superiority this gave, morale within the armed forces remained comparatively low. This was mainly due to the army's involvement in national politics, periodic purges of officers by whichever faction was in the ascendant, and an underlying current of military uncertainty and unease. A lackadaisical attitude often adopted by both officers and men reflected itself in the indifferent condition of weapons and equipment. On the other hand, the state of training, which had remained at a consistently low level for years, was improving, and had done so noticeably since the recent arrival of more Soviet instructors.

A semi-political organization, known as the People's Liberation Army, loosely modelled on the lines of the Chinese militia of Mao Tse-tung, was tolerated by the ruling generals as they thought that it might be of use to them. Elements of this force had been mobilized in October 1966, when a few rifles had been issued to them, but as this body was completely untrained and almost undisciplined it had no influence on the course of the war or the political stability of the régime. There was also a youth organization, known as Futtawa, which had been given some Soviet encouragement, but never amounted to anything. In mid-May university students were ordered to form themselves into small infantry units, each about 150 strong, as a home defence element, but this project did not get very far either. In fact, all these organizations were little more than shambles, characterized by their loud political clamour.

The 500-strong Asifa, of Fatah, which had set up a sabotage school on Syrian territory near the Sea of Galilee, had been brought under the control of the Second Bureau of the Government. Also in Syria was the small group of about 100 PLA terrorists, which Ahmed Shukairy had placed under 'national command'. The Syrian Government in particular regarded this PLA contingent with deep suspicion because it was paid with Egyptian money, had Egyptian arms and explosives, and looked to Nasser for guidance. On 3 June Major-General Ahmed Suweidani, the Syrian Chief of Staff, officially assumed control of these 'Palestine Forces', nominating an officer to command them, but their surly acquiescence in this curb was only temporary and partial. The PLA unit was quickly sent into Jordan.

SYRIAN STRATEGY

For years the unsettled inward-looking Syrian officers had blindly put their faith in the apparently super-strong defences in the west overlooking Israel. They were more concerned with changing, or securing, their Governments by force or trick than with developing a strategy commensurate with the loudly-voiced Arab intention of utterly crushing Israel. At least one-third of the regular army was permanently entrenched facing Israel, and at least another third—perhaps the best third—was in or near Damascus to protect the Government of the day from internal subversion. Egyptian staff officers had arrived to try to persuade the Syrian armed forces to operate in accordance with Nasser's concept of how the Unified Arab High Command should function, but they were not successful in asserting their influence over the Syrians as was General Riad with the Jordanians. This, possibly because the Soviet Military Mission, having supplied the arms and equipment, insisted upon some say in how they were to be used, and partly because of a reluctance on the part of nearly all political leaders and senior officers to co-operate fully with them. The Syrians were little pleased by the recent UAR-Jordanian Defence Pact, about which it had not been consulted, and the Syrian Baathists in particular were deeply antagonistic towards Hussein. It seems that the Egyptians had no influence at all on the strategy or the conduct of the war in Syria, and that the Syrians, until they decided that the war was lost and accepted a cease-fire, followed the Soviet advice to defend strongly their static south-western wall.

It is doubtful whether there were any realistic plans to mount a hard campaign against Israel, but there can be no doubt that fanciful ones existed on paper, and that the Syrians were prepared to put them into practice should the opportunity to do so easily and cheaply ever present itself. The main plans for the Syrian offensive (code-named Nazzar, meaning Victory) provided for a divisional force to attack over the Benot Yacov Bridge[1] to take Safad, with another divisional force to attack south of the Sea of Galilee to take Tiberias. There was also to be a brigade-sized diversion towards Dan. In fact, some preparations had already been made, in that the Syrian units concentrated near Mishmar Hayarden had been issued with rubber dinghies and rafts to cross the Jordan, while many of the mines and obstacles immediately east of the Benot Yacov Bridge, which was in 'no man's land', had been removed. By the end of D Day, which according to some documents was supposed to be the 7 June 1967, these three Syrian columns were expected to have captured all eastern Galilee as far west as Safad and north-west to touch the south-eastern tip of the Lebanon. However seriously meant these contingency plans might have been, Syria never envisaged having to fight alone, but only in conjunction with offensive moves into Israel by other Arab armies, when it might be possible to take advantage of a weakly defended northern Israel. It is interesting that there was a Syrian contingency plan

[1] Full Hebrew name is Gesher Benot Ya'acov (Bridge of the Daughters of Jacob).

to occupy northern Jordan east of the River Jordan as far south as Mafraq. The Iraqi brigade that had been briefly sent into Syria was withdrawn when Hussein and Nasser made their defence pact. The respective Baathist parties of Syria and Iraq were exceptionally abrasive towards each other.

THE GOLAN PLATEAU

The Israeli fighting against the Syrians took place entirely on what has now come to be known as the Golan Plateau,[1] an elongated stretch of high ground about 40 miles long extending from the slopes of Mount Hormon in the north to the River Yarmuk in the south. Rising abruptly from the Jordan Valley and the Sea of Galilee in the west, it reaches eastwards to the Rakkad River, a tributary of the River Yarmuk. It is at its maximum width in the centre, being some 16 miles from a point just south of the Benot Yacov Bridge over the River Jordan to Boutmiye, a large village on the eastern edge. Both to the north and south of this meridian the plateau tends to narrow in shape almost to blunt points. The best and easiest approach to the Golan Plateau is from the north-east, from the direction of Damascus, as the other directions all present difficulties. The Mount Hormon massif (rising to 9,232 feet above sea level) blocks the north of the plateau; the deep ravines of the River Rakkad in the south-east, and of the River Yarmuk in the south, form natural obstacles to vehicles; and the mountain escarpment overlooking the Jordan Valley presents a formidable barrier (looking up from the Huleh and Upper Jordan Valleys, these heights appear a huge unbroken wall of rugged, cliff-like rock). The western edge of the Golan Plateau, which overlooked Israeli territory, can be divided into three sectors. That in the north extends from Tel Azzaziat almost to the Benot Yacov Bridge, in which sheer rocky heights rise up from the Huleh Valley to over 2,000 feet. Seemingly impregnable and impassable, they present few openings; such as exist are mere slits of ravines let into the cliff faces and even the more gradual parts of the slopes

---

[1] Until 1967 this area, especially its western edge, was usually referred to as the 'Syrian Heights', but the expressions Golan Heights and Golan Plateau are now accepted nomenclature.

are studded with huge basalt boulders. In the central sector, from the Benot Yacov Bridge south to the Sea of Galilee and then along its eastern shore to Koursi on the Wadi Samak, the

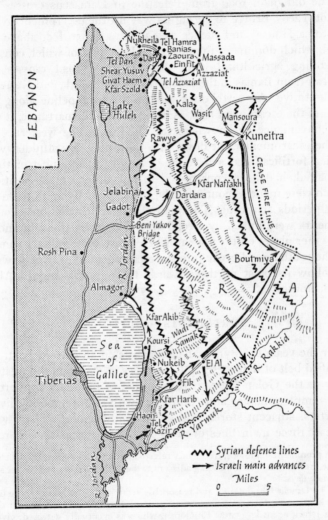

mountainous slope up to the plateau, although rising to nearly 3,000 feet, tends to be more gradual, especially in the north-east part, where the level stretch of the Beteiha Plain leads to more convenient slopes beyond. The tiny southern sector, from Koursi to the River Yarmuk, has the steepest slopes of all; the sheer cliffs rise abruptly to nearly 1,400 feet above the shore of the lake.

The old main road from Palestine to Damascus crosses the Benot Yacov Bridge to zigzag its way up the escarpment to the Customs House[1] and thence to Kuneitra, 2,850 feet above sea level, which dominates the plateau, a large part of which consists of rolling agricultural land. Another main road crosses the plateau from Banias in the north, through Massada and Kuneitra to Boutmiye. An earth track follows the oil pipeline along the edge of the escarpment and, as it comes into the narrative, it can for convenience be known as the Oil Road. The western edge of the escarpment right down into the valley was studded with Syrian fortifications; a network of supply roads, most of them asphalted, had been constructed to link up the main positions which were manned continuously, the soldiers living in them for long periods at a time. The many military installations around Kuneitra were linked by a road system, as were those in one or two other places on the plateau where there were military camps. In the south a road broke into the escarpment by way of Tawafik to follow its crest north-eastwards through Fik and El Al to reach Boutmiye.

SYRIAN DISPOSITIONS

Over the years the Syrians had constructed an extremely strong fortified belt of defences[2] up to 10 miles in depth on the western edge of the Golan Plateau. It consisted of mutually supporting gun emplacements and bunkers, with underground living quarters, adjacent stores, and connecting trenches. There were at least three main lines of defence, but in places they were in

---

[1] A prominent landmark, frequently referred to by the Israelis as the Customs House, from a stout stone building adjacent to the bridge that has been in use since Mandate days.

[2] The Israelis had detailed and reasonably accurate—although not quite up to date—maps and information about the Syrian defences, largely secured for them by an Israeli agent known as Eli Cohen, who was eventually detected, given a well-publicized trial and publicly hanged in Baghdad on 18 May 1965. The normal Israeli intelligence services had, of course, supplemented Cohen's information, especially in regard to the detailed lay-out of the defences, the terrain and possible tank routes.

terraced formation to fit in with the contours of the escarpment. Good use had been made of the basic rocky terrain, supplemented where necessary with concrete. The main artillery positions were to the rear of the forward defence lines, overlooking and able to support any of them, and placed to allow the guns to lift their fire to fall on Israeli settlements in the valley below. It was estimated that the Syrians had 265 artillery pieces on the western edge of the Golan Plateau, as well as about 100 anti-aircraft guns concentrated in small groups near headquarters. These forward defences were permanently manned by three infantry brigades, each having a unit of T-34s and SU-100s, as an integral part of the formation. Additionally there were 30 World War II German Panzer tanks, of 1943 vintage, with 75-mm guns, scattered in fixed positions, mainly in the northern part of the defensive belt. Other formations were positioned close to Kuneitra, the Syrian military headquarters for this front.

Worried, no doubt, by rising Israeli anger at their sheltering and sponsoring Arab terrorists, and perhaps also in eager anticipation of easy conquests, during the period of rising tension the Syrians had moved other formations on to the Golan Plateau. A fresh infantry brigade[1] came to support the two northernmost infantry brigades, another was sent south to the region of Fik and El Al, another was positioned about 10 miles from Kuneitra, and yet another infantry brigade at about the same distance to the north of the town. This brought the total of Syrian infantry brigades on the plateau up to eight, at least one of which was a reserve one. One armoured and one mechanized brigade had been moved westwards from Kuneitra into the centre of the plateau, while another armoured and a mechanized brigade came in to take their places. All told the Syrians had some 260 tanks and self-propelled guns (not all 'runners'), and over 40,000 soldiers, in three armoured and five infantry brigades and seven National Guard battalions, on the Golan Plateau.

---

[1] Syrian infantry brigades identified were the 8th, 11th, 19th, 32nd and 90th. GOC Northern Command, Press Conference, 17 June 1967.

ISRAELI STRATEGY

Feeling an especial animosity towards the Syrians because of their pitiless and systematic shelling of Israeli settlements and agricultural workers in the Huleh and Upper Jordan Valleys over the years and continual interference with the National Water Conduit, the Israelis had prepared offensive plans to take at least the Golan Plateau for strategic safety. The basic Israeli plan was to penetrate at as many points as possible through the Syrian defensive belt, and then exploit as opportunity offered. Armoured thrusts were to aim at Banias, Massada and Kuneitra, primarily to gain control of that road.

FIRST DAYS OF THE WAR

The Israeli General Staff was alarmed at the sudden build-up of Syrian forces on the Golan Plateau, fearing that it might be a prelude to an offensive. As it did not want to fight on more than one front at a time, particular care was taken not to initiate any action or offer any provocation either just before 5 June, or immediately after that date, when the Israelis were more than fully involved with the Egyptians and Jordanians. On the First Day of the war (5 June) the Syrians were uncharacteristically quiet, there being no shelling of Israeli territory at all. The only action occurred when Syrian aircraft dropped a few bombs during the early morning on some Israeli frontier settlements and an airstrip, but the Syrian planes were quickly chased away by Israeli interceptors and did not return. This happened before the Syrian air force was struck by the Israeli air forces at its home bases.

However, on the Second Day of the war (6 June), they may have felt encouraged by the false claims of Egyptian and Jordanian thrusts into Israel and other imaginary successes. Although much of their air force had by this time been put out of action, the Syrians began moves preliminary to their Nazzar offensive by recommencing shelling into Israel and making a tentative ground attack. Beginning at 0545, artillery and mortar fire was directed from Tel Azzaziat, a notorious feature on the border held by the Syrians, on to both Shear Yushuv and Tel

Dan, about a mile and a half to the west and north-west respectively. This barrage continued until 0700, when two small forces of Syrian infantry, each of company strength, moved across the border into the attack under cover of fire from tanks on the adjacent Banias Ridge. These assaults were held by the local defence forces. At 0720 Israeli aircraft appeared and poured cannon fire and napalm on to the attackers, which together with artillery fire, caused them to retreat hastily.

Syrian shelling continued throughout the Second Day of the war and also on the Third (7th) and Fourth (8th) Days too. Shells fell on such places as Kibbutz Dan and Kfar Szold in the north, Gadot and Rosh Pina in the centre, and Ein Ger, Haon and Tel Kazir in the south. Many civilians took to their shelters, and some had to remain there for up to 120 hours. The bombs and shells caused crops to catch fire, and as the shelling was intensified and was replied to in kind by the Israelis, more crops, scrub and vegetation were set alight on both sides of the border. The scene was marked by many tall pillars of smoke in daylight and by flickering firelight during darkness.

ISRAELI DISPOSITIONS

Once the Egyptian and Jordanian fronts had been largely resolved and the final result was no longer in doubt, Israeli attention quickly turned to Syria. Israeli formations and units began to concentrate in the north under the command of Brigadier David Elazar, GOC Northern Command. These consisted mainly of U and O Armoured Brigades, both of which had just been fighting the Jordanians as part of the Peled Ugda, and Q Paratroop Brigade, which had been in action in Jerusalem with the Narkiss Ugda, and which on the late evening of the Third Day (7th) had moved near to Tiberias, on the Sea of Galilee. Other formations included E Infantry Brigade, in position just south of the Sea of Galilee, which had made a feint southwards into Jordanian territory on the Second Day (6th); B Armoured Brigade,[1] not yet committed to action, which had one Sherman battalion and a mechanized infantry battalion, and which had

---

[1] 'One of the last reserve formations to be mobilized on 24 May.' (*Tanks of Tammuz*.)

concentrated near Givat Haem in the north; and the famous
(1st) Golani Brigade, with three mechanized infantry battalions,
an element of which had taken part in the fight for Nablus.
There was also I Infantry Brigade deployed from Mishmar
Hayarden to the north. The Golani Brigade is one of the exceptions to the Israeli security rule of concealing actual brigade
designations–perhaps because its commander and officers were
too extravert. Certainly its morale was extremely high. Other
units of armour, infantry and specialists came rushing up during
the last hours of the fighting, but they had to content themselves
with a supporting or a mopping-up role. In all Brigadier Elazar
initially was able to muster about 250 tanks, almost as many as
the Syrians, and slightly less than 20,000 men for his assaulting
force–this latter number swelled to about 30,000 by the cease-
fire.

ISRAELI PLAN OF ATTACK

Brigadier Elazar was ordered to prepare to attack the Syrians at
0700 on the Third Day of the war (7th), using whatever troops
he had at his disposal in Northern Command, but mainly owing
to unfavourable meteorological conditions that could have
impeded air support the project was postponed.

During the night (of the 7th and the 8th) additional forces
arrived, including elements of A, O and U Armoured Brigades.
Brigadier Elazar had set H-Hour to be at 1000 on the Fourth
Day (8th) but it was postponed, only minutes before this time,
by a political decision, and cancelled at 0100 on the Fifth Day
(9th). However, the political decision was reversed and Brigadier
Elazar received orders to start the offensive at 0700 on that day.
Brigadier Elazar's outline plan was to use the Golani Brigade,
supported by two companies of Shermans from A Armoured
Brigade, to penetrate the northern part of the Syrian front in the
region of Tel Azzaziat to clear the extreme north-west corner and
to occupy the Banias Ridge, while the remainder of A Armoured
Brigade broke through near Kfar Szold, its task being to seize
Zaoura and then exploit through Kala to Kuneitra. O Armoured
Brigade was to be in reserve in this area, ready instantly to exploit
success, reinforce thrusts, or make new ones if required. In the

centre sector the Sherman and mechanized infantry battalions of U Armoured Brigade were to attack towards Rawye. I Infantry Brigade was to open a tank path for it, and also to attack Tel Hillal and Dardara. Two companies of paratroops with a company of Shermans from U Armoured Brigade were to break through towards Darbashiyeh, in two columns, and another two companies from Q Paratroop Brigade, with a company of Shermans from U Armoured Brigade, were to make for Jelabina. Right in the south the remainder of U Armoured Brigade (only one company), and Q Paratroop Brigade concentrating near the southern tip of the Sea of Galilee, were ready to break into the Golan Plateau near Tel Kazir. E Infantry Brigade was ordered to cross the River Jordan in the neighbourhood of Korasin, near where it runs into the Sea of Galilee.

The main Israeli thrusts were to be made against the hardest terrain in the northern sector of the Syrian defensive belt, which was less strongly defended, while the slightly less difficult centre sector around the Benot Yacov Bridge, which was far more strongly held, was left alone, it being the intention to assault those defensive positions from the rear once the breakthroughs in the north had been achieved. The paramount aim was that of swift and deep penetration to seize Kuneitra, which dominated the northern part of the plateau, and then to exploit south, or east, as opportunity offered.

The Fifth Day (Friday, 9 June)

From dawn on the morning of the Fifth Day waves of Israeli aircraft pounded the Syrian defences at 10-minute intervals, using their special concrete dibber bombs against the stone and concrete emplacements. Mostly they failed to penetrate or cause material damage although the weight of the attacks and the terrific blast tended to stun the defenders. Napalm was also dropped freely, but had only a limited effect as the Syrians had affixed guttering to many of their defence works to catch the flaming material and prevent it from falling or seeping inside. During the early hours of the morning, although raging fires fitfully lit up the countryside and frequent flares were projected by the Syrians, Israeli engineers worked to clear lanes through the minefields on their own side of the border, and made ready to cross to the Syrian side to perform a similar task. On this part of the frontier spring rains invariably displaced or even washed away many mines, so minefields had to be automatically resown, which the Israelis had conscientiously done. Although the Israelis did not know this at the time, the Syrians, with characteristic Arab slothfulness, had failed to carry out this annual chore and so their minefields were largely ineffective. The Syrians had, too, deliberately lifted many of their own mines from around the Benot Yacov Bridge area, intending to advance along this axis if opportunity offered. Along most of the front an artillery duel, which had begun at dawn, developed in intensity, but died down at about 0900. At about 1000, when the Syrians spotted Israeli units moving to their start-lines, it broke out again furiously, and a heavy rain of shells fell on the Israeli side of the border.

A ARMOURED BRIGADE BATTLE

At 1000 A Armoured Brigade consisting of one Sherman battalion and one mechanized infantry battalion, which were organized into three combat teams, moved out from Givat Haem (less two companies) with a tank unit leading along a single track through the Israeli minefield; they aimed to hit the border between Tel Azzaziat and Kfar Szold. For part of the time the Israeli vehicles were under direct observation by the Syrians, who brought down heavy artillery fire on them; despite aircraft intervention, casualties were caused to men and vehicles. The Second-in-Command of the leading battalion was killed while still on Israeli soil. As this column neared the border eight bulldozers led the way, clearing the route of mines; five of them were hit and disabled before Syrian territory was reached. The piece of terrain selected for this formation to break through was extremely difficult. A point was chosen where there were not quite so many scattered basalt boulders on the lower slopes, and some patches of ground between the boulders were firm and passable (although with difficulty) for vehicles. With infantry patrol protection Israeli engineers crept down to the stream that formed the frontier and probed for mines.

The immediate objectives of A Armoured Brigade were to take Zaoura and Kala. The leading Shermans crossed the border at 1130 and almost immediately came upon the first Syrian defensive position, garrisoned by a platoon, known as Gur El Askar, which was on a north–south supply road that led from Tel Azzaziat to Kanaba. Immediately the tanks fired full at the defences as they charged over them at speed, but there was no return fire, as the defenders, dazed from the aerial pounding, had withdrawn. This sharp movement had brought the Israeli Shermans on to the supply road. With two reconnaissance vehicles probing ahead, they turned southwards along it, but within minutes bumped into a second and stronger Syrian position a little higher up the escarpment at Namush. Again the Shermans, with all guns firing, rushed at the post, managing to destroy an anti-tank gun before it could fire a shot, and literally overrunning the defences. The tanks continued on a few hundred yards, leaving the following mechanized infantry to deal with the garrison at Namush, who either surrendered or disappeared into the escarpment rocks eastwards, leaving piles of equipment behind them. The leading Israeli tanks were now climbing steeply along the narrow supply road. They had not gone very far past Namush when they came under anti-tank fire from a position about 1,000 yards ahead, near the village of Ukda, some 1,500 feet above and overlooking Kfar Szold. The Shermans quickly fired back and then tried to bypass this enemy position by sheering off along a side track, which however brought them back on to the main supply road, out of sight from the Ukda emplacements but within sight and range of a major position at Sir Adib on the Oil Road. Heavy Syrian anti-tank fire came down on the Israeli tanks from this position, which was about half way up the escarpment. The route thus far had been so winding and the contours of the escarpment so confusing that this tank unit mistook Sir Adib for Zaoura,[1] and the leading officers were surprised that it was not being subjected to heavy aerial bombardment according to plan. Several tanks were hit and more were damaged in the interval while an air strike was called for on Sir Adib. Once the air strike had pounded the

---

[1] 'It soon became clear that Biro had mistaken Sir Adib for Zaoura.' (*Tanks of Tammuz*.)

Syrian positions, the Shermans, with all guns firing, charged at the emplacements, which were gained but at some cost in vehicles and men. In this charge the Battalion Commander was wounded. When Sir Adib was reached there followed a period of doubt and indecision, during which the officer who had just taken over command of the unit was killed. It was suddenly appreciated that Sir Adib lay just below, but hidden from the strongly-defended Kala on the crest.

The commander of A Armoured Brigade had decided that when Namush was taken the leading Sherman combat team would continue the advance towards Kala, in a south-easterly direction, which it had done. The second Sherman combat team was to turn off north-eastwards to assault Zaoura, on the crest, which it had also done. His Brigade HQ and the other combat team turned northwards just after Namush and followed a track parallel to that taken by the second Sherman combat team, so that they would be right behind it when it assaulted Zaoura. Somehow the Brigade HQ had taken the wrong supply road, and found itself moving southwards instead of northwards. Eventually it arrived right behind the leading Sherman combat team held up before Sir Adib. Once Sir Adib had been taken it moved northwards along the Oil Road towards Zaoura.

The second Sherman combat team had successfully overrun two smaller enemy positions on the lower slopes as it climbed up the supply road towards Zaoura but it was brought to a halt when an anti-tank gun disabled the leading tank, which then blocked the roadway. Other tanks promptly took to small side tracks and forced their way upwards until they were close enough to charge the enemy position with all guns firing. This initiative by individual tank commanders saved the situation and kept the momentum of the advance going. The position at Zaoura was in two parts, the lower one in and just below the village itself and the other a little way above the village on the actual crest. The Sherman tanks forced their way forwards and upwards, overcoming anti-tank guns with the aid of heavy air strikes, until the Shermans were able to open fire on the village. At this moment the combat team arrived moving up the Oil Road, and was shot at by tanks, the lower positions soon being overrun. Next the Shermans moved into the village and, under the cover of an air strike, encircled and successfully assaulted the upper position. By 1600 Zaoura was in Israeli hands, and the first foothold had been made on the plateau. One combat team was deployed ready to hold any counter-attack, while two companies of tanks were sent southwards on the supply road that led from Zaoura to Kala, where the first Sherman combat team was still fighting desperately.

While Zaoura was being successfully reduced, the Sherman combat team left behind at Sir Adib was having a rough passage. Another officer took over after the commander was killed, pulled it together and started to advance towards Kala. The supply road from Sir Adib to Kala climbs steeply as it twists up the escarpment, and it was blocked by 'dragons' teeth' anti-tank obstacles about one mile below Kala. To the south of this road block was a large anti-tank gun position, while a still larger defensive complex to its immediate north overlooked it. There remained only 23 Shermans[1] in three companies, nearly 20 having been lost already by enemy action, mechanical failure or from sliding backwards or sideways owing to the steepness of the gradients. An air strike was called down on the north position, after which the Shermans successfully assaulted the Syrian position.

Next, under covering fire from the Shermans, now in position on the high ground to the north of the road, the remainder of the combat team approached the road block, using smoke to screen their movement from the anti-tank guns firing at them from the south of the roadway. Half the Shermans remained below the road block to engage the Syrian guns, while the others, one by one, quickly scuttled through it, to become immediately involved in a comparatively short range fire-fight with Syrian T-34s, Su100s and anti-tank guns positioned between the stone houses in Kala village itself, which was actually on the crest of the escarpment. Once through the road block they charged straight away uphill with all guns firing hard. Owing to difficulties of intercommunication[2] between tanks, it was a fight in which individual initiative played a big part.

Unfortunately an air strike could not be brought down to

---

[1] *Tanks of Tammuz.*

[2] 'Radio contact between tanks was poor.' (*Tanks of Tammuz.*)

cover this dangerous advance, because the Israeli commander had difficulty in making identification signals as his equipment had been shot away. Only two Shermans made the outskirts of Kala village, there to be pinned down. Information came through that a Syrian tank company of seven T-54s was moving from Wasit towards Kala, and it entered Kala at about the same moment as the two Israeli Shermans. This tense situation lasted for almost an hour, and it was not until about 1800 that Israeli aircraft could be brought into action to pound the enemy armour, which soon began to withdraw. Heavy air attacks were then made on Kala, which gave the attackers a breathing space, but they were unable to exploit this situation. At about 1830 the tanks of the combat team of A Armoured Brigade from Zaoura came southwards along a supply road into Kala, which they quickly cleared. The remaining Syrians either surrendered or escaped eastwards. Having fought two very hard battles, one at Zaoura and the other at Kala (each lasting nearly four hours), A Armoured Brigade had by nightfall gained a bridgehead—a wedge about five miles wide—on the Golan Plateau, after having broken completely through the defensive belt.

THE GOLANI BRIGADE BATTLE

A little farther to the north the Golani Brigade, consisting of three infantry battalions in half-tracks, with two attached companies of Shermans from A Armoured Brigade, was later off the mark; it did not cross the border into Syria until 1400. There had been delays in forming-up, changes of start-lines and vehicle casualties caused by Syrian artillery fire when still on Israeli soil, which had meant last-minute reorganization. The first main obstacle was the formidable Tel Azzaziat, the feature on the border dominating the whole of the northern part of the Huleh Valley, which had such good fields of fire westwards that the only practical way of assaulting it was from the east (that is, from Syrian territory), so it was decided to break across the border immediately to its south to get on to the supply road leading north to Tel Azzaziat, on which were two covering positions. One was known as Bourj Buvil, and the other immediately above it, on a separate feature, was known as Tel Fakhr;

these were to be assaulted simultaneously. The Tel Fakhr position, about three miles inside Syrian territory, was in two parts, the northern and the southern sectors, each consisting of concrete emplacements, bunkers, underground quarters and stores, and connecting trenches each surrounded by a triple barbed wire fence. They were originally protected by covering minefields, and although some of the mines had been displaced or washed away, enough remained to make it distinctly dangerous for assaulting vehicles. Mines were also set within the wire fencing. A Golani battalion advanced on Tel Fakhr in half-tracks from the south-west, first attacking and overrunning the southern position known as Bahgait and then wheeling to assault the main position from the east with covering tank support, but as soon as it crossed the border it came under heavy anti-tank fire, which disabled several half-tracks. One company, after suffering casualties in this approach march, changed direction and charged straight for the Syrian position. Instead of using bangalore torpedoes or explosives to blast a way through the wire fencing, several of the Israeli soldiers jumped from their half-tracks and draped themselves over the wire to form a living bridge with their bodies, over which their comrades scrambled into the compound. Fierce hand-to-hand fighting developed as the Syrians fought back strongly. The defenders emerged from their bunkers after a while and launched a counter-attack in which both the commanding officer and battalion second-in-command were killed. In this close-quarter fighting, as the Israelis were actually inside the enemy positions, it was not possible to give fire support or call down an air strike. The fighting lasted from about 1515 until 1830, and was regarded by the Israelis as one of the two most hard fought battles of this war—the other being Ammunition Hill in Jerusalem. When this battle died down the Golani Brigade[1] counted nearly 60 Syrian bodies in the posts and took 20 prisoners, but their own casualties amounted to just over 100, of whom nearly 30 were killed. Most of the Syrians escaped eastwards during the final charges when they realized how the battle was going.

Next a Golani company turned on Bourj Buval, the small post

---

[1] Press Conference, Tel Aviv, 17 June 1967.

on the supply road just below Tel Fakhr, which was found to be deserted. A Golani battalion then concentrated upon Tel Azzaziat, which was first smothered with several heavy air strikes that included the dropping of napalm. The remaining opposition was quickly overcome, many of the Syrian defenders being able to slip away eastwards in the confusion. Another Golani unit had advanced to attack Tel Fakhr simultaneously; in this case the fighting lasted from about 1625 until 1645, when the position was overrun by the Israelis. The Golani Brigade[1] had broken through the upper part of the Syrian defensive belt and secured strong footholds on the side of the escarpment.

OTHER ACTIONS

A few miles to the south, opposite Notera, after Israeli engineers had spent the morning and part of the afternoon clearing lanes through minefields on the Israeli side, the HQ, with AMX tanks of U Armoured Brigade, crossed the border and with elements of E Infantry Brigade clearing the way, commenced to climb up the supply road that led to Rawye, which was not quite on the crest of the escarpment. Full air support was given. After overrunning two small Syrian positions the AMX unit assaulted and entered Rawye at about 1800. Once having occupied this position, the Israelis deployed ready to hold any counter-attack. Three AMXs had been disabled by anti-tank fire.

Half-a-dozen miles farther south still a similar action was being taken by other companies of E Infantry Brigade in half-tracks, supported by a company of AMXs. After lanes through the minefields had been cleared, this force crossed the border just north of the drained Lake Huleh, forcing its way over the first, small Syrian defensive positions to get on to the supply road. It then moved in two columns on parallel supply roads, and by 1800, with ample air support, had assaulted and seized the emplacements near the village of Darbashiyeh, two-thirds of the way up the escarpment. Fortifications near Dardara had been

---

[1] The Golani Brigade claims to have captured 13 enemy posts in the Syrian fighting, to have mopped-up Kuneitra after A Armoured Brigade had swept through it, and to have planted an Israeli flag on one of the peaks of Mount Hormon. Press Conference, Tel Aviv, 17 June 1967.

assaulted at 0930 and taken by 1120. Tel Hillal was taken by 1235. These positions were captured by a unit of I Infantry Brigade, operating independently of the U Armoured Brigade advance. During the last hour before darkness this force spread out laterally along the supply roads on the lower slopes of the heights, clearing out small Syrian positions that dominated Kibbutz Shamir below in the Huleh Valley.

Still farther south, after lanes through the minefields had been cleared, two companies of Q Paratroop Brigade, supported by a company of Shermans from U Armoured Brigade, moved towards the frontier near Mishmar Hayarden to break through on to the supply road system. They had been ordered to take Jelabina by night, H-Hour being set for 2400.

COMMENTS ON THE FIFTH DAY'S FIGHTING

By the evening of the Fifth Day the Israelis had gained a five-mile-wide bridgehead on the top of the escarpment, between Zaoura and Kala, and had penetrated the defended mountain wall in five other places, all in the northern part of the Syrian defensive belt. The Israeli success was considerable, but was not as great as they had hoped. Having to fight two hard battles during the afternoon, at Zaoura and Kala, had retarded its programme. Brigadier Elazar had also hoped that the Golani Brigade would have made a much quicker advance and occupied the Banias Ridge at least by nightfall, but this formation had been delayed, first in crossing the frontier to move into action and then by having to fight the battle of Tel Fakhr. While the paratroops and the infantry had been able to penetrate the outer Syrian defences and force their way some distance up the escarpment, it had been hoped that all, or at least some of them, would have completely broken through the defensive belt to emerge on the top of the plateau itself. The whole operation seems to have been delayed by hidden problems of preparing, organizing, briefing, reconnaissance and resupply, as well as of switching formations around. There was also disappointment that the troops concentrated near the southern side of the Golan Plateau were not able to commence their assaults that day, which might have drawn Syrian troops away from the vital northern

sector. In any event, by cracking these extremely formidable
defences the Israelis had done splendidly by any standards.
Their successes were due largely to the great width of the frontal
break-in which tended to immobilize the Syrian command
system, the deadening weight of their aerial bombardment, good
artillery and mortar support, the determination of all ranks to
keep the momentum of the advance going, and the outstanding
initiative and leadership of the junior commanders and individuals in the forward waves.

The Israeli air force had begun to pound the Syrian defences
at daylight, continuing throughout the day practically without
ceasing. At 0940 it concentrated upon the Syrian artillery positions on the edge of the escarpment, and then switched to soften
up the forward positions just before the first assaults went in.
Once the Israeli attacks were launched aircraft were allocated
to direct ground support, some remaining overhead all the time
to be on instant call to take action when requested by the ground
troops. Other aircraft took on interdiction tasks at targets on the
plateau and to the east of Kuneitra, disrupting supply columns
and scattering the small groups of tanks that were sent forward.
By afternoon scores of dense pillars of smoke were rising from
the plateau and the escarpment as vehicles and stores were hit
and set on fire.

It had not been an easy day for the Israelis, as despite being
stunned by aerial and artillery bombardment the Syrian soldiers
generally stood fast and fought back. Each post had to be actually
overrun by tanks, and the trenches and bunkers physically
cleared by the following infantry with small arms fire and grenades before the defenders would surrender or try to escape.
The Syrian defence had proved to be tough and so rigid
that none of its elements had any sort of a counter-attack role,
not even a local one. The defenders were supposed to stay within
their fortifications, the theory being that even if any of the
attackers managed to get past them, they would become ever
more deeply enmeshed as they pushed farther into the defensive maw, until they were pulverized and eliminated by cross-
fire from other positions.

During the advance a number of Israeli vehicles became
ineffective; some were disabled by mines and accurate anti-tank

shooting, while several of the 24-year-old Shermans and half-tracks found the steep gradients and rocky going too much for their engines, transmissions and other mechanical parts. Others cast tracks and yet others slithered down steep gradients, often being brought to a jarring halt only by the large basalt boulders. The Sherman's stout armour was able to absorb a great deal of anti-tank fire and still keep going; some tanks were hit as many as a dozen times in the Syrian fighting. Generally, the half-tracks made out rather better than the Shermans mechanically, although their rubber tracks did not obtain such good purchase on the rocky ground as did steel ones.

Only a small proportion of the Syrian artillery fire was directed against the Israeli formations when they were first detected and seen to be moving up to their start lines. The main weight of their shells continued to fall on Israeli settlements in the middle distance, as it had been doing intermittently since dawn. This was fortunate for the Israelis, as had the whole of the Syrian artillery been concentrated on them at this juncture they would have suffered a great many more casualties, and perhaps some units would have been so badly knocked about that they would not have been able to continue the advance as they did. The Syrians seemed to realize their mistake too late, as they did not switch all their artillery fire on to the attackers until most of the vehicles had crossed the border and were entering the broken country at the foot of the escarpment, which gave more cover. It is not clear why the Syrians missed such an opportunity to inflict casualties. Perhaps it was just slow reaction. Perhaps they regarded these moves as feints, expecting the main attack to come in the obvious region around the Benot Yacov Bridge, where the terrain was more favourable. Perhaps they were puzzled as to the true objectives of the Israelis. Or they may have had great faith in the strength of their defences in this sector. The Israelis claim to have monitored during this phase several Syrian radio messages from the battlefield in Russian, one of which ('Stop firing at the settlements—fire at the enemy') gave rise to the suspicion that Soviet advisers might be helping to direct the defensive battle. There seems to be no explanation for these messages in Russian, nor any evidence that Soviet personnel were involved in the fighting or in directing the Syrian forces.

One would think that the risk of Soviet personnel being made prisoner, with consequent international implications, was too great for the Soviet Union to take. As far as is known, all Soviet personnel with the Syrian forces were recalled to Damascus on the first day of the war, to remain there under the immediate control of the Soviet Military Mission.

As night fell the forward Israeli units deployed and made ready to repulse an anticipated Syrian counter-attack, which did not materialize. During the night the Israelis refuelled their vehicles, and brought up supplies and ammunition, while mechanics worked furiously patching up tanks and vehicles, replacing tracks and carrying out other repairs on the spot. Throughout the hours of darkness, although the battlefield was fitfully illuminated by fires, many Israeli vehicles that had fallen out slowly rejoined their units in the forward positions.

The Sixth Day (Saturday, 10 June)

The Syrians had not launched any counter-attacks during the night but had contented themselves with spasmodic shelling, despite Israeli counter-bombardment and air activity. Starting at 0001, men of Q Paratroop Brigade with Shermans of U Armoured Brigade advanced across the frontier making for Jelabina, which they took by 0430 after a hard fight. At dawn the Israelis made fresh advances into the Golan Plateau in the north, when good progress was made in the face of continued stiff Syrian opposition, followed later by other penetrations into the southern part. At about 1100 a series of explosions in the Syrian-held parts of the plateau—particularly noticeable because there was no Israeli bombing at that moment—signalled the end of the main organized Syrian resistance. The Syrians realized that they were beaten. At least four brigades, possibly five, withdrew in reasonably good shape; they were those in reserve around Kuneitra which had not been in ground contact with the Israelis. They included one armoured and one mechanized brigade, the others being infantry. A large part of the other armoured and mechanized brigades, elements of which were in direct contact with the advancing Israelis, also withdrew fairly successfully, although many vehicles and much equipment had to be hastily abandoned. Many Syrian units along this front escaped on foot, large numbers of soldiers abandoned their arms and equipment and got away across country over the northern hills, while others surrendered, although organized resistance did not really cease until about 1430. Israeli activity had stopped at about 1400. In this theatre, unlike that of the Sinai, distances were much smaller and the terrain was more conducive to escape and avoiding detection from the air. The Israeli advance, still mainly frontal, facilitated the Syrian withdrawal.

A ARMOURED BRIGADE BATTLE

We left A Armoured Brigade holding the bridgehead on the edge of the plateau between Zaoura and Kala, anticipating a Syrian counter-attack. Vehicles were refuelled, and ammunition replenished. Many stragglers caught up. As no hostile Syrian move was made, the latest intelligence was evaluated after midnight, fresh orders were given, and the brigade, abandoning Zaoura, moved to concentrate around Kala. At dawn, under cover of an air strike, the brigade moved out from Kala towards Wasit. At Wasit, about five miles distant, the Israelis were halted by enemy fire from the emplacements there, and also by fire from some T-54s of the Syrian armoured brigade. Further air strikes, followed by flanking assaults, overran these positions, and the Syrian armour withdrew. After regrouping, A Armoured Brigade continued to advance along the road to Mansoura, a further five miles to the east. Progress was slow owing to Syrian tank and artillery fire, and on the more open parts of the plateau the Israelis began to take casualties. The leading Israeli Shermans approached Mansoura and engaged the enemy tanks on the outskirts of the village and the guns in the defensive positions. There was no return fire as the tank crews, gunners and soldiers had deserted their posts minutes before. The Israelis found about a dozen enemy T-54s, T-34s and SU100s, mostly with their engines still running.

It was now a race for Kuneitra. Passing through Mansoura in battle order, the Shermans moved across the open country but it was 1430 before the Israeli armour entered Kuneitra, to find it abandoned, some 27 hours after the operation had commenced.

Practically all the Syrian troops had hastily decamped in vehicles about three hours earlier. Israeli tanks quickly drove through the camp complex, but not a shot was fired. A few civilians had been left behind and some soldiers had been unable to get away with the main body, but they had hidden inside buildings. An armoured patrol was sent southwards along the road to Boutmiye. It arrived without incident at 1630, while the remainder of the brigade deployed to the east of Kuneitra, blocking the road to Damascus, which was only 40 miles distant.

THE GOLANI BRIGADE BATTLE

To the north, near Tel Azzaziat and Tel Fakhr, the exhausted Golani Brigade, which had fought so well and desperately the previous day but had advanced no further before nightfall, had also deployed to meet an anticipated counter-attack, but the Syrians remained in their defences within gun-shot to the north and north-east. Considerable Syrian shelling came from the direction of the Banias Ridge. During such darkness as there was (several fires were burning on this part of the battlefield), and while the Golani Brigade was preparing for the next advance, the whole of O Armoured Brigade, consisting of two Sherman battalions and one mechanized infantry battalion, moved from just north of Rosh Pina right up to the border near Tel Azzaziat. O Armoured Brigade supported the Golani Brigade in an advance before dawn from Tel Azzaziat and Tel Fakhr towards Banias. The Sherman tanks of O Armoured Brigade successfully attacked another fortified feature, known as Tel Hamra, which was about one mile due west of Ramat Banias. Resistance was strong and the town of Banias was not entered by the Israelis until about 1000. Once on the plateau, where the terrain was more favourable to vehicular movement, O Armoured Brigade with one Golani unit moved quickly uphill from Banias against the Syrian positions at Ein Fit, which they overran. Then these two units moved south to Zaoura, which had been taken and briefly held by A Armoured Brigade the previous day. The Syrian positions had not all been cleared, but they were ironed out by a combination of air strikes and artillery fire, and armoured and infantry assaults. Many of the defenders fought back aggressively. Once the Zaoura complex had been reduced, the Israeli unit moved eastwards along the road towards Massada. The time was now about 1100. The Syrian explosions had puzzled the Israelis who, expecting stiff opposition, asked for an air strike and more artillery support before assaulting the Massada defences. Demolitions prevented the Israelis from moving along the road; they had to use the tracks to the south of Zaoura. Massada was taken in the late afternoon. When the Israelis finally entered they found only a few wounded and stragglers who had been left behind. The whole area was littered with abandoned weapons, equipment and vehicles. The Sherman battalion and two companies of the Golani Brigade were next ordered to probe northwards towards the Mount Hormon massif. Later in the afternoon Golani soldiers planted an Israeli flag on one of its southern peaks.

Now that Massada was secured a Golani battalion was ordered to move as fast as it could to Kuneitra. It arrived there to make contact with A Armoured Brigade at about 1500, and it was given the task of searching and clearing the camps and the town. The other Golani battalion (with the other Sherman battalion of O Armoured Brigade after Ramat Banias, Tel Hamra and the town of Banias had been reduced and occupied) began to clear the Banias Ridge. This completed, the force moved into the small north-western pocket of Syrian territory that reached to the Lebanese frontier, and which included strong but deserted positions around Nukheila. In this extreme northern region the Druze, most of whom had stayed in their villages and encampments, began during the late afternoon to collaborate openly with the Israelis. By then they had realized that most of the Syrian soldiers had left and that those who remained were fugitives.

OTHER ACTIONS

The two battalions of U Armoured Brigade which had taken Rawye, a strong point part way up the escarpment, on the previous evening, made preparations during the night to continue their advance at dawn. Under cover of air strikes and artillery support they fought their way upwards along a narrow supply road to the top of the plateau, which they reached at about 1000, although not without casualties. Once on the Golan Plateau proper, they deployed and moved along the axis of the road to the north-east, making for Kanaba and Wasit. When they approached the fortified village of Kanaba the Shermans deployed and made a flanking assault, only to find the fortifications and village deserted. Wasit, only about four miles from Kanaba, had just been occupied by a unit of A Armoured Brigade, which had then moved on to Kuneitra. Once Kanaba was found to be empty, U Armoured Brigade was order to change direction and move due south to seize and hold Kfar Naffakh, about eight miles away on the main Benot Yacov Bridge–Kuneitra road. Difficulties were encountered in an attempt to press through the village of Koasset, so the brigade was rerouted by way of the Oil Road. The Shermans advanced in battle order, to be halted by some 15 Syrian tanks near a feature called Tel Shiban, which necessitated a detour. U Armoured Brigade finally took Kfar Naffakh at about 1430. A formal assault with covering artillery support was made, and once again the Syrian positions were discovered to be deserted. The defenders had withdrawn two hours previously, and only a few stragglers were captured. The reconnaissance company of U Armoured Brigade was sent along this road eastwards. It made contact with A Armoured Brigade at Kuneitra at about 1600. The Sherman and the mechanized infantry battalions set up a series of strong road blocks to trap any Syrian troops withdrawing eastwards, to interdict supply vehicles and meet counter-attacks. But these measures were too late as the majority of the soldiers who had manned the forward defences had already retreated. However, some stragglers were captured.

Paratroops in half-tracks, who had reached Darbashiyeh the previous evening, at dawn continued their fight to reach the summit of the plateau, which they achieved just before 1100. Once on the plateau this formation turned south-east along a supply track making for Kfar Naffakh, on the main Benot Yacov Bridge to Kuneitra road. The leading elements of this force reached Kfar Naffakh just after 1300, to make contact with the main body of U Armoured Brigade. H Armoured Brigade, fresh from its operations near Jerusalem, arrived on the

Syrian front during the night and moved up to Darbashiyeh
(which had just been taken by paratroops) where it was intended
that it should remain as the Command Reserve; but with A and
U Armoured Brigades making for Kuneitra, it was ordered to
move along the Oil Road towards Boutmiye, where it made
contact with Israeli paratroops who had been landed there by
helicopter. It then went on to occupy the nearby village of Rafid.

The battalion from Q Paratroop Brigade, which had captured
Jelabina early in the morning, and the two companies of E
Infantry Brigade, which had taken Dardara, Tel Hillel and other
positions nearby, with their attached tanks, continued at dawn
their respective advances to the top of the escarpment against
strong opposition. Both managed to reach the Oil Road by about
1000, after suffering casualties. Intending to assault the very
strong Syrian defences covering the Benot Yacov Bridge from
the rear, once the plateau had been gained, these two Israeli
forces made contact with each other and began moving south.
One column moved along the Oil Road and the other along
parallel supply routes lower down the side of the escarpment,
clearing the Syrian positions as they went by drenching them
with heavy fire. Extremely stiff at first, Syrian resistance abruptly
slackened and became more disjointed after 1100, but it was
almost 1300 before a unit of E Infantry Brigade was ready to
mount an assault from the north-east on to the main fortifications around the Customs House near the Benot Yacov Bridge,
which was taken by 1400. The Israelis found the defences
almost deserted. They occupied them without opposition and
captured such Syrians as had been unable to get away.

This vital communication point secured, the main part of this
Israeli force, consisting of the paratroop battalion and the two
companies of Shermans, moved eastwards along the road to
Kuneitra. When it came to within three miles of Kfar Naffakh,
now occupied by U Armoured Brigade, it was ordered to halt
and set up a strong road block. A reconnaissance element made
contact with U Armoured Brigade at Kfar Naffakh at 1500. Two
companies of paratroops in half-tracks, with a company of Shermans, were sent south-westwards along the supply roads leading
down into the Jordan Valley to clear and take possession of all
Syrian fortifications in that area. The two companies from E

Infantry Brigade had been left to hold the Benot Yacov Bridge; one of them, with some Sherman tanks, was ordered to move south on the supply road near the foot of the escarpment along the east bank of the River Jordan, achieving this by getting behind the Syrian positions.

Farther south still, at 1400, another company from E Infantry Brigade, with half-a-dozen Shermans, crossed the border near the northern tip of the Sea of Galilee and remained there as a block on the east bank of the River Jordan. Even farther to the south, other companies of E Infantry Brigade, moving north from Ein Ger along the shore of the Sea of Galilee, cleared the Beteiha Plain (taking prisoner the few Syrians unable to escape) and at about 1800 made contact with other elements of the same formation in blocking positions.

THE SOUTHERN SECTOR

In the southern sector of the Golan Plateau the Israelis were faced with the problem of assaulting steep heights that rose almost abruptly from the Sea of Galilee and the Yarmuk Valley, and which came to a jagged point in the corner where Israeli, Syrian and Jordanian territory met. Along the crest of this cliff-like escarpment a Syrian military supply road linked the defensive positions. The strongest positions were Kfar Harib, overlooking the settlement of Ein Ger and another known as Amrataz A-Din dominating the Harib Pass, through which one of the few routes passed up to the plateau; Nukeib, blocking a possible northward advance from Ein Ger; and Tawafik, on the slopes of the cliff blocking the mouth of the Yarmuk Valley. Other strong positions on the crest included Fik and El Al, on the supply road leading through them on to Boutmiye. Brigadier Elazar had intended to make a night attack, but this was called off for political reasons and he did not receive permission to advance until 1130. He set H-Hour for 1300, when a unit of mechanized infantry rushed the mouth of the Harib Pass, which controlled the routes upwards, to find it deserted. The Israelis remained there, holding this key communication bottleneck for a while, by which time other Israeli units concentrated near the Sea of Galilee were ready to attack the extreme south-western tip of the Golan Plateau, not knowing that the Syrians had already withdrawn from these positions. These troops consisted mainly of one battalion from Q Paratroop Brigade, two battalions from E Infantry Brigade and one Sherman battalion from U Armoured Brigade. They had crossed the River Jordan and were on their start-lines immediately south of Tel Kazir.

The Israeli troops had intended to start the battle with an aerial and artillery barrage at 1200 but were suddenly puzzled by the quietness over the Syrian positions. Suspecting a trap, the commanders feared that the assault might involve costly battles such as those at Kala and Tel Fakhr. In their hesitation they postponed the preliminary barrage. The imminent fall of Kuneitra decided the issue. The order to advance was given at 1300. An infantry battalion moved up the steep slopes towards Tawafik under cover of air and artillery support. The infantry-men scrambled upwards on foot. Tawafik and then Amrataz A-Din were taken by 1415. A company of Shermans followed, starting to ascend the escarpment at 1430. The Israelis now held the key to the Yarmuk Valley.

The pilots of five accompanying Israeli helicopters, who had been flying low over the area, reported that the Syrian positions appeared empty. Two helicopters, sent to find out more, returned with the information that no vehicles were near the positions. The time had come for bolder and quicker measures, so about 100 paratroops were packed into the helicopters and put down near the Kfar Harib defences. These were deserted, and were occupied by about 1600. Returning to the valley, the helicopters lifted a further detachment of paratroops, this time setting them down near Fik, which was also found to be deserted. Fik was astride the supply road on the crest of the escarpment, and once it was occupied by the Israelis their tanks and half-tracks began climbing up the road through the Harib Pass, the leading vehicles reaching Fik[1] at about 1700. On the plateau proper the going was reasonable for vehicles and fairly good progress was made. The Israeli commanders in this sector, because of prickly opposition, remained cautious lest their

---

[1] Just after the Israeli vehicles had passed through Fik a detachment of naval commandos arrived there, having come on their own initiative from Haifa looking for a fight. The sailors were disappointed.

forward troops be ambushed. From Fik another detachment of paratroops was lifted forward by helicopters and put down near El Al, about six miles ahead. El Al was deserted too, and was held by the paratroops until the leading Israeli vehicles arrived. This leap-frogging movement, of lifting troops by helicopter to take and hold positions ahead until the vehicles containing other troops arrived, continued for the remainder of the way. The advance quickened as the terrain became even more favourable for vehicular movement and, indeed, the majority of the paratroops were able to remain in their half-tracks during the latter stages of this advance. A reconnaissance unit of five jeeps with recoilless rifles, which had been landed by helicopter at Kafr Harib, was able to dash into Boutmiye in time to ambush a Syrian column at about 1800.

After El Al had been occupied a detachment of E Infantry Brigade, advancing north from Ein Ger, first of all took Nukeib, overlooking Ein Ger itself, that almost perpetually Arab-dominated and besieged Israeli outpost. Once Nukeib was occupied, an infantry company from the same brigade, which had moved forward into Ein Geddi, advanced along the eastern shore of the Sea of Galilee into Koursi, a Syrian village, where the few inhabitants who remained frantically waved pieces of white cloth in surrender. Crossing the Wadi Samak, this company continued on to enter Kafr Akib, where a similar situation obtained. It halted about four miles farther on, when it made contact with the Israeli company that had moved southwards from Almager.

COMMENTS ON THE SIXTH DAY'S FIGHTING

Despite the terrible pounding the Syrians were receiving, and although their main defensive belt had been penetrated at several points, they generally held fast and fought back until they were overrun or ordered to withdraw. Daylight brought more Israeli air strikes in support of ground troops who were struggling to extend the penetrations made. Right up until 1430 the Israelis suffered many casualties and had to fight every inch of the way forward. By 1100 the Syrian Command system had broken down but resistance continued.

During the afternoon the Israeli General Staff had been urging its commanders to advance as far and as fast as they could so as to occupy the maximum amount of Syrian territory before the cease-fire came into effect. All Israeli aggressive air activity ceased at about 1400 and by evening, just before the cease-fire became operative at 1830, the whole of the Golan Plateau was in Israeli possession. After repeated calls by the UN this cease-fire line began where the forward Israeli soldiers stood at that moment. In fact, the Israelis, in anticipation, had in some places—for obvious reasons—stopped on good tactical features.

COMMENTS ON THE SYRIAN FIGHTING

There is little doubt that the Israeli ground troops' successes, praiseworthy as they were, could not have been achieved without complete Israeli control of the air, and the consequent massive close air support. It was officially stated that the Israeli air force flew more sorties against the Syrians than on all the other fronts together; while no precise figure has been quoted, they must have numbered well over 1,000. In fact, there was seldom a moment when Israeli aircraft were not over the battlefield, making air strikes, dropping napalm, firing rockets and cannon shells, or waiting on the 'cab rank' to hit opportunity targets or be called upon to help the ground troops. The Syrian air force did not come into the picture at all, and the Israelis bombed freely to within 25 miles of Damascus—a self-imposed limitation. This is in no sense derogatory to the ground forces, as the achievement of the Israeli soldiers in breaking through the strong Syrian defensive belt was a military epic in itself. For a day and a half the Syrians fought back well, as is evidenced by the Israeli casualties, which are quoted as 152 killed and 306 wounded. The hardest fought battles, by Israeli agreement, were at Kala by A Armoured Brigade and at Tel Fakhr by the Golani Brigade. The Israelis estimate that the Syrians lost about 1,000 killed and that at least three times that number were wounded. The Israelis took 560 prisoners. They claim to have put 70 Syrian tanks out of action and to have captured another 40 intact. Thus of the original 260 tanks on the Golan Plateau at the start of the war, the Syrians successfully withdrew about 150—nearly two-thirds–and about the same proportion of their armoured personnel carriers and other vehicles. Israeli tank losses are not released but must have numbered over 100 armoured vehicles (mainly Shermans and half-tracks); of this total a large proportion were repaired, so the actual figure lost might be nearer 30. Many Israeli tanks and half-tracks, especially those in O and U Armoured Brigades which had been in action against the Jordanians, were about at the end of their mechanical tether, and perhaps less than one-third were 'runners' by the cease-fire. Of the 265 Syrian guns on the plateau when the war began, the Israelis claim to have knocked out over 150, mainly by aerial action, and to have captured another 50 intact, which again means that the Syrians were able to recover about 60. There were also over 900 artillery pieces of different sorts that never got on to the Golan Plateau at all.

At least half the Syrian force on the Golan Plateau disintegrated, including the infantry brigades manning the forward belt of fortifications and part of the armoured and mechanized brigades that had advanced westwards from Kuneitra. With few exceptions the Syrian fighting spirit seems to have remained surprisingly high even after 1100, when several arms, fuel and supply dumps were simultaneously blown up to prevent them falling into Israeli hands. The order to retreat had gone out during the morning, probably at about 1030, and as it percolated downwards the officers were the first to leave. They escaped in any available vehicles, which partly explains why only 560 (mostly wounded) were captured. Once the officers had gone, the soldiers became involved in the mad scramble. Most of them also managed to withdraw in vehicles, and the remainder took to the countryside on foot.

The Syrian army had suffered a staggering and costly defeat. The part that remained intact had been withdrawn to defend Damascus. The Israelis had won a splendid victory, through good junior leadership, good exploitation and freedom of the air. They had swept away the formidable Syrian Western Wall, the vaunted defensive barrier against any Israeli threats.

CHAPTER 8

The Naval War

The navies of Israel and the Arab States involved played a very minor and unspectacular part in this war. The Israeli Navy, the poor relation of the Israeli Defence Forces, was accorded only a small fraction of the defence budget. Its scope was considered limited as ships are slow-moving vessels compared with modern aircraft; the far longer time they take to cover the comparatively short distances in the Middle East was a negative factor in this fast-moving war. Nonetheless, a small, compact and hard-hitting naval force had been developed by the Israelis consisting of approximately 3,000 personnel, mainly regulars, and about 24 ships. It was based on Haifa, with smaller facilities at Ashdod (planned to be developed as a submarine base) and Eilat.

Israel possessed two submarines of the S Class, both British of World War II vintage. One, the *Rahav*, which had a modern sonar system and depth-charge launchers for anti-submarine work, was reported unable to submerge because of a technical fault discovered on the eve of the war, while the other, the *Tanin*, which for some reason had been put 'in mothballs', had to be hastily prepared for service.[1] The *Haifa*, formerly the *Ibrahim Al Awal*, which had been captured from the Eygptians on 31 October 1956 during the Sinai Campaign, was classed as an 'anti-submarine frigate', although it had formerly been a British destroyer. The *Eilat*, *Yaffo* and *Noga* were the three other destroyers of the Israeli Navy, all former British ships. There were also a 100-ton coastguard cutter, built in Germany, which had two 20-mm anti-aircraft guns, and a

---

[1] On 18 May 1967 the Israelis took over a British T Class submarine at Portsmouth; it had improved sonar devices and was fitted with mountings for machine guns for a surface role (something the Royal Navy did not normally cater for). Named the *Leviathan*, it immediately went out on exercises with British naval ships, and did not reach Israel in time to take part in the war.

British-built 46-ton Seaward Patrol Craft, with a four-inch gun and two 20-mm anti-aircraft guns, as well as three old American landing craft.[1] Of its flotilla of 12 motor torpedo boats (MTBs), three had been built in Italy, six in France and three in Britain. Each carried two torpedoes, a 40-mm gun and two 20-mm anti-tank guns.

As from 19 May frantic efforts had been made to bring the Israeli naval ships as up to date as possible. Radar installations were fitted to those without them, more anti-aircraft guns were installed, and a few trawler-type ships were pressed into temporary service for routine protective coastal patrols, so as to enable the regular naval ships to form an offensive flotilla. The Israeli merchant marine was fast developing, already having over 80 ships registered at Lloyd's. The *Haifa*, then being refitted in Haifa harbour, was hastily finished and put to sea in time.

In numbers, ships and fire-power the Israeli Navy could not match that of the Egyptians, who had the largest naval force of any Mediterranean Power, so its tasks were to protect the Israeli coastline from attack, prevent either saboteurs or troops being landed from the sea on Israeli soil or behind advancing Israeli troops, and to persuade the Egyptians to send as many of their ships south through the Suez Canal—thus there would be less to take action against Tel Aviv and the population centres of the coastal plain. The majority of the Israeli ships were based on Haifa, and normally only three MTBs were stationed at Eilat; as a deceptive measure four other LCTs were sent overland to Eilat to arrive in daylight, to be launched in full view of Akaba, and to be seen moving south down the gulf. However, they went only just out of sight, where they waited until darkness, when they returned without lights and were moved back inland a few miles. The next, and following, days the same procedure was carried out with the same LCTs, giving the impression that the Israelis were mustering all their small craft for an assault on Sharm El Sheikh. This deception was successful and caused both a build-up of the garrison at Sharm El Sheikh and several Egyptian ships to be sent southwards through the Suez Canal.

[1] They were respectively a landing craft (infantry), a landing craft (mechanized) and a landing craft (tank).

THE EGYPTIAN NAVY

The Navy had been commanded since January 1966 by Brigadier[1] Schlomo Erell. The previous Commander IDF Navy had been Brigadier Yochai Ben-Nun, who had gained almost legendary fame in Israel for his exploits in the War of Independence.[2] It was he who had developed and trained the small unit of naval commandos and frogmen. Although he had left the Navy to become Director of the Department of Oceanography Research at Haifa, he retained his connexions with the naval commando unit, continuing to enthuse it with daring and unconventional ideas and techniques.

THE EGYPTIAN NAVY

By comparison with that of Israel, the Egyptian Navy was large and modern, having about 11,000 personnel, mostly short-service regulars, and over 100 craft of various sizes. These vessels included 12 submarines of the Soviet V and R Classes, eight destroyers (six of the Soviet Skoryo Class and two of the British Z Class), 12 coastal anti-submarine vessels, 10 minesweepers, 32 MTBs and eight other miscellaneous vessels of Soviet, British or American origin. Pride of place was given to the 18 Soviet missile boats, of which 10 were of the Osa Class and eight of the Komar Class. Both carried the Soviet Styx[3] surface-to-surface missile, which had a range of over 20 miles and was the standard armament on all Soviet fast patrol boats. The 160-ton Osa Class missile boat had two pairs of launchers, while the 100-ton Komar Class had only a single pair, both craft having speeds of about 40 knots.

The Commander-in-Chief of the Egyptian Navy and Chief of Naval Staff was Rear-Admiral Soliman Izzat. His Navy's tasks were to protect the Egyptian coastline from any Israeli naval depredations, to bombard Israel and to support from the sea any land invasion into Israel, and to be responsible for the

---

[1] The Israelis retain the same ranks for all three services, in this case 'Aluf' or brigadier.

[2] During the War of Independence in 1948 Yochai Ben-Nun had badly damaged the Egyptian destroyer, the *Emir Farouk*, by loading a small motor boat with explosives, aiming it at the ship, and himself jumping clear just before the moment of impact.

[3] The NATO code-name.

Gulf of Akaba and the route south to the Yemen. Normally less than a quarter of the Egyptian ships were south of the Suez Canal at any one time, but the Israeli deception measures caused him to order another ten vessels southwards. In fact, two destroyers passed through the Suez Canal on 4 June, the last Egyptian ships to do so. The main Egyptian naval bases were at Port Said and Alexandria. There were smaller naval facilities at Port Suez, Hurghada on the Gulf of Suez, and Safaga and Koseir on the Red Sea, as well as at Hodeida in the Yemen. Once hostilities commenced Nasser loudly warned all international shipping to keep clear of the triangle between Port Said and Haifa.

OTHER ARAB NAVIES

None of the other Arab navies became involved in hostilities with Israel. All were tiny and ineffectual, perhaps with the exception of that of Syria, based on Latakia; it had a total strength of about 1,500 ratings, and possessed four Komar Class missile boats, six coastal escorts, three Soviet MTBs, two Soviet minesweepers and three French patrol boats. It could have taken some offensive action had the inclination been present. The Lebanese Navy, with only one 100-ton patrol vessel, an old American landing craft and three French MTBs, was another matter, as was the Iraqi Navy, which consisted mainly of 12 MTBs, all in the Persian Gulf.

THE NAVAL WAR

Both the Israeli and Egyptian navies remained quiet during the daylight hours of the First Day of the war, but as soon as darkness fell some Israeli ships moved towards Egypt. Brigadier Erell, of course, knew by this time that the Egyptian Air Force had been smashed, but Admiral Izzat did not. As an Israeli destroyer and two MTBs approached Port Said, and were still some 15 miles away, two Osa missile boats suddenly came towards them at speed. The Israelis waited until they were about 1,000 yards distant and then opened fire, registering several hits. Without firing a shot the two Egyptian vessels turned about and

returned into Port Said harbour. This incident happened at
0240 (on the Second Day) and the Israelis claimed to have
caused considerable damage.

That same first night two parties of Israeli frogmen were put
ashore, one at Port Said and the other at Alexandria. The Israelis
estimated correctly that the Egyptians had four missile boats,
three anti-submarine craft (which were really frigates) and three
MTBs in Port Said harbour. The small group of Israeli frogmen
managed to get into the harbour but were unable to locate any
of the ships they were looking for. They discovered two oil-
tankers, which were not touched, the Israeli explanation being
that the explosion would most probably have killed many
civilians living close to the dock. All the Israeli frogmen returned
safely.

The other small party, of six frogmen, was less fortunate.
Carried by submarine to a point just off the Ras El Tin naval
base at Alexandria, the frogmen rowed ashore in a small dinghy
and successfully penetrated the anchorage where, it is claimed,
they sank a number of vessels, including an Osa missile boat,[1]
and damaged others. The Israeli submarine returned at the
appointed time to pick up the frogmen but, after waiting as long
as it could, it had to submerge and withdraw just before dawn.
The Israelis state that the submarine returned and waited on each
of the two following nights in the hope that the frogmen might
have been able to get away. An account given me by a senior
Egyptian officer differs slightly from that of the Israelis. The
Egyptians claim that the Israeli submarine was detected just
after the frogmen had disembarked from it, and that they fired
at it, causing it to submerge hurriedly. They kept the incident
quiet for three days in the hope that the Israeli submarine
would return. A naval force of two missile boats and four MTBs
lay in wait each night, but it failed to show up. The Israeli
frogmen only slightly damaged one dry dock and one small ship.
An Egyptian account of the capture of the frogmen, later given
in *Al Ahram*, was that four of them, detected in the sea near the
yachting harbour to the east of Alexandria at about noon on the
Second Day, were picked up by MTBs, and that the other two

---

[1] Two days later *Al Ahram* reported the loss of one missile boat without giving
details.

were caught at about 1400 (both Egyptian local times) at a place not stated. The Israeli account is that the frogmen, having missed their rendezvous on the first night, returned to shore to hide during the day in the hope of being able to swim out the following night. Towards the end of the day, however, they were discovered, and they surrendered to the Egyptian police to evade local mob justice. These six Israeli sailors were eventually exchanged after the war.

After hovering in the vicinity of Port Said all night, the Israeli destroyer and MTBs withdrew to the open sea just before dawn. Their commanders knew that the Egyptians still had aircraft left at airfields beyond the Israelis' reach, and they could not be sure that they might not be attacked by them and sunk. Early on the morning of the Second Day (6th), the Egyptian missile boats slipped out of Port Said harbour and sailed westwards along the coast to Alexandria, where they were effectively removed from the scene, as they carried insufficient fuel to enable them to sally out from Alexandria to bombard the Israeli coast and return. If they refuelled at sea they would be exposed in daylight at some stage to the Israeli Air Force. Only from Port Said had it been possible for the missile boats to reach Israel and return to base during the short hours of darkness.

To the south on the evening of the Second Day (6th), just after darkness had fallen, an Egyptian naval force of two destroyers and six MTBs moved from Sharm El Sheikh slowly up the Gulf of Akaba, but turned back before reaching a point where three Israeli MTBs were lurking in ambush about 20 miles south of Eilat.

On the afternoon of the Third Day (7th) the Israelis detected an Egyptian submarine near Rosh Hanikra, close to the Lebanese–Israeli border. It was attacked by three Israeli destroyers, which dropped depth-charges, and a large oil slick appeared on the surface. As has been related, three Israeli MTBs from Eilat arrived and sailors went ashore at Sharm El Sheikh at 1430 to hoist the Israeli flag.

On the Fourth Day (8th) another Egyptian submarine was detected near Haifa. When depth-charges were dropped near it an oil slick was observed. Later that day, the Israelis say, yet another Egyptian submarine approached their coast near Ashdod, but withdrew when fired upon. For their part the Egyptians emphatically deny that any of their submarines went near Haifa or the northern Israeli coast during the war.

During the nights of the Fourth and Fifth Days (the 8th and 9th), when the Egyptians realized just how badly the war was going for them, they withdrew all the craft, both naval and merchant marine, that they could from Port Said to Alexandria. The Suez Canal was blocked by ships sunk on President Nasser's direct orders, and the Egyptian ships that had been at Hurghada, Safaga and Koseir sailed off southwards to the safety of Hodeida in the Yemen.

The Israeli Navy had done its duty quietly and competently, but the opportunity for glory had not occurred. The projected combined naval and air assault on El Arish, scheduled for the first night, in which the Navy might have had a chance to excel, had been cancelled, partly because Jordan had unexpectedly entered the war and troops had to be diverted to the Jordanian Front, and partly because of the successful advance of the Tal Ugda. The Egyptian Navy had not once bombarded Israel's long and vulnerable coastline. Most of the credit for this, of course, should fall to the Israeli Air Force.

THE ATTACK ON THE 'USS LIBERTY'

On the Fourth Day (Thursday, 8 June) the *USS Liberty*, a communications vessel crammed full of electronic equipment, was sighted steaming north-eastwards by two Israeli MTBs in the Mediterranean a few miles north of the Sinai coast. They instantly identified it as an Egyptian ship, its silhouette being somewhat similar to that of the known Egyptian supply vessel, *El Quseir*, and they asked for Air Force assistance. This information was, of course, relayed immediately to the main operations room at GHQ. A few minutes later another message identified the ship as American. The MTB commanders were sharply ordered to check to make sure. The US Naval Attaché in Tel Aviv was contacted, and he confirmed that there should be no American ships in that particular stretch of water. The next report from the MTBs was that the ship was a Soviet one, but the Israeli commanders were told to look again, as the Soviet

Embassy in Tel Aviv also denied that there were Soviet vessels in that area of the Mediterranean.[1]

Meanwhile, the Israeli Air Force had come into the picture. A flight of three Mirages sighted the ship and, commencing at 1405, swooped down on the *USS Liberty*, raking it with cannon fire. At this moment the American vessel was 12 nautical miles north of El Arish. The aircraft made six strafing runs over the ship and then flew away. Twenty minutes later the two MTBs, which had been watching in the background, made for the ship at a fast speed with all their machine-guns firing. When they got closer they loosed off two torpedoes. One missed completely but the other struck the *USS Liberty* squarely amidships, tearing a gaping hole some 40 feet across in its side at the water-line. Suddenly the MTB attack stopped. The Israelis were now close enough to realize that this was indeed an American ship, although by this time the American flag had been shot away. The whole attack had lasted about 30 minutes, during which 34 Americans had been killed and 75, including the captain, wounded. Fires were blazing in several parts of the ship, and later 821 hits were counted–Israeli Air Force and Naval marksmanship had been good. Once they realized that they had attacked an American vessel, the Israelis put a helicopter at the disposal of the American Naval Attaché, who immediately flew out to the damaged *USS Liberty*, but he was refused permission to go aboard. After hovering around ineffectually for a while he dropped his visiting card, wrapped in a handkerchief, on to the deck and flew back to Tel Aviv.

Within half-an-hour of the end of the attack the fires on board had been put out. Refusing all offers of Israeli help, the *USS Liberty* turned and steamed slowly northwards, listing heavily to starboard, its watertight compartments keeping it afloat. It was joined in due course by the *USS Little Rock*, a cruiser, which escorted it to Malta, where it was put into dry dock for repairs. Its casualties were taken aboard the *USS America*, an aircraft carrier.

Later that day the US Defence Department in Washington issued a statement confirming that the *USS Liberty* had

---

[1] The Soviet Union did not have Naval or Service Attachés accredited to Israel, but its Embassy staff, of over 120, was the largest in the country.

departed from Rota, in Spain, on 2 June for the eastern Mediterranean, and had arrived at a point 12 nautical miles north of El Arish at the time of the attack. The reason for the ship's presence was 'to ensure communications between US Government Posts in the Middle East and to assist in relaying information concerning the evacuation of American citizens from countries of the Middle East'. No advance warning of its arrival had been given to any of the warring Middle East states.

The Israeli Government apologized and offered full compensation claiming that it was a case of mistaken identification. The US Government accepted, but sent a Navy Board out to investigate. The theory that the Israelis thought this was an Egyptian deception ruse, in which an Egyptian ship was flying an American flag in order to get close in to bombard El Arish, then in Israeli hands, is the most probable and acceptable of several improbable explanations.

CHAPTER 9

Reaction and Retrospect

After the period of rising tension, there was a feeling almost of relief in Israel once hostilities commenced. Quiet determination mingled with some apprehension as people anticipated casualties at the front and the bombing of population centres. Rumours circulated that the Egyptians were manufacturing poison gas. In the Arab countries there were belligerent speeches and arrogant joy. On the First Day Syria, Jordan, the Lebanon, Algeria, Kuwait and the Sudan all declared war on Israel, while Algeria sent a brigade post-haste to Egypt.[1] Saudi Arabia announced that its troops were entering Jordan on their way to fight the Israelis, Morocco said it was sending soldiers to the Middle East, and in Tunisia mobs attacked the Embassies of Britain and America. All day the Arabs issued false and boastful communiqués, while they ignored feeble bleats from the UN. All day the Israelis tried to hide their successes.

Britain was anxious about its Middle East oil supply, and also the possible adverse effect an Arab victory might have on the explosive Aden situation. Nasser broke off diplomatic relations with America. Israel was disappointed by the unexpected coolness of France, an ally it had come to rely upon heavily for material and diplomatic support. India, and a number of Afro-Asian states, openly condemned Israel as the aggressor, as did the Soviet Union. Both America and the Soviet Union feared escalation, so much so that Mr Kosygin, the Soviet Premier, used the 'hot line'[2] between Moscow and Washington to tell President Johnson that the Soviet Union would not intervene if America would not, which tended to give the impression that the Soviet view was that Egypt would quickly become the victor.

---

[1] 'Boumedienne rushed 5,000 troops overland to aid Egypt, but they got stuck in Libya.' (*David's Sling*.)

[2] This was the first time the 'hot line' had ever been used since its installation, in August 1963, after the Cuban missile crisis.

On the Second Day Egypt announced the closure of the Suez Canal to cut off oil supplies to Western nations, Iraq and Kuwait said they would send no more oil to Britain or America, and Syria and the Lebanon stopped oil flowing through their pipelines. Iraq, Syria and the Sudan broke off diplomatic relations with Britain and America. In the afternoon the UN Security Council reassembled in an emergency session and called upon the countries concerned to cease fighting. Syria and Iraq rejected this appeal, while Egypt did not bother to reply. Israel said it would stop fighting if the others would do the same. Jordan agreed to a cease-fire, but the Israelis would not accept this as the Jordanian forces were commanded by an Egyptian general. The Soviet Union suddenly became extremely displeased with Nasser when it learned of his attempts to implicate Britain and America by alleging that their aircraft were fighting alongside those of Israel, and it immediately changed its attitude. Premier Kosygin was again on the 'hot line' to President Johnson, this time saying that the Soviet Union would now work within the UN for an immediate and unconditional cease-fire. It had become obvious to the Soviet Military Mission in Egypt that not only was Egypt not going to win the war quickly, but perhaps was not going to win it at all, and these thoughts were passed on to Moscow. By evening the rough extent of the Israeli air victory was all but common knowledge.

On the Third Day Radio Cairo stopped its boastful propaganda and martial music, replacing them with readings from the Koran. Egyptian communiqués admitted that UAR Forces had fallen back to the 'second line of defence', and that Egyptian troops had been withdrawn from Sharm El Sheikh to 'rejoin the main body'. In the evening General Rabin announced that Israeli forces were in complete possession of the Sinai, Sharm El Sheikh, East Jerusalem and the West Bank, leaving the world at large in no doubt as to the extent of their victory. Nasser summarily dismissed Colonel Salah Nasr, his Chief of Intelligence,[1]

---

[1] It is of interest to note that in an interview with the Editor-in-Chief of the American magazine *Time* in May 1969, in answer to a question that it was said he was getting misleading information from his military (during this war), President Nasser replied: 'I was not handling military matters before the 1967 War. Now I am handling them directly. I am confident I am not being misled.'

and detailed General Murtagi, GOC Sinai, to take command of all the Egyptian forces in the field, which did not really alter much. In the UN the Soviet representative put a resolution to the Security Council to demand an immediate cease-fire, which was accepted unanimously. Again Israel said it would agree if the others conformed, and this time Jordan accepted the cease-fire, but Egypt, Iraq and Syria still refused.

On the Fourth Day the Israelis implemented the cease-fire with Jordan, which they delayed until they captured Jericho. In the morning King Hussein spoke over Radio Amman to his people, admitting the Jordanian reverses and expressing disappointment at the failure of the Egyptian and Iraqi Air Forces. He was the first Arab leader to tell the Arabs at least some of the true facts. Radio Cairo still made feeble but false boasts, claiming, for example, to have shot down 25 Israeli aircraft the previous day. Nasser accepted the UN resolution for a cease-fire, which came into effect at about 2000. That evening Nasser conferred with his Defence Minister, Field-Marshal Amer, and senior generals, when they urged him to resign.[1] Much argument ensued, and the meeting ended by Nasser saying he would make a speech to the nation the next day. The 'hot line' between Moscow and Washington was again used in the afternoon, this time by President Johnson, who after the *USS Liberty* incident hastened to tell Premier Kosygin why US ships and aircraft were racing into the eastern Mediterranean.

The Fifth Day was notorious for Nasser's 'resignation' speech, made on Egyptian television in the evening, in which he said: 'We cannot hide from ourselves the fact that we have met with a grave setback in the last few days . . . I am willing to assume the entire responsibility . . . I have decided to give up . . . every official post and every political role and return to the ranks of the public.' He named Zakaria Mohiedin, a former Premier and Director of Security Police, as the new President. The immediate reaction was that the citizens of Cairo in mass took to the streets, demanding that he stay in office. The spontaneity and sincerity of these demonstrations had been questioned, as they required considerable organization, but the fact remains that they were

---

[1] *The Sandstorm.*

effective. Professing to be moved by this response, Nasser said that he would defer his decision until the next day. The 'set-back' was not explained in any detail, and the Egyptians were still largely unaware of their disasters–indeed, they only really learned of their enormity when survivors straggled home. At dawn the Israelis turned the force of their arms against Syria, promptly causing that country to ask the UN for a cease-fire.

On the Sixth Day the Soviet Union broke off diplomatic relations with Israel and threatened to impose sanctions if Israeli troops did not stop advancing into Syrian territory. A cease-fire with the Syrians came into effect at about 1830, when the occupation of the Golan Plateau was completed. In Cairo Nasser said he would accept the people's will to remain President, and the National Assembly granted him full powers to carry through the necessary political and military reconstruction.

On the first day after the war, Sunday, 11 June, the freighter *Dolphin* reached Eilat, the first Israeli ship to pass through the Straits of Tiran since the Egyptian blockade. The Chairman of the Suez Canal Authority announced that the Canal was closed owing to the sinking of several ships in it, but he would not name them or give their nationalities. In fact, Nasser had ordered certain Egyptian ships and barges to be sunk at the northern end near Port Said, just south of Ishmailia and near Port Suez, to ensure that it was really blocked. Fourteen foreign ships (including four British) were trapped in the Great Bitter Lakes. Syria demanded an emergency meeting of the UN Security Council, as it alleged that Israeli troops were still advancing towards Damascus, but the UN hesitated. In Cairo, fortified by popular acclaim, Nasser turned on those who had suggested he resign, dismissing his Defence Minister, Shamseddin Badran, Field-Marshal Amer and eight senior officers who included the Commanders of the Air Force and the Navy, and General Murtagi, GOC Sinai. More 'resignations' followed. Nasser then elevated General Fawzi, the Chief of Staff, to Field-Marshal Amer's former post of Deputy Supreme Commander, with the new title of Chief of the Armed Forces, while General Riad, fresh from his defeats in Jordan, became Chief of Staff.[1] Also dismissed

---

[1] General Riad was later killed by shell fire on 9 March 1969, during an artillery duel across the Suez Canal.

was Ahmed Said, Director of Broadcasting Services, who had become noted for his extravagantly optimistic boasts, claims and threats.

Compiling a short balance sheet, in six days of fighting the Israelis had occupied about 26,000 square miles of Arab territory for the cost of 778[1] soldiers (and 26 civilians) killed, 2,586 soldiers (and 195 civilians) wounded and 21 taken prisoner (of whom five were killed by mobs). Israel also took over 11,500 prisoners, the majority of whom were Egyptian; of these about 6,000 were released almost immediately, most of the remainder being held against the exchange of 16 Israeli prisoners. On 15 June 1967 the Israelis opened Athlith Camp to journalists. They were holding there 5,499 Arab prisoners, mainly Egyptian, who included nine generals, 10 colonels and 300 officers. A month later they claimed to have ferried another 6,000 Egyptians, who had been picked up from the desert, across the Canal. Israeli equipment losses had been more than made up by captured material which was quickly taken into use. For example, Egyptian cannon shells seized at El Arish were used by Israeli aircraft to strike at Syrian positions during the last two days of the war. The Arabs continue to be evasive about their losses, but the Israelis estimated them to amount to about 15,000 killed and 53,000 wounded. Moshe Dayan, for example, said on 4 August 1969 that during the Six Day War Israel suffered 3,336 casualties (of whom 778 were killed). Presumably he was referring to military losses only.

The Israelis were now faced with the problem of administering a large Arab population. A census conducted just after the war showed about 33,000 Arabs in the Sinai (mainly at El Arish), 350,000 in the Gaza Strip (about 120,000 in Gaza and 175,000 in refugee camps), 70,000 in East Jerusalem, 600,000 on the West Bank, and 6,400 (practically all Druze) on the Golan Plateau. The Bedu in the Sinai do not seem to have been included in these figures. About 150,000 Arabs had fled eastwards across the River Jordan, far less than was originally estimated. Taking into account some 300,000 Arabs already living in Israel before the war, the final figures showed that there were now 1,385,000

---

[1] The first figure issued, of 679 Israeli servicemen killed, was later amended.

Arabs in Israel or Israeli-occupied territory, compared with 2,365,000 Jews.

The Israeli Defence Force had come out of the war very well, but nonetheless certain disciplinary measures were taken. Several officers who had failed were removed from their commands or staff appointments, other regulars were relegated to the reserve. Many of these removals, however, were covered by normal retirements and the reorganization of the officer-cadre. A few, officers and soldiers, were court-martialled for poor behaviour in action. The Israelis do not release any figures on disciplinary matters, or give them any publicity. Officers and soldiers who had not come up to scratch in battle were mostly forgiven for their shortcomings in the magnanimity of victory, and also because it was thought necessary to keep up the façade of Israeli martial invincibility to over-awe the Arabs. Rewards were also given to those who had done well, consisting of some 51 Chief of Staff 'Mentions in Dispatches'.[1]

In the defeated Arab armies, with the exception of that of Jordan, there were wholesale dismissals, demotions, transfers and punishments, that weakened the structure and further damaged morale. In the Egyptian forces, in the weeks following the war, some 750 senior officers were removed and an equal number transferred to office jobs or positions in the nationalized industries. This was also done in part deliberately to ensure that the armed forces did not attempt to seize power. The whole upper command and staff structure was torn apart to such an extent that the Soviet Military Mission, which was trying to rebuild the Egyptian armed forces, intervened to insist that those Egyptian officers who had done well on the Soviet training courses be brought back. Many soldiers were punished and degraded which tended further to dampen morale.

President Nasser and King Hussein remained in power in their respective countries, as did General Jadid for a few months more. Nasser formed a new Cabinet and Hussein reshuffled his,

---

[1] This war prompted the Israelis to try to put their honours and decorations on a more formal system. Bravery decorations in three classes are being instituted. Israeli Servicemen have been awarded a 'campaign' ribbon for each of the three wars that have been fought since 1948, which are worn on the left breast in the conventional military manner.

while Jadid dismissed the Commander of the Southern Front and certain other army officers, as much to strengthen his own position in the country as for any other reason. There were comparatively few dismissals or punishments in the Jordanian Army. Although General Majali's title was changed, Major-General Khammish, the Chief of Staff, was retained in his position to reorganize the shattered force. By 10 July Nasser and Hussein were again hob-nobbing in Cairo. One by one UN observers reappeared and quietly positioned themselves on some of the cease-fire lines, and General Odd Bull returned to his former headquarters at Government House in Jerusalem. Despite protests, the Israelis triumphantly incorporated Arab East Jerusalem to form a united city, but they were rebuffed by France when, on 27 June, President de Gaulle issued a statement condemning Israel for starting the war. The period of Israeli–French friendship and co-operation had come to an end. Other old scores were paid off, and Colonel Hatoum, who had led an unsuccessful *coup* against the Syrian Government in February 1966, and had fled to Jordan, returned to Syria during the war to offer his services, hoping that all was forgotten and forgiven in this moment of Arab crisis. It was not—and the Syrians executed him.

A rather odd fact is that some 75,000 Jews still remain in Arab countries, the largest number, 50,000, being in Morocco. In Libya, just after the war, about 20 Jews were killed by mobs, and the authorities allowed over 3,000 to leave, but despite the adverse conditions some 1,000 stayed on. About 1,000 Jews still remain in Egypt (mainly held in camps), about 2,500 in Iraq and some 5,000 in Syria. None of these countries would allow any to leave—they are held as bargaining counters. About 7,000 Jews live in more reasonable conditions, but in doubtful security, in the Lebanon, and ask only to be left alone. There were about 13.5 million Jews in the world, of whom about 2.3 million were in Israel, 5.2 million in the USA and 1.2 million in Europe.[1]

The 'suicide' of Field-Marshal Amer was a direct outcome of the war. After he was summarily dismissed by Nasser, many other Egyptian officers who had been similarly treated began

---

[1] *David's Sling.*

to meet at his house in Cairo. It was later alleged[1] that plots were hatched to kidnap Nasser and take over the Government, and also that anti-Nasser literature was handed out. Amer was placed under house-arrest on 27 August 1967, and his suicide occurred on 15 September. Considerable speculation was aroused as to whether it was really suicide or whether he had been killed at Nasser's instigation. The official explanation of his death was extremely unsatisfactory.

On 20 June, little more than a week after the war, Marshal Zakharov, the Soviet Chief of Staff, appeared with a large Military Mission in Cairo, where he remained for a fortnight, apart from two short visits to Syria. His task was obviously to hold a post mortem and to arrange for the Egyptian forces to be re-equipped with Soviet arms. The importance of this project was underlined when the Soviet President, Podgorny, visited Cairo from 21 to 24 June. On the 25th the first plane-load of new Soviet arms arrived, to be followed at increasingly frequent intervals by others.

On 1 July there was fighting between Israeli and Egyptian troops when an Egyptian detachment crossed the Canal about 10 miles south of Port Said; on the 3rd the Israelis admitted the first act of sabotage in their occupied territories, when Egyptian commandos derailed a train in the Sinai; on the 5th two Israeli officers were killed by Egyptian mortar fire near the Suez Canal, on the 8th four Egyptian MiGs appeared over the Sinai for the first time since the war to clash with two Israeli planes; and on the 12th occurred the first big artillery duel across the Canal, in which Israeli soldiers were wounded. On the same day, the 12th, the Israeli destroyer, *Eilat*, sank two Egyptian MTBs.

On 15 July Israeli and Jordanian forces again exchanged fire across the cease-fire line. In the third week of that month a Soviet naval force of 13 warships visited Egyptian ports to emphasize how solid was the Soviet backing of Nasser. On 26 August an Egyptian SU-7 was shot down by the Israelis over the Sinai, and on 21 October the Israeli destroyer, *Eilat*, was sunk by an Egyptian Komar Class missile boat, evoking retaliatory Israeli shelling of the Suez oil refineries. The cease-

---

[1] The state trials did not commence until January 1968.

fire, which had been of such short duration, was now little more than a fiction, and despite the good intentions and the endless talk of settlements, lasting solutions and peace plans, hostilities had been resumed and an undeclared war between Israel and the Arabs was once again in full progress, extracting its daily toll of casualties.

After the post-mortem results have been studied, and all arguments and excuses analysed, the conclusion must be that the Third Arab-Israeli War was a crushing victory for the Israelis and a humiliating defeat for the Arabs. Skilful propaganda and public relations techniques displayed the successes and martial qualities of the Israelis in their best light to the world, at the same time carefully hiding the few chinks in their armour, while the ensuing sulky silence of the Arabs obliterated many of their good points and minor successes. The Suez Canal remained closed, not only to the Israelis but to everyone else, thus preventing Arab oil passing through it to the West, while the Straits of Tiran and the Gulf of Akaba had been opened to the Israelis.

Many contributed to the Israeli victory, not the least the well-trained individual Israeli soldier, who was always clear in his own mind what he was fighting for, which was to preserve the existence of Israel. He was ably led by his regimental officers, and well directed and supported by a capable General Staff, which contributed more than any other group or individual to victory by evolving suitable strategy, developing leadership, pursuing good training techniques and formulating tactical solutions. After the First Day both President Nasser and King Hussein, and their respective General Staffs, lost control over the progress of the war, but the Israeli General Staff retained a firm grip over its conduct throughout.

Moshe Dayan, the Defence Minister, made the biggest impact on world opinion, and to him perhaps has gone too much credit for winning the war. There was no doubt that he was the right man for the right job, who did the right things at the right time, bringing life and hope to the Israeli Forces and the nation at a critical moment; he both inspired and gave confidence, but he came on to the military scene at the eleventh hour. All plans and preparations had been made by the quiet, unassuming Chief of

Staff and his staff officers. But Moshe Dayan brought the colourful leadership that was essential and, once he took over his appointment, all decisions and emphasis were his. A Defence Minister does not normally interfere in the day-to-day conduct of a war, but lets his Chief of Staff implement his decisions through conventional channels. Moshe Dayan, not a brilliant staff officer but more a commander-type, did this. A senior officer who worked with him during this war told me that Dayan had a 'flair for battle' and that he was a 'lucky general'. He did not shirk responsibility, nor did it worry him, as he had the confidence of his convictions. In this respect Dayan and Rabin complemented each other perfectly, forming a winning leadership. Once the die was cast the conduct of the war was entirely in their hands. His 'intuition' led him to put a greater emphasis on the Jerusalem Front. He was right, as the entry of Jordan into the war was unexpected by most Israelis, and caused a hasty revision of plans on the First Day as reserve troops were switched from the Sinai Front to Jerusalem. Jerusalem was extremely important to the Israelis, and Moshe Dayan clearly saw that it was little use gaining huge tracts of Sinai desert at the cost of the loss of New Jerusalem, or parts of it. Once the possibility of seizing East Jerusalem presented itself he gave special attention to this battle, holding Brigadier Tal back for two days at El Arish until the Jerusalem battle had been resolved. Moshe Dayan had his priorities right, and it was well for Israel that he had.

The other main character, Premier Eshkol, does not seem to have come out so well. Usually he is depicted as hesitant and indecisive at a critical moment in Israeli history, but this is not a fair picture.[1] He was rather overtaken by internal politics and overshadowed by the publicity-conscious Moshe Dayan, but his character and determination, which had achieved economic stability for Israel, were underestimated by the Arabs and the Soviet Union. Their faulty assessment allowed the Israelis, despite overt escalation, to gain a decisive surprise and thus to demolish yet another preconception.

The preponderance of Arabs over Israelis (usually quoted at

---

[1] Levi Eshkol died in office on 26 February 1969.

anything from 110 million to 52 million, depending on the source and context) can be misleading as the great majority was silent, parochial and passive. In more realistic terms the Arabs were able only to muster between 300,000 and 400,000 soldiers against Israel. Israel, however, mustered some 270,000, was able to choose the place and time of attack and operated on interior lines of communication. As the Arabs were dispersed and operating on exterior lines of communication, the seeming disparity in numbers was much diminished. On the battlefields the Arabs and Israelis were often nearly equal in numbers. The Israeli policy was to 'put all their best goods in the shop window and sell them first' – in short, to hit hardest with the best they had. For example, only 14 brigades, or elements of 14 brigades, have been identified in action in this war on all fronts, which means that over half the 'teeth' formations (Israel mobilized 32 brigades) never saw any action at all. The brigades that went into action were the best trained and equipped they had, while those that were less well equipped, less well trained or perhaps had morale or other problems, were held back. Had circumstances demanded their use, they would undoubtedly have been fed on to the battlefield in their order of capability.

Soviet influence with the Arabs increased with defeat, but only because the Soviet Union is the only power willing and able to supply them with arms. Soviet shortcomings were many (especially their lack of experience in desert warfare) and contributed to the Israeli victory. But their main weakness lay in their intelligence, and also their failure to appreciate and evaluate accurately the calibre and morale of the Israeli leaders and armed forces. The Russians did not get the 'feel of the nation'. No Israeli military attaché had been permitted in Moscow since 1949, and so there was no Soviet opposite number in Tel Aviv; the Soviet Union had to rely upon Arab reports instead of being able to assess the situation for itself at first hand. The Unified Arab High Command, under General Ali Amer, designed to mobilize and direct the efforts of 110 million Arabs against Israel, was a completely ineffectual piece of Arab political superstructure, it having been undermined by the activities of the PLO. Such co-operation as briefly existed between Arab states had been promoted directly by President Nasser. The Unified Arab High

Command simply proved a known fact—that the Arabs were not united.

In retrospect the Third Arab-Israeli War was a bright and glorious page in Israeli history. But the prospect may be a darker one.

Index

The Words: Arab(s); Egypt(ian)(s); Israel(i)(s); Jordanian(ian)(s); Nasser; Syria(n)(s) are not included as they appear on so many pages

FORMATIONS, AIRCRAFT, WEAPONS AND VEHICLES

INDEX